T0149211

ODD WORDS

FOR CROSSWORD AND PEOPLE IN PUZZLES

ODD WORDS

FOR CROSSWORD AND PEOPLE IN PUZZLES

FIFTH EDITION

Ben Bougard

iUniverse

ODD WORDS FOR CROSSWORD AND PEOPLE IN PUZZLES
FIFTH EDITION

iUniverse books may be ordered through booksellers or by contacting:

iUniverse
1663 Liberty Drive
Bloomington, IN 47403
www.iuniverse.com
1-800-Authors (1-800-288-4677)

Because of the dynamic nature of the Internet, any web addresses or links contained in this book may have changed since publication and may no longer be valid. The views expressed in this work are solely those of the author and do not necessarily reflect the views of the publisher, and the publisher hereby disclaims any responsibility for them.

Any people depicted in stock imagery provided by Thinkstock are models, and such images are being used for illustrative purposes only. Certain stock imagery © Thinkstock.

ISBN: 978-1-4917-9518-7 (sc)
ISBN: 978-1-4917-9519-4 (e)

Print information available on the last page.

iUniverse rev. date: 07/11/2016

A hobbit - BILBO
A little, musically - POCO
A people of Mexico - SUMA
A sound - SCHWA
A thousand years - CHILIAD
Abalone - ORMER
Abandoned calf - CADE
Abbot's staff - CROSIER
Abnormal loss of
    hair - ALOPECI
Aborigine of Japan - AINU
Abounding in shrubs - BOSKY
About 1.3 cu.yds. - STERE
Abraham's wife - SARAH
Abruzzi bell town - ATRI
Absolute rule - IMPERIUM
Absorbed-dose units - RADS
Abstract artist - ARP
Abstract being - ENS or ESSE
Abstract painting - OPART
Abstract rumor - CANARD
Abusive phrase - EPITHET
Abyss - ABYSM
Acacia tree - BABUL
Acclimation - ECLAT
Accustomed - WONT
Achilles' victim - HECTOR
Acid in tone - ACERB
A hobbit - BILBO
A little, musically - POCO
A people of Mexico - SUMA

A sound - SCHWA
A thousand years - CHILIAD
Abalone - ORMER
Abandoned calf - CADE
Abbot's staff - CROSIER
Abnormal loss of
    hair - ALOPECI
Aborigine of Japan - AINU
Abounding in shrubs - BOSKY
About 1.3 cu.yds. - STERE
Abraham's wife - SARAH
Abruzzi bell town - ATRI
Absolute rule - IMPERIUM
Absorbed-dose units - RADS
Abstract artist - ARP
Abstract being - ENS or ESSE
Abstract painting - OPART
Abstract rumor - CANARD
Abusive phrase - EPITHET
Abyss - ABYSM
Acacia tree - BABUL
Acclimation - ECLAT
Acid of apples - MALIC
Acidity - ACOR
Acorns coat - TESTA
Act of God - FORCE MAJEURE
Actual being - ESSE
Acupressure - SHIATSU
Adding machine
    inventor - PASCAL
Address the moon - ULULATE

Adriatic peninsula - ISTRIA

Adriatic seaport - ANCONA,
BARI, RIMINI
or TRIESTE

Adriatic wind - BORA

Adroit, generally - HABILE

Adult doodlebug - ANTLION

Adult insect - IMAGO

Advances degree - PHD or SCD

Advantage - BEHOOF

Adventure tale - GEST
or GESTE

Aegean area - IONIA

Aegean island - DELOS
or SAMOS

Aerospace material - BERYLIUM

Aesir ruler - ODIN

Afghan city - HERAT

Afloat - NATANT

Afore - ERE

African antelope - ADDAX,
BONGO, ELAND,
GEMBOK, GNU,
IMPALA, KOB, KUDU,
LICHI, NYALA, ORIBI,
ORYX, RHEABOK,
STEENBOK, SUNI,
TETEL, TOPI or TORA

African arid region – SAHEL

African badger - RATAL

African caftan- DASHIKI

African capital - ACCRA

African evergreen - COLA

African fever - LASSA

African fox - ASSE or CAMMA

African gorge - OLDUVAI

African ground squirrel - XERUS

African knife - PANGA

African language – SWAZI

African lemur - MACACO

African lily - AGAPANTHUS

African lute - OUD

African mammal - RATAL

African monkey - GUENO

African musical
instrument - MBIRA

African nation - DJIBOUT

African nomad - BERBER

African ox - ZEBU

African palm tree - RAFFIA

African plant - ALOE

African pullover - DASHIKI

African river - UBANGI

African rodent - HYRAX

African ruminant - OKAPI

African shirt - DASHIKI

African sorcery - OBEAH

African spear - ASSEGAI

African spear tree - ASSEGAIS

African stork - ARGALA
or MARABOU

African tableland - KAROO

African timber tree - ODUM

African tongue - RUNDI

African tree - SHEA
African tunic - DASHIKI
African village - KRAAL
African wildcat - SERVAL
African witchcraft - OBEAH
Again, in music - BIS
Agaves plant - SISAL
Agaves root - AMOLE
Aging - SENESCENT
Agouti or coypu - CAVY
Agricultural
    pesticide - LINDANE
Air dwellers of
    folklore - SYLPHS
Air: pref. - ATMO
Airplane controls - AELERONS
Airplane engine
    housing - NACELLE
Air sacs in the lungs - ALVEOLI
Airtight - HERMEDIC
Aladdin parrot - IAGO
Alarm bell or signals - TOCSIN
Alaskan or Aleutian isle -
    ADAK, ATKA or ATTU
Alaskan knife - ULUL
Alaskan National
    Park - DENALI
Alaskan volcano - KATMAI
Alcoholic cakes - BABAS
Ale holder - TUN
Alencon - LACE
Aleutian island - ADAK

Alfonso's queen - ENA
Algerian cavalryman - SPAHI
Algerian port - ORAN
Algonquian chief - SACHEM
Algonquian
    leaders - SAGAMORES
Alkene - OLEFINE
Alligator shirt maker - IZOD
Allowance for waste - TRET
Alloy of lead & tin - TERNE
Alloy of silver &
    gold - ELECTRUM
Alluring woman - HORIS
Alluringly plump - ZAFTIG
Almond poison - AMARINE
Alms box - ARCA
Aloe fiber - PITA
Alpine peak - EIGER
Alpine region: var. - TIROR
Alpine river - AARE
Altar cloth - DOSSAL
Altar enclosure - BEMA
Altar of stars - ARA
Altar screen - REREDOS
Aluminum coin of
    Israel - AGORA
Amateur newsletter - FANZINE
Amazon bird - HOATZIN
Amazon dolphin - INIA
Amazon estuary - PARA
Amazon feeder - NEGRO
Amazon native - TUPI

Amazon port - BELEM

Amazon rain forest - SELVA

Amazon valley people - TUPI

Ambrosia of
immortality - AMRITA

American chameleon - ANOLE

American dogwood - OSIER

American hog - DUROC

American Indian
grouping - TUPI

American larch - TAMARACK

American lizard - AMOLE

American saint - SETON

Amerind - ERIE or OTOE

Ammonia compound -
AMIDE or AMINE

Ammonia derivative - IMIME

Among other
things - INTERALIA

Amorous glance - OEILLADE

Amtrack Train - ACELA

Amulet - MOJO

An amino acid - ARGININE,
LYSINE or SERINE

An archangel - URIE

Anatomical cavity - FOSSA

Anatomical duct - VAS

Anatomical folds - PLICAE

Anatomical
intersection -CHIASMA

Anatomical network - RETE

Ancient - HOARY

Ancient: Pref. - PALEO

Ancient African city - UTICA

Ancient African
kingdom - NUMIDIA

Ancient ally of Sparta - ELIS

Ancient alphabetic
character - RUNE

Ancient Arabian
kingdom - SHEBA

Ancient ascetic - ESSENE

Ancient assemblies - FORA

Ancient Balkan
region - THRACE

Ancient Biblical
country - ARAM

Ancient Biblical land - ELAM

Ancient box - CIST

Ancient British Celts - ICENI

Ancient capital of
Lydia -SARDIS

Ancient catapult - ONAGER

Ancient Caucasian - OSSET

Ancient Celtic tribe - ICENI

Ancient chariot - ESSED

Ancient Chinese capital - XIAN

Ancient Chinese poet - LIPO

Ancient Chinese money - TAEL

Ancient city of Edom - PETRA

Ancient city of
Mesopotamia - EDESSA

Ancient city on the
Nile - MEROE

Ancient country in Africa - NUMIDIA

Ancient country in the Peloponnesus - ELIS

Ancient Dead Sea country - MOAB

Ancient Egyptian city - TANIS

Ancient Egyptian diety - PTAH or SHU

Ancient Egyptian gold - AMENRA

Ancient Egyptian papers - PAPYRI

Ancient Ethiopian capital - MEROE

Ancient fertility god - BAAL

Ancient fertility goddess - ASTARTE

Ancient fiddle - REBEC

Ancient German - GEAT

Ancient gold coin - AUREUS

Ancient Greece - HELLAS

Ancient Greek belts - CESTI

Ancient Greek city or state - ELEA or POLIS

Ancient Greek coin - OBOL or STATER

Ancient Greek colony - IONIA

Ancient Greek council - BOULE

Ancient Greek courtesan - HETAERA

Ancient Greek covered walks - STOAS

Ancient Greek dialect - EOLIC or IONIC

Ancient Greek district or region - IONIA or LACONIA

Ancient Greek Geographer - STRABO

Ancient Greek goddess - ENYO

Ancient Greek marketplace - AGORA

Ancient Greek Mystic - ORACLE

Ancient Greek Physician - GALEN

Ancient Greek Poet - SAPPHO

Ancient Greek portico - STOA

Ancient Greek region - AEOLIA

Ancient Greek sage - SOLON

Ancient Greek sculptor - SCOPAS

Ancient Greek serf - HELOT

Ancient Greek soldier - HOPLITE

Ancient Greek tunic - CHITON

Ancient Greek weight - MINA

Ancient hall of music - ODEA

Ancient Hebrew coin - GERAH

Ancient Hebrew lyre - ASOR

Ancient Hebrew kingdom - SAMARIA

Ancient Hewbrew stringed Instrument - NABLA

Ancient Hebrew prophet - ELIAS

Ancient Hebrew
vestment - EPHOD

Ancient idol - BAAL

Ancient Incan capital - CUZCO

Ancient inscription - RUNE

Ancient Irani - MEDE

Ancient Irish god - LUG

Ancient Israeli
fortress - MASADA

Ancient Italian
area - ETRUSCAN

Ancient Italian deity - FAUN

Ancient Italian town - ELEA

Ancient Italic people - SABINES

Ancient Jewish sect
member - PHARISEE

Ancient King of
England - HAROLD

Ancient kingdom - EDOM

Ancient kingdom on the
Nile - NUBIA

Ancient laborer - ESNE

Ancient letter - RUNE

Ancient lute - REBEC

Ancient marketplace - FORA

Ancient markings -
OBELI or RUNE

Ancient metal collar - TORC

Ancient Mexican - TOLTEC

Ancient Mexican
resident - OLMEC

Ancient mid east
kingdom - MOAB

Ancient Nile kingdom - NUBIA

Ancient ointment - NARD

Ancient oracle site - DELPHI

Ancient Palestinian - ESSENE

Ancient paper - PAPYRUS

Ancient part of Iran - MEDIA

Ancient people - OSSET

Ancient Persian - MEDE
or ELEAMITE

Ancient Phoenician
city - SIDON

Ancient Phoenician
seaport - TYRE

Ancient rabbi - HILLEL

Ancient region of
France - ALSATIA

Ancient Roman historian - LIVY

Ancient Roman port - OSTIA

Ancient Roman
province - RAETIA

Ancient sage - SOLON

Ancient Scandinavian
poets - SKALDS

Ancient Semitic
country - EDOM

Ancient Spanish
kingdom - NAVARRE

Ancient stone tool - EOLITH

Ancient stringed
instrument - PSALTERY

Ancient strong box - ARCA

Ancient Syrian city -
ALEPPO or ELBA
Ancient Syrian
kingdom - MOAB
Ancient temple - NAOS
Ancient Theban supreme
god - AMENRA
Ancient tome - CODEX
Ancient Tuscan
nation - ETRURIA
Ancient Turkish city - EDESSA
Ancient Umbrian
city - SPOLETO
Ancient warship - TRIEME
Ancient wine flask - OLPE
And others: abbr. - ETAL
Andes plateau - PUNA
Andes tuber - OCA
Andean shrub - COCA
Andorran coin - PESETA
Angel - SERAPH
Angel of the highest
order - SERAPH
Angle measurer - ALIDADE
Angle symbol - THETA
Angler's bars - HERLS
Anglo-Saxon coin - ORA
Anglo-Saxon laborer - ESNE
Anglo-Saxon spear - GAR
Anglo-Saxon tax -
DANEGELD or GELD
Anglo-Saxon Theologian - BEDE

Animal fat - ADIPOSE
Animal's backbone - CHINE
Animal's breadbasket - MAW
Anise liqueur - PERNOD
Ankle bone - TALUS
Ankle bones - TALI or TARSI
Annealing oven - LEHR
Annuity scheme - FONTANE
Another name for the
Furies - DIRAE
Ant - EMMET
Antarctic penguin - ADELIE
Antarctic predators - SKUAS
Antelope of Tibet - GOA
Anticlimax - BATHOS
Antigone's uncle - CREON
Antilles Island - SABA
Antipathy - ODIUM
Antiquated - FUSTY
Antique coin - ACU
Antiquity - ELD
Antitoxins - SERA
Ants, old style - EMMETS
Anvil - INCUS or OSSICLE
Apertures - STOMATA
Apathy - ACEDIA
Apparition - EIDOLON
or WRAITH
Appetite - EDACITY
Apple, e.g. - POME
Apple acid - MALIC

Apollo's birth place - DELOS
Apollo's nymph - DAPHNE
Apollo's twin sister - ARTEMIS
Apse dome - CONCHA
Apteryx - KIWI
Aquatic nymph - NAIAD
Aquatic rodent - COYPU
Aqualung
    inventor - COUSTEAU
Aquarium bottom
    feeder - LOACH
Aquarium fish - DANIO,
    GOURAMI, NEON,
    TETRA or WRASSE
Arab boat - DHOW
Arab chieftain - EMEER
Arab commandoes - FEDAYEEN
Arab garment - HAIK
Arab headdress - KAFFIYEH
Arab land - OMAN
Arab market place - SOUK
Arab robes - ABAS
Arab Satan - EBLLS
Arabian cloak - BURNOOSE
Arabian coast vessel - DHOW
Arabian gazelle - ARIEL
Arabian port - ADEN
Arabian Sea feeder - INDUS
Arabic father - ABOU
Arabic letter - ALIF
Arbitrary penalty - AMERCE
Arbor - PERGOLA

Arboreal lemur - INDRI
Archaic bidding - HEST
Archangel - URIEL
Archetype - PARADIGM
Architectural pier - ANTA
Arctic bird - SKUA
Arctic goose - BRANT
Arctic gull - XEMA
Arctic jacket - ANORAK
Arctic whale - NARWHAL
Area of expertise - METIER
Arenas - STADIA
Argentine grassland - LLANO
Argentina port - PARANA
Argo captain - AENEAS
Argonne forest river – AISNE
Argue frivolously - CAVIL
Arguments - POLEMICS
Arikara - REE
Arizona Indian - PIMA
Arm bones - RADII or ULNAE
Arm of the Amazon - PARA
Arm pit - AXILLA
Armadillo - APAR
Armadillo armor - SCUTE
Armless, backless
    seat - TABORET
Armor piece - TASSE
Armor plate - TUILLE
Armored breastplate - CUIRASS
Armpit - AXILLA

Army victuals - MRES

Aromatic herb - HYSSOP

Aromatic herb - HYSSOP

Aromatic plant - CHIA
or NARD

Aromatic resin - MYRRH

Arrange in threes - TERNATE

Arrogance - HUBRIS

Arrow poison - CURARE,
INEE or UPAS

Arsenic sulphide - REALGAR

Art deco Artist - ARTE

Artemis's twin - APOLLO

Article of food - VIAND

Artificial Intl
language - ESPERANTO

Artificial rubber - BUNA

Artist's studio - ATELIER

Artist's surface - GESSO

Artistic movement - DADA

Artistic prayer - ORANT

Arrow smith's wife - LEORA

Artistic taste - VIRTU

Arum plants - AROIDS

As - QUA

As above - ADEM

As written - SIC

As written musically - STA

Ascetic - ESSENE

Ashy substance - CALX

Asia Minor - ANATOLIA

Asia Minor region - AEOLIA

Asian ass - ONANGER

Asian boat - SAMPAN

Asian citrus - POMELO

Asian deer - SIKAS

Asian fish - LOACH

Asian fruit - LOQUAT

Asian gazelle - GOA

Asian goat -TAHR

Asian holiday - TET

Asian language - LAO or SHAN

Asian legume - SOYA

Asian long horned
sheep - ARGALI

Asian mountain goat - TAHR

Asian mushroom - SHIITAKE

Asian mustard plant - MASABI

Asian noodles - RAMEN

Asian nurse or
nursemaid - AMAH

Asian ox - GAUR, YAK
or ZEBU

Asian palm - ARECA or BETEL

Asian range - ALAI

Asian River between China &
Russia - AMUR or LENA

Asian sea - ARAL

Asian snake - KRAIT

Asian soy product - MISO

Asian starlings - MYNAS

Asian tree - ASAK

Asian weight - TAEL

Asiatic herb - ORACH

Assail persistently - BELABOR

Assam or Oolong -TEA

Assam silkworm - ERIA

Assembly place of old - AGORA

Assert - POSIT

Assyrian city - ARBELA

Assyrian god - ASHUR

Assyrian god of war - ASUR

Astringent - ACERB

Astrinent compound - TANNIN

Astronomer's light
    ratio - ALBEDO

Astronomical unit - PARSEC

At full speed - AMAIN

At last: Fr. - ENFIN

Athenian hangout - STOA

Athenian law giver - DRACO

Athenian lawmaker or
    sage - SOLON

Athenian magistrate - ARCHON

Athenian solon - DRACO

Atlantic clam - QUAHOG

Atheletes foot – TINEA

Atlantic fish - LING,
    MENHAGEN or SCUP

Atlantic food fishes - PORGIES

Atlantic mackerel - CERO

Atlas' seven
    daughters - PLEIADES

Atmospheric pressure
    unit - TORR

Atomic number
    1 - HYDROGEN

Atomic number 2 - HELIUM

Atomic number 5 - BORON

Atomic number 7 - NITROGEN

Atomic number 10 - NEON

Atomic number 16 - SULFER

Atomic number 23 - ARSENIC

Atomic number 26 - IRON

Atomic 30 - ZINC

Atomic number 45 - RHODIUM

Atomic #46 - PALLADIUM

Atomic number 50 - TIN

Atomic number 54 - XENON

Atomic number 55 - CESIUM

Atomic number 56 - BARIUM

Atomic number 68 - ERGIUM

Atomic number
    74 - TUNGSTON

Atomic number 75 - RHENIUM

Atomic number 77 - IRIDIUM

Atomic number 86 - RADON

Atomic number 96 - CURIUM

Atomic particle - MESON
    or NEUTRON

Attachment to a fishing
    line - SNELL

Aunt, Sp. - TIA

Auricular - OTIC

Aurora's Greek
    counterpart - EOS

Austerlitz name change - ASTAIRE

Austria - WIEN

Australian Alps - TIROL

Australian bird - ARARA

Australian cockatoo - GALAH

Australian cuckoo - KOEL

Australian horse - WALER

Australian lizard - MOLOCH

Australian sheep dog - KELPIE

Authentic - ECHT

Authorative edict - UKASE

Avatar of Vishnu - RAMA

Avifauna - ORNIS

Away - FRO

Away from one's mouth - ABORAL

Awkward - SPLAY

Awns - ARISTAS

Ax handle - HELVE

Axiom - TENET

Ayla's creator - JEAN AUEL

Babe in the woods - NAIF

Baby barracuda - SPET

Baby beaver - KIT

Baby bird - EYAS

Baby food - PAP

Baby oyster - SPAT

Babylonian goddess - ISHTAR

Babylonian numeral - SAROS

Babylonian sky god - ANU

Babylonian sun god - SHAMASH

Babylonian tower - ZIGGURAT

Baccarat variation - CHEMIN DE FER

Bacchanalian cry - EVOE

Bacchante - MAENAD

Backs - DORSA

Bacterium - AEROBE

Bactrian beast - CAMEL

Bad blood - ANIMUS

Bad: pref. - MAL

Bad imitation - ERSATZ

Bad luck - HOODOO

Bad taste in art - KITSCH

Bad Tempered - WASPISH

Bad tempered old woman - HARRIDAN

Badger kin - RATEL

Bagpipe kin - MUSETTE

Baja seaport - ENSENADA

Bake eggs - SHIRR

Balance - STASIS

Balcony - MIRADO

Balderdash - FLUMMERY

Baldness - ALOPECIA

Balearic Island - IBIZA

Balkan capital - TIRANA

Ball of yarn - CLEW

Ball point pen inventor - BIRO

Ballerina - DANSEUSE

Ballerina step - PAS

Ballerina's rail - BARRE

Ballet jump - ENTRECHAT
    or PAS DE CHAT

Ballet leap - JETE

Ballet movement or
    pose - CHASSE,
    ELANCE or PLIE

Ballet position - ECARTE

Ballet stars - ETOILES

Ballet step - PAS

Balloon probe - SONDE

Ballroom dance - SALSA

Balm for aches &
    pains - ARNICA

Balsam burner - CENSER

Baltic Sea barge - PRAM

Baltic Sea capital - TALLIN

Baltic Sea port - RIGA

Bamako's land - MALI

Bambi's aunt - ENA

Banana kin - ABACA

Bank of France - RIVE

Bantu language - XHOSA

Bantu native - ILA

Barbary ape - MAGOT

Barbary sheep - AOUDAD

Barbed-wire barricade - ABATIS

Bard's song - MADRIGAL

Barge - HOY

Bark cloth - TAPA

Barley beards - ARISTAS
    or AWNS

Barracuda - SPET

Barrel maker - COOPER
    or STAVER

Barrio grocery - BODEGA

Based on the number
    six - SENARY

Basic sugar - SUCROSE

Basket fiber or
    material - RAFFIA

Basket making need - ISTLE

Basketry willow - OSIER

Basswood - LINDEN

Bast fiber - RAMIE

Basutoland - LESOTHO

Bat-eared fox - ASSE

Bat haven - ANTRE

Bat wood - ASH

Bathsheba's husband - EURIAH

Battery inventor - VOLTA

Battery type - NICAD

Battlefield fence - ABATIS

Battlement opening - CRENEL

Battleship nickname - BIGMO

Bauble - GEWGAW

Bauxite component - ALUMINA

Bavarian leatherwear -
    LEDERHOSEN

Bay - LAGUNA

Bay of the White Sea - ONEGA

Bay window - ORIEL

BC/Alaska River - STIKINE

Beak - NEB

Bean, for sprouting - MUNG

Bear young - YEAN

Beard of rye - AWN

Bearded - BARBATE

Beat - ICTUS

Beatify - BLESS

Beautiful woman of
    paradise - HOURI

Beaver hat - CASTOR

Become rigid - OSSIFY

Bed canopy - TESTER

Bed covering - DUVET

Beehive - SKEP

Beet variety - CHARD

Beethoven dedicatee - ELISE

Beethoven opus - EROICA

Beetle - CHAFER

Beetle wings - ELYRA

Before: pref. - ANTE

Before birth - INUTERO

Begum's spouse - AGHA

Behold, to Caesar - ECCE

Beige - ECRU

Beijing coin - YUAN

Being - ESSE

Belgian port city - GHENT
    or OSTEND

Belgian princess - ASTRID

Belgian waterway - OISE

Belgium River - YSER

Believer in God - DEIST

Belladonna lily - AMARYLLIS

Bellflower - LOBELIA

Bell like instrument - CELSTRA

Bell shaped hat - CLOCHE

Bell tower - CAMPANILE

Bell town - ATRI

Bellini opera - NORME

Belly - WAME

Belly button - AMPHALOS

Belly muscles - RECTI

Below: Pre. - INFRA

Bend in a ships timber - SNY

Benedictine title - DOM

Benefactor Yale - ELIHU

Benign tumor of the skin - WEN

Berber nomads - TUAREG

Bern's river - AARE

Berry parts - ACINI

Best vision spot - FOVEA

Bet to lose every trick in
    cards - MISERE

Betel palm - ARECA

Beyond: Prefix - META

Bible prophet - JOEL

Biblical book - HOSEA,
    JONAH or PROVERBS

Biblical bushel - EPHA

Biblical herdsman - AMOS

Biblical incense - MYRRH

Biblical judge - ELI

Biblical king - ELAH

Biblical kingdom - ELAM
or MOAB

Biblical land - OPHIR

Biblical liar - ANANIANS

Biblical lion - ARI

Biblical mount - HOREB,
NEBO or SINAI

Biblical place of exile - HARA

Biblical prophet - AMOS,
HOSEA, PESGAH
or ISAIAH

Biblical queen - ESTHER

Biblical spy - CALEB

Biblical twin - ESAU

Biblical weed - TARE

Biblical witch's home - ENDOR

Big baboon - MANDRILL

Big bird - RHEA

Big bug - CICADA

Big name in tea - TAZO

Big Sur retreat - ESALEN

Billiard table cloth - BAIZE

Binary compound - OXIDE

Binary star in Perseus - ALGOL

Biochemical catalyst - OXIDASE

Biological bristle - SETA

Biology classes - GENERA

Biology lab stain - EOSIN

Birch family
tree - HORNBEAM

Bird beak - NEB

Bird bill part - CERE

Bird droppings - GUANO

Bird of Greenland - ERNE

Bird of prey - ELANET

Bird with a crest - HOOPOE

Birds - ORNIS

Bird's wing - PINION

Birth a lamb - YEAN

Birth sack - CAUL or VEIL

Birthmark - NEVUS

Birthplace of Apollo - DELOS

Birthplace of Buddha - NEPAL

Birthplace of
CAMUS - ALGERIA

Birthplace of Jules
Verne - NANTES

Bishop of Rome - POPE

Bishoprics - SEERS

Bishop's headdress - MITRE

Bishop's permission - EXEAT

Bishop's staff - CROSIER

Bit of mosaic - TESSERA

Bitter - ACERB

Bitter vetch - ERS

Bitter vetches - TARES

Bizarre - OUTRE

Black and white diving
bird - MURRE

Blackbird - MERLE or OUSEL

Black cuckoo - ANI

Black- current liqueur - CASSI

Black fish - TAUTOGS

Black footed albatross - GOONEY

Black forest tree - BAUM

·Black gibbon of Asia - SIAMANG

Black grape - ZINFANDEL

Black gum tree - TUPELO

Blackjack - COSH

Black sea arm - AZOY

Black sea port - ODESSA, ORDU or VARNA

Black tailed gazelle - GOA

Black tea - BOHEA

Black vulture - URUBU

Blacksheep - ROUE

Blackstone - ONYX

Black-tailed gazelle - GOA

Blackthorn fruit - SLOE

Bleach - ETIOLATE

Bless - SAIN

Blessing - BENISON

Blindfold a falcon - SEELS

Blissful - ELYSIAN

Blissful state - NIRVANA

Blister - BLEB

Blithe - JOCUND

Bloated - TUMID

Block of Earth's crust - MASSIF

Blood: Pref. - HEMA

Blood clots - EMBOLI

Blood of the gods - ICHOR

Blood pigment - HEMA

Blood sucking fly - TABANID

Blood vessel network - RETE

Blood vessels - VENAE

Bloodstone - HELIOTROPE

Blossom-bearing stems - SCAPES

Blue dye - ANIL, ANILIN or WOAD

Blue grass genus - POA

Blue-gray - BLAY

Blue myrtle - LILACS

Blue Nile source - TANA or TSANA

Blue sky - WELKIN

Blue-violet - PERSE

Blue wildflower - GENTIAN

Boadicea's people - ICENI

Boatman on the river Styx - CHARON

Bobby's blackjack - COSH

Bobolink - ORTOLAN

Body - SOMA

Body cavities - ANTRA

Body duct - VAS

Body of beliefs - ETHOS

Body of poetry - EPOS

Body of work - OEUVRE

Body sacs - BURSA

Bog plant - SUNDEW

Boil down - DECOCT

Bolero composer - RAVEL

Boletus mushroom - CEPE

Bolivian Indian - MOXO

Bollard - KEVEL

Bombastic - OROTUND

Bombay suburb - THANA

Bombay today - MUMAI

Bon mot - EPIGRAM

Bone cavities or
    chambers - ANTRA

Bone cavity - FOSSA

Bone: Fr. - OSTE

Bone inflammation - OSTEITIS

Bone material - APATITE

Bone: Pref. - OSTE

Bones - OSSA

Bony - OSTEAL

Boobook baby - OWLET

Book after Amos - OBAD

Book after Chronicles - EZRA

Book after Daniel - HOSEA

Book after Exodus - LEV

Book after Ezekiel - HOSEA

Book after Ezra - NEH
    or NEHEMIAH

Book after Gal. - EPH

Book after Hosea - JOEL

Book after Job - PALMS

Book after John - ACTS

Book after Joel - AMOS

Book after Jonah -MICAH

Book after Judges - RUTH

Book after Leviticus - NUM

Book after Mark - ST.LUKE

Book after Micah - NAHUM

Book after Neh - ESTH

Book after Num. - DEUT

Book after Proverbs - ECCLES

Book before Amos - JOEL

Book before Daniel - EZEKIEL

Book before Esth - NEH

Book before
    Habakkuk - NAHUM

Book before Jeremiah - ISAIAH

Book before Jobe - ESTHER

Book before Joel - HOSEA

Book before John - LUKE

Book before Judges - Joshua

Book before Nehemiah - EZRA

Book before Nehum - MICAH

Book before Num - LEV

Book before Obadiah - AMOS

Book before Philemon - TITUS

Book before Romans - ACTS

Book before Titus - TIM

Book of Hymns - PSALYER

Book of prophecies - HOSEA

Book of reprints - OMNIBUS

Book of Sayings - ANA

Book size - OCTAVO

Bookbinder's leather - ROAN

Bookbinding leather - ROAN

Bookplate - EXLIBRIS

Books with eight
    pages - OCTAVOS

Boorish person - CHURL

Boot wheel - ROWEL

Bordered by a ridge - VALATE

Borden's spokes cow - ELSIE

Boredom - ENNUI

Boring oration - SCREED

Boring tool - WIMBLE

Borneo Sea - SULU

Borodin prince - IGOR

Botanic structure - OVULE

Botanical bristle - SETA

Botanical cell - CYST

Botanical garden - ARBORETA

Botanical opening - STOMA

Botanical sac - ASCUS

Both: pref. - AMBI

Bothered - ATE

Bottle holding 3 magnums of
Champagne - REHOBOAM

Bottle in
    wickerwork - DEMIJOHN

Bounce over water - DAP

Bounce playfully - DANDLE

Bound bundle of sticks - FAGOT

Bovine hybrid - CATALO

Bovine stomachs - OMASA

Bowed, in music - ARCO

Boxlike sled - PUNG

Braided bread - CHALLAH

Brain membrane - DURA
    or DURAMATER

Brain passage - ITER

Branch of the Amazon - PARA

Branches - RAMI

Branch training
    trellises - ESPELIER

Brandy letters - VSOP

Brazilian airline - VARIG

Brazilian macaw - ARA

Brazilian palm - ASSAI

Brazilian rattler - MARACA

Brazilian river - TIETE

Brazilian rubber tree - ULE

Brazilian seaport - BAHIA,
    BELEM, NATAL,
    or SANTOS

Brazilian state - BAHIA

Brazilian timber tree - SATINE

Breakfast cereal - MUESLI

Breakfast roll - BIALY

Breastbones - STERNA

Breastplate - AEGIS,
    CUIRASS or EGIS

Breathing affliction - APNEA

Breed of sheep - CHEVIOT

Brew - DECROCT

Bribe - SOP or SUBORN

Bric-a-brac shelves - ETAGERE

Brief insight or
    summary - APERCU

Bright star - ALGOL

Brightly colored fish - OPAH

Brightly colored parrot - LORY

Brilliance - ECLAT

Brilliantly colored
	lizard - AGAMA

Brindled cat - TABBY

Bring forth sheep or
	young - YEAN

Bring forward as
	proof - ADDUCE

Bristle: Prefix - SETI

Bristle like part - SETAE

Bristly - SETOSE

British farm structure - BYRE

British lunch - TIFFIN

British medical
	journal - LANCET

British sonar - ASDIC

Brit's morning
	break - ELEVENSES

Brit's fireplace - INGLE

Brittany seaport - BREST

Brittle resin - COPAL

Broad bean - FAVA

Broad winged hawk - BUTEO

Broken down horse - JADE

Brood of pheasants - NIDE

Brook trout - SALTER

Broom of twigs - BESOM

Brother of Castor - POLLUX

Brother of Electra - ORESTES

Brother of Ethan Allen - IRA

Brother of Esau - JACOB

Brother of Fidel - RAUL

Brother of Hector - PARIS

Brother of Iphigenia - ORESTES

Brother of ISIS - OSIRUS

Brother of Jacob - EDOM
	or ESAU

Brother of Miriam - AARON

Brother of Moses - AARON

Brother of Ophelia - LAERTES

Brother of Osiris - SET

Brother of
	Polynices - ETEOCLES

Brother of Prometheus - ATLAS

Brother of Saud - FAISAL

Brother of Seth - ABEL

Brother of Tamar - ABSALOM

Brother of Thor - Tyr

Brother of Van Gogh - THEO

Brown bear - URSID

Brown ermine - STOAT

Brown fur - NUTRIA
	or STOAT

Brown pigment - SIENNA

Brown tint - SEPIA

Brownish songbird - LINNET

Brunei coin - SEN

Brunei's locale - BORNEO

Brynhild's beloved - SIGURD

Buckthorn - CASCARA

Buckwheat porridge - KASHA

Buddhist angels - DEVAS

Buddhist
	enlightenment - SATORI

Buddhist holy city - LHASA

Buddhist language - PALI

Buddhist monk - BONZE

Buddhist movement - CHAN

Buddhist people - LAO

Buddhist religious center
in Japan - NIKKO

Buddhist sacred
mountain - OMEI

Buddhist Satan - MARA

Buddhist Shrine - STUPA

Buddhist teachings - DHARMA

Buddhist temple - WAT

Buddhist tower - PAGODA

Buddhist who has obtained
Nirvana - ARHAT

Buckwheat porridge - KASHA

Buffalo, for one - BOVID

Buffalo of the Celebes - ANOA

Bug group - HETEROPTERA

Bug repellent - DEET

Build a nest - NIDIFY

Bulgarian coin - LEV

Bulgarian seaport - VARNA

Bulletin board runners - SYSOPS

Bullfighter's cloak - CAPA

Bullfighter's march - PASEO

Bulrush - TULE

Bundle of nerves - RETE

Bundle of twigs - BESOM
or FAGOT

Bung - SPILE

Bunny tail - SCUT

Burgundy wine - MACON

Burial urn - OSSUARY

Burmese rice dish - SELA

Burmese tribesman - SHAN

Burn balm - ALOE

Burn suddenly - DEFLAGRATE

Burn with a ray - LASE

Burp - ERUCT

Burrowing rodent - PACA

Bur sera resin - ELEMI

Burst open - DEHISCE

Bush baby - GALAGO

Bush cricket - KATYDID

Buster Brown's dog - TIGE

Butcher bird - SHRIKE

Butcher's scraps - OFFAL

Butterfly - SATYR

Cabot's ship - MATHEW

Cacophony - DIN

Cactus - SAGUARO

Cactus features - AREOLAE

Cactus plant - OPUNTIA

Cadmus' daughter - INO

Caesar's dog - CANIS

Caesar's horse - EQUUS

Caesar's wife - UXOR

Cain's brother - ABEL or SETH

Cake - GATEAU

Calla - ARUM

Calcareous rock deposit - TUFFA

Calculating machine inventor - PASCAL

Calcutta cloth - DHOTI

California bulrush - TULE

California oaks - ROBLES

California resort city - OJAI

California town - APTOS

California volcano - LASSEN

Calligraphy line - SERIF

Caliph - IMAM

Called - YCLEPT

Calvary - GOLGOTHA

Calyx part - SEPAL

Cambodia (once) - KHMER

Camel - BACTRIAN

Camel kin - GUANACO

Camel's hair fabric - ABA

Cameo stone - SARDONYX

Camping place for troupes - ETAPE

Campus life - ACADEME

Canaanite commander - SISERA

Canaanite deity - BAAL

Canal to the Baltic - KIEL

Canary Island - TENERIFE

Canary's cousin or relative - SERIN

Canary's nose - CERE

Candies fruit - GLACES

Candle ingredient - STEARIN

Cannabis - BHANG

Canonical hour - COMPLINE, MATIN, NONES or SEXT

Canopy - TESTER

Canopy for a boat - TILT

Cant - ARGOT

Cantina tidbit - TAPA

Canvas coating - GESSO

Capacitance unit - FARAD

Cape fox - ASSE

Capek play - RUR

Caper - DIDO

Capillary's cousin - TABULE

Capital of Afghanistan - KABUL

Capital of Albania - TIRANA

Capital of American Samoa - PAGO PAGO

Capital of ancient Elam - SUSA

Capital of ancient Laconia - SPARTA

Capital of ancient Syria - ANTIOCH

Capital of Angola - LUANDA

Capital of Antigua - ST. JOHN

Capital of Armenia - YEREVAN

Capital of Aruba - ORANJESTAD

Capital of Assyria - NINEVEH

Capital of Azerbaijan - BAKU

Capital of Bahrain - MANAMA

Capital of Bali - DENPASAR

Capital of Bangladesh - DACCA or DHAKA

Capital of Belarus - MINSK

Capital of Belgium - BRUSSELS

Capital of
Benin - PORTO-NOVO

Capital of Bihar - PATNA

Capital of Boeotia - BETA

Capital of Bolivia - LA
PAZ and SUCRE

Capital of Bosnia - SARAJEVO

Capital of
Botswana - GABORONE

Capital of Brittany - RENNES

Capital of Bulgaria - SOPHIA

Capital of
Burundi - BUJUMBURA

Capital of Cambodia - RIEL

Capital of
Cameroon -YEOUNDE

Capital of Chad - N'DJAMENA

Capital of Chile - SANTIAGO

Capital of Colombia - BOGOTA

Capital of Congo - KINISHASA

Capital of Costa Rica -
SAN JOSE

Capital of Crete - CANEA
or HERAKLION

Capital of Croatia - ZAGREB

Capital of Cyprus - NICOSIA

Capital of Delaware - DOVER

Capital of Dominica - ROSEAU

Capital of Drome - VALENCE

Capital of East
Flanders - GHENT

Capital of Egypt - CAIRO

Capital of Ecuador - QUITO

Capital of Eritrea - ASMARA

Capital of Estonia - TALLINN

Capital of Ethiopia -
ADDIS ABABA

Capital of Fiji - SUVA

Capital of Georgia - TBILISI

Capital of Ghana - ACCRA

Capital of Guam - AGANA

Capital of
Guyana - GEORGETOWN

Capital of
Haiti - PORT-AU-PRINCE

Capital of Hejaz - MECCA

Capital of Honduras -
TEGUCIGALPA

Capital of
Hungary - BUDAPEST

Capital of Iceland - REYKJAVIK

Capital of Idaho - BOISE

Capital of India - NEW DELHI

Capital of Indonesia - JAKARTA

Capital of Iraq - BAGHDAD

Capital of Isere - GRENOBLE

Capital of Jamaica - Kingston

Capital of Jordan - AMMAN

Capital of Kansas - TOPEKA

Capital of Kazakhstan -
    AQMOLA, ASTANA or
    ALMAATA
Capital of Kenya - NAIROBI
Capital of Korea - SEOUL
Capital of Laconia - SPARTA
Capital of La Manche - STLO
Capital of Laos - VIENTIANE
Capital of Latvia - RIGA
Capital of Lesotho - MASERU
Capital of Libya - TRIPOLI
Capital of
    Liechtenstein - VADUZ
Capital of Lithuania - VILNUS
Capital of Lombardy - MILAN
Capital of Lorraine - METZ
Capital of Lydia - SARDIS
Capital of Macedonia - SKOPJE
Capital of Majorca - PALMA
Capital of Maldives - MALE
Capital of Mali - BAMAKO
Capital of Malta - VALLETTA
Capital of Manche - ST LO
Capital of Mauritius -
    PORT LOUIS
Capital of Minorca - MAHAN
Capital of Mongolia -
    ULAN BATOR
Capital of Montana - HELENA
Capital of Morocco - RABAT
Capital of
    Mozambique - MAPUTO

Capital of Muscat - OMAN
Capital of
    Nepal - KATHMANDU
Capital of New Jersey
    TRENTON
Capital of New South
    Wales - SYDNEY
Capital of New Mexico -
    SANTA FE
Capital of Niger - NIAMEY
Capital of Nigeria - ABUJA
    or LAGOS
Capital of North
    Carolina - RALEIGH
Capital of North
    Dakota - BISMARK
Capital of Okinawa - NAHA
Capital of Oman - MUSCAT
Capital of Oregon - SALEM
Capital of
    Pakistan - ISLAMABAD
Capital of Phoenicia - TYRE
Capital of Piedmont - TURIN
Capital of Portugal - LISBON
Capital of Puerto Rico -
    SAN JUAN
Capital of Qatar - DOHA
Capital of
    Queensland - BRISBANE
Capital of Roman Britain -YORK
Capital of Rwanda - KIGALI
Capital of Samoa - APIA

Capital of
Saskatchewan - REGINA

Capital of Saudi
Arabia - RIYADH

Capital of Schleswi-
Holstein - KIEL

Capital of Senegal - DAKAR

Capital of Shensi - SIAN

Capital of Sicily - PALERMO

Capital of
Slovakia - BRATISLAVA

Capital of South
Dakota - PIERRE

Capital of Spain - MADRID

Capital of St.
Kitts - BASSETERRE

Capital of
Suriname - PARAMARIBO

Capital of
Swaziland - MBABANE

Capital of Switzerland - BERN

Capital of Syria - DAMASCUS

Capital of Taiwan - TAIPEI

Capital of Tanzania - DAR
ESSALAAM

Capital of Tasmania - HOBART

Capital of
Thailand - BANKOCK

Capital of the
Bahamas - NASSAU

Capital of the
Comoros - MPRONI

Capital of the
Crimea - SIMFEROPOL

Capital of the Dominican
Republic - SANTO
DOMINGO

Capital of the Netherlands
Antilles - WILLEMSTAD

Capital of the
Punjab - LAHORE

Capital of the Ukraine - KIEV

Capital of Taiwan - TAIPEI

Capital of Texas - AUSTIN

Capital of Tibet - LHASA

Capital of Timor - DILI

Capital of Togo - LOME

Capital of Transfer - UMTATA

Capital of Tunisia - TUNIS

Capital of Turkey - ANKARA

Capital of Uganda - KAMPALA

Capital of
Uruguay - MONTEVIDEO

Capital
Uzbekistan - TASHKENT

Capital of Valise - SION

Capital of Vanuatu - VILA

Capital of
Venezuela - CARACUS

Capital of
Vermont - MONTPELIER

Capital of Vietnam - HANOI

Capital of Western Samoa - APIA

Capital of
Wisconsin - MADISON

Capital of
　　Wyoming - CHEYENNE
Capital of Xizang - LHASA
Capital of Yemen - ADEN
　　or SANA
Capital of Zambia - LYSAKA
Capital of
　　Zimbabwe - HARARE
Capital on the AAR - BERN
Capital on the Casouab - BAKU
Capital on the Songka
　　River - HANOI
Capital on the Vltava - PRAGUE
Capital once know as
　　Salisbury - HARARE
Capri or Elba - ISOLA
Captive of Hercules - IOLA
Capuchin monkey - SAI
Caravansary - SERAI
Car amide - UREA
Carbon compound - ENOL
　　or KETONE
Card game - ECARTE
Cardiac contraction - SYSTOLE
Cardinal flower - LOBELIA
Cardinal's cap - BIRETTA
Carefree - BLYTHE
Carefree episode - IDYLL
Caret-shaped letter - LAMBDA
Cargo derrick - STEEVE
Caribbean dance music
　　or style - SOCA

Caribbean island -
　　ARUBA or SABA
Carmen composer - BIZET
Carnelian - SARD
Carnivorous mammal - RATEL
Carnivorous plant - SUNDEW
Carpathian range - TATRA
Carpet fiber - ISTLE
Carried by the wind - EOLIAN
Carrion - OFFEL
Carthaginian queen - DIDO
Cartilage disc - MENISCI
Cascade of ruffles - JABOT
Case for a small article - ETUI
Caspian feeder - URAL
Caspian sturgeon - BELUGA
Cassava root - MANIOC
Cassia plant - SENNA
Castle's back gate - POSTERN
Castle's stronghold - KEEP
Castor's mom - LEDA
Castorum - BEAVER URINE
Cat genus - FELIS
Cat nip - NEPETA
Cat's monogram - TSE
Categorized groups - TAXA
Catamount - PUMA
Cataplasm - POULTICE
Catapult - BALLISTA
Caterpillar hairs - SETAE
Cathedral city - ELY

Catholic calendar - ORDO

Catkin - AMENT

Catlike - FELID

Catlike mammal - CIVET

Cato's course - ITER

Cattle genus - BOS

Cattle, old style - KINE

Cattle plague - MURRAIN

Caucho-ule - RUBBER TREE

Cautious - CHARY

Cave or cavern - ANTRE

Caveman's flint - EOLITH

Cavern on the way to
Hades - EREBUS

Cavity - FOSSA

Cedar of the
Himalayas - DEODAR

Ceiling feature - TRAVE

Celebes buffalo or ox - ANOA

Celestial being with three pairs of
wings - SERAPH

Celestial dog - CANIS

Celestial shadow - UMBRA

Cell body - SOMA

Cell constituent - RNA

Cell division process - MITOSIS

Celtic Mayday - BELTANE

Celtic Neptune or sea god - LER

Celtic spirit - BANSHEE

Center of activity - LOCI

Central American
bird - QUETZEL

Central American tree - EBO

Central Asian mountains - ALTA

Central point - NODE

Century plant - AGAV,
ALOE or MAGUEYS

Ceramic blue - SMALT

Cereal fungus - ERGOT

Ceremonial chamber - KIVA

Ceremonial Feast - POTLATCH

Cereal grass - RAGI

Certain alloy - TERNE

Certain Asian soldier - ROK

Certain bacterium - AEROBE

Certain bird - TRILLER

Certain Bison - WISENT

Certain church calendar
day - FERIA

Certain cleaner - SALSODA

Certain consonant -
LABIAL or LENIS

Certain cotton - PIMA

Certain cue used in
singing - PRESA

Certain electronic
tubes - TRIODES

Certain epoch - EOCENE

Certain fruit - POME

Certain gemstones - SPINELS

Certain group - NONET

Certain Indian - CADDO

Certain Japanese
American - SANSEI

Certain muscle - TENSOR

Certain rabbits - LAPINS

Certainly - IWIS

Cete or cetacean - ORC
or WHALE

Chain of connected
ideas - CATANAS

Chair back - SPLAT

Chalcedony - SARD

Chalice - CALIX

Chalice veil - AER

Chalk or marble - CALCITE

Chameleon - ANOLE

Chan portrayer - OLAND
or TOLER

Chancel - BEMA

Change: Pref. - META

Chanted hymn - CANTICLE

Channel - GAT

Channel Island - SARK

Chanticleer - ROOSTER

Chantilly's river - OISE

Chapter of the Koran - SURA

Characteristic spirit - ETHOS

Charged lepton - MUON

Charged particle - ANION,
CATION, ION
or PROTON

Charging policy - PRIX FIXE

Charlemagne's
capital - AACHEN

Chat idly - PRATE

Chattering bird - DAW

Chauvinistic patriot - JINGO

Cheekbone - MALAR

Cheep wine - PLONK

Cheerful - JOCUND

Cheese variety - STILTON

Chef's hat - TOUQUE

Chef's thickening agent - ROUX

Chemical compound - ALKALI,
AMINE, ENOL, ESTER,
HALIDE, ISOMER,
OXIDE or STEROL

Chemical nuclide - ISOMER

Chemical salt - CITRATE
or ARSENAT

Chemical suffix - ENE or ENOL

Cherub superior - SERAPH

Chest for valuables - ARCA

Chestnut coating - BUR

Chewing-gum
ingredient - CHICLE

Chicken - TREPID

Chicken breed - WYANDOTTE

Chickle source - SAPODILLA

Chickpea - GRAM

Chief Vedic god - INDRA

Child of Ra - SHU

Childbirth - PARTURITION

Childish - PUERILE

Chilian deset - ATACAMA

Chilean seaport - ARICA

Chills & fever - AGUE

Chilly - ALGID

Chimpanzee - BONOBO

China/Russia border
River - AMUR

Chinawood oil - TUNG

Chinese coin - TAEL

Chinese coins - YUANS

Chinese cuisine - HUNAN

Chinese deer - SIKA

Chinese division - MIAO

Chinese dynasty - CHI,
CHOU, HSIA
or LIAO

Chinese fruits - LITCHIS

Chinese gooseberry - KIWI

Chinese house idol - JOSS

Chinese ideal or "way" - TAO

Chinese industrial
area - WUHAN

Chinese isinglass - AGAR

Chinese money - YUAN

Chinese noodle dish - LOMEIN

Chinese official
residence - YEMAN

Chinese pagoda - TAA

Chines pasta - LOWEMIN

Chinese philosopher - LAOTSE

Chinese poet - LIPO

Chinese port - AMOY or LUDA

Chinese pottery - CHUN

Chinese puzzle - TANGRAM

Chinese seaport - AMOY
or LUDA

Chinese secret society -TONG

Chinese tea - CHA, LAPSANG
or SOUCHONG

Chinese weight unit -
LIANG or TAEL

Chipped stone - EOLITH

Chiromancer - PALMIST

Chitinous body - CARAPACE

Chivalrous
undertaking - EMPRISE

Choise dish - VIAND

Choise tea - HYSON

Choler - ANGER

Chopin piece - ETUDE
or MAZURKA

Choral composition - ARIOSA

Chorus girl - CHORINE

Christ stopped at - EBOLI

Chronic liar - ANANIAS

Church book - PSALTER

Church calender - ORDO

Church council - SYNOD

Church cup - CALIX

Church desk - AMBO

Church music - MOTET

Church oil - CHRISM

Church part - APSE or NAVE

Church
passageway - NARTHEX

Church roster or tribunal - ROTA

Church screen - RERADOS

Church yearbook - ORDO

Circle - COTERIE

Circle dance - HORA

Circuit - AMBIT

Circuit courts - EYRES

Circular - GYRAL

Circular window - ROUNDEL

Circumference - AMBIT

Citrus garden - ORANGERY

City in Afghanistan - HERAT

City in Africa - MOMBASA

City in Alabama - SELMA

City in Alaska - SITKA

City in Asia - MANILA

City in Belgium - AALST, LIEGE or YPRES

City in Bolivia - LA PAZ or ORURO

City in Brazil - NATAL

City in Brittany - BREST

City in central China - SIAN

City in China - XIANGTAN

City in Denmark - ARHUS or ODENSE

City in Egypt - ZAGAZIG

City in Ethiopia - HARAR

City in Finland - ABO or ESPOD

City in France - METZ or STLO

City in Germany - BREMAN, KIEL or TRIER

City in Greenland - THULE

City in Hokkaido - SAPPORO

City in India - POONA

City in Iran - QOM or TABRIZ

City in Israel - LOD or EILAT

City in Italy - MANTUA, TORINO or UDINE

City in Japan - OSAKA or OTARU

City in Judah - ADAR

City in Kansas - IOLA

City in Kirghizia - OSH

City in Korea - TAEGU

City in Kyrgyzstan - OSH

City in Lombardy - LODI

City in Macedonia - EDESSA

City in Magdeburg - ELBE

City in Maine - SACO

City in Mexico - OAXACA

City in Moravia - BRNO

City in Morocco - CEUTA or FE

City in Nebraska - LINCOLN

City in New York - ORLEAN

City in Nigeria - EDE, IWO, IFE, KANO or LAGOS

City in Northern Italy - MANTUA '

City in Norway - BERGAN

City in Ohio - ELYRIA

City in Oregon - SALEM

City in Pakistan - LAHOR
City in Portugal - OPORTO
City in Provence - ARLES
City in Romania - ARAD
City in Russia - KIROV
    or TULA
City in RWANDA - KIGALI
City in Siberia - OMSK
City in Sicily - ENNA
City in South Korea - TAEGU
City in Spain - LEON
City in Sweden - UPPSALA
City in Switzerland - BASEL
City in Syria - ALEPPO
City in Texas - PAMPA,
    ODESSA or WACO
City in Transylvania - CLUV
City in the
    Newtherlands - BREDA
City in the Ukraine - LVOV
City in Thessaly - Larissa
City in Transylvania - DEVA
City in Tuscany - LUCCA,
    PISA or SIENNA
City in Utah - OREM
City in Vietnam - HAIPHONG
City in Wisconsin -
    EAUCLAIRE or NEENAH
City in Yorkshire - LEEDS
City near
    Amsterdam - HAALEM
City near Bremen - EMDEN

City near Dallas - DENTON
City near Lake Nassar - ASWAN
City near Moscow - KIROV
City near Padua - ESTE
City near Provo - OREM
City near San Marino - RIMINI
City near the Caspian
    Sea - AMUL
City near Venice - UDINE
City north of Leon - OVIEDO
City north of Triest - UDINE
City of ancient Ionia - SMYRNA
City of ancient
    Palestine - SAMARIA
City of ancient Rome - OSTIA
City of Ishikar Bay - OTARU
City of Moravia - BRNO
City of Panama - COLON
City of Spain - GRENADA
    or ORENSE
City of the Mudhens - TOLEDO
City of the Philistines - GATH
City of Yemen - ADEN
City on Crow
    Creek - CHEYENNE
City on Great South Bay - ISLIP
City on Lac Leman - GENEVA
City on Lake Michigan - GARY
City on Lake
    Winnebago - NEENAH
or OSHKOSH
City on Long Island - RYE

City on Minorca - MAHON

City on Puget Sound -TACOMA

City on Seneca Lake - GENEVA

City on the Aare - BERNE

City on the Adige - TRENT

City on the Aire - LEEDS

City on the Aker - OSLO

City on the Alabama - SELMA

City on the Allegheny -
GENEVA or OLEAN

City on the Amazon
delta - BELEM

City on the Arkansas - TULSA

City on the Arno -
FLORENCE or PISA

City of the Bay of Biscay
LAROCHELLE

City on the Bay of Haifa - ACRE

City on the Black sea - YALTA

City on the
Bosporus - ISTANBUL

City on the Brazos - WACO

City on the Cauca - CALI

City on the Clyde - GLASGOW

City on the Colorado - YUMA

City on the
Columbia - ASTORIA

City on the Cuyahoga - AKRON

City on the Danube -
BUDAPEST, LINZ, NOVI,
SAD, ULM or VIENNA

City on the Delaware -
CAMDEN, EASSTON or
TRENTON

City on the Dnieper - KIEV

City on the Douro - OPORTO

City on the Dvina - RIGA

City on the Ebro - LOGRONO
or SARAGOSSA

City on the Erie canal - ITHICA

City on the
Euphrates - BABYLON

City on the Ganges - AGRA,
ALLAHABAD, BENARES
or PATNA

City on the Grand - LANSING

City on the
Guadalquivir - CORDOBA

City on the Han - SEOUL

City on the Hari Rud - HERAT

City on the Hudson - ALBANY,
NYACK, TROY
or YONKERS

City on the Humboldt - ELKO

City on the Ij - AMERSTAM

City on the Ijsslemeer - EDAM

City on the Illinois - PEORIA

City on the Inn - St.MORITZ

City on the Irtysh - OMSK

City on the Isere - GENOBLE

City on the Jumna -
AGRA or DELHI

City on the Ligurian
Sea - GENOA

City on the Loire - BLOIS,
NANTES, NEVERS,
ORLEANS or TOURS

City on the
Merrimack - NASHUA

City on the Meuse - LIEGE,
NAMUR or SEDAN

City on the Mississippi -
MEMPHIS, MOLINE or
ST. PAUL

City on the Missouri -
OMAHA or PIERRE

City on the Mohawk - UTICA

City on the Moselle - EPINAL,
METZ or TRIER

City on the Mures - ARAD
or MURESUL

City on the Nile - THEBES

City on the Oder - BRESLAU
or WROCLAW

City on the Ohio - CINCINATI

City on the Oka - OREL

City on the Orne - CAEN

City on the Orsk - URAL

City on the Penobscot -
BANGOR or OROONO

City on the
Potomac - ARLINGTON

City on the Po - CREMONA,
TORINO or TURIN

City on the Raccoon -
DES MOINES

City on the Red - HANOI

City on the Red
Cedar - LANSING

City on the Rhine - ARNHEM,
BASLE, BERN, BONN,
COLOGNE, MAINZ
or WEISBADEN

City on the Rhone - ARLES,
AVIGNON, GENEVA
or LYONS

City on the Rio Grande - EL
PASO or LAREDO

City on the Roaring
Fork - ASPEN

City on the Ruhr - ESSEN

City on the Saone - LYON

City on the Salt - MESA

City on the
Savannah - AUGUSTA

City on the Seine - PARIS
or ROUEN

City on the
Shannon - LIMERICK

City on the Skunk - AMES

City on the Smokey Hills -
ABILENE or SALINA

City on the Somme - AMIENS

City on the Songka - HANOI

City on the
Squamscott - EXETER

City on the Styr - LUTSK

City on the
Susquehanna - ONEONTA

City on the Tanaro - ASTI

City on the Tanshui - TAIPAI
City on the Thames - ETON
City on the Tiber - ROME or OSTIA
City on the Tigris - AMARA or BAGHDAD
City on the Trinity - DALLAS
City on the Truckee - RENO or TAHOE
City on the Ural - ORSK
City on the Vardar - SKOPJE
City on the Vire - ST LO
City on the Vistula - WARSAW
City on the Vltava - PRAGUE
City on the Volga - SAMARA
City on the Willamette - EUGENE or SALEM
City on the Yamuna - AGRA
City on the Yangtze - CHUNG KING
City on the YODO - OSAKA
City on the Yonne - SENS
City Southwest of Frunze - OSH
Civet cousin - GENET or RASSE
Civilian clothes - MUFTI
Clairvoyant - FEY
Clan - GENS or SEPT
Clan chief - THANE
Clan of the Cave Bear, Author - AUEL
Clarion call - TANTARA

Clarified butter - GHEE
Classes - GENERA
Classical theaters - ODEA
Clavier - PIANO
Claw - CHELA
Clay-rich soil - MARL
Cleaving tool - FROE
Cleopatra's eye makeup - KOHL
Cleopatra's maid - IRAS
Cleric's vestment - AMICE
Clerical cap - BIRETTA
Clerical garment - RABAT
Clerical wear - ORALES
Clever prank - DIDO
Click beetle - ELATER
Cliff-base pile - SCREE
Climber's gear - CRAMPON
Climber's spike - PITON
Climbing palm - RATTAN
Climbing plant - CLEMATIS or
Clinging mollusk - LIMPET
Clinging vine - CIPO
Clinophobe's fear - SLEEP
Clique - COTERIE
Clone part - RAMET
Clot - COAGULUM
Cloth fibre - RAMIE
Cloth made from bark - TAPA
Cloth ridge - WALE
Clothe - ENDUE
Clown fish - ANEMONES

Cloy - PALL
Clump of wool - TOD
Coachman - JEHU
Coal dust - CULM
Coarse clothes - STAMMEL
Coarse fern - BRACKEN
Coarse hominy - SAMP
Coarse round basket - SKEP
Coarse rug - DRUGGET
Coarse, twilled cotton
    fabric - CHINO
Coarse woolen fabric - CADDIS
Coastal dune - DENE
Coatings - PATINAE
Coat of fur - PELAGE
Coat-of-Arms border - ORLE
Cobra's cousin - MAMBA
Cockeyed - AGEE
Cocktail flavoring - ORGEAT
Coconut fibre - COIR
Coconut flesh - COPRA
Cod's cousin - HAKE
Code of the
    Samurai - BUSHIDO
Coerse - DRAGOON
Coffeecake - KUCHEN
Cognac letters - VSOP
Coin - SPECIE
Coin of ancient
    Rome - SESTERCE
Coin of Cairo - PIASTER
Coin of Helsinki - EURO

Coin of Indian or
    Pakistan - PAISA
Coined money - SPECIE
Coins of Iceland - AURAR
Coins of old Italy - SOLDI
Cold - ALGID
Cold confection - BOMBE
Cold-weather gear - ANORAK
Cold winds - SARSARS
Collected sayings or
    Anecdotes - ANA
Collection - COTERIE
    or OMNIBUS
Collection of poems - DIVAN
Collection of primative
    poetry - EPOS
Collection of writings - ENOCH
College teacher - DOCENT
Colonial blackbirds or
    cuckoos - ANIS
Colorado peak - LAPLATA
Colorado River feeder - GILA
Colorful chalcedony - AGATE
Colorful fish - OPAH or TETRA
Colorful lizard - AGAMA
Colorful moth - LUNA
Colorful parrot - KORIKEET
Colorful perch - DARTER
Colorful pullover - DASHIKI
Coloring process - BATIK
Colorless liquid - ALDOL
Columbian conifer - PINO

Columbine - AQUILEGIA

Column base - PLINTH

Column support - ORLO
or SOCLE

Column type - ANTA

Come forth - DEBOUCH

Comet's head - COMA

Comic verse - DOGGEREL

Command - BEHEST

Commemorative
vase - AMPHORA

Common - VULGATE

Common compound - OXIDE

Common mineral - BLENDE

Common people - PLEBS

Commonplace - PROSAIC
or PROSSY

Communal cuckoo - ANI

Communion cup - AMA

Compacted coal - CANNEL

Complex image - FATA
MORGANA

Complication - NODUS

Complications - NODI

Component of fertilizer -UREA

Compound containing Element
5 - BORATE or BORIDE

Computer code - EBCDIC

Computer language - ALGOL

Computer Screen - VDU

Concave arches - TORIC

Concealed - PERDU

Concerning - ANENT

Concert hall - ODEON
or ODEUM

Concerto solo - CADENZA

Concise summary - PRESCIS

Conflicting drama - AGON

Conger - EEL

Congo River - EBOLA or UELE

Conic section - PARABOLA

Coniferous forest - TAIGA

Connection - NEXUS

Connective tissue - FACIA

Connoisseur - EPICURE

Consort of Opps - SATURN

Consorty of shiva - SHAKTI

Consort of Siva - SATI

Conspicuous success - ECLAT

Constellation near
Scorpius - ARA

Constriction of the
pupil - MIOSIS

Construe - EDUCE

Constituent of
DNA - ADENINE

Constituent of living cells - RNA

Container for
bones - OSSCIARY

Containing copper - CUPRIC

Containing gold - AURIC

Containing iron - FERRIC

Contemporary - COEVAL

Control freak - SVENGALI

Controversial - ERISTIC

Convent - PRIOY

Converging points - FOCI

Convert into soap - SAPONIFY

Convex at both
edges - GIBBOUS

Convex moulding -
OVOLO orTORI

Convincing - COGENT

Convocation of witches - ESBAT

Cooked cereal - KASHA

Cooked pheasant - SALMI

Cooked salad - SALMAGUNDI

Coot - SCOTER

Copper film - PATINA

Copycat - EPIGONE

Coral, e.g. - POLYP

Coral reef - CAY

Cordage fibre - ISTLE, JUTE,
RAMIE or SISAL

Corday's victim - MARAT

Corduroy feature - WALE

Core group - CADRE

Cormorant - SHAG

Corn lily - IXIA

Cornea's companion - SCLERA

Corner of the eye - CANTHUS

Corner stone - QUOIN

Corner stone tablets - STELAE

Cornmeal bread - TORTILLA

Cornmeal mush - SAMP

Cornmeal patty - HOECAKE

Corduroy rib - WALE

Cornice bracket - CORBEL

Corpulent - OBESE

Correct text - EMEND

Corrigenda - ERRATA

Corsican patriot - PAOLI

Corymb - CYME

Costly victory - PYRRHIC

Cosmetic material - ORRIS

Cote d'azur menu - SCAD

Coterie - SET

Cotton cloth - CHINO

Cotton fabric - KHADDAR,
LENO or PEMA

Cotton fiber - NOIL

Cotton thread - LISLE

Cotton type - PIMA

Cottonwood tree - ALAMO

Counsel - REDE

Counter stroke - REPOSTE

Country between France &
Spain - ANDORRA

Couple - DYAD

Course rug - DRUGGET

Court call - ADIN

Court decree - ARRET

Court order - MANDAMUS

Courtyard - QUAD

Cover an enbankment - REVET

Covered walk - STOA

Covered with hair - PILAR

Cow barn - BYRE

Cow corn - SILAGE

Cow genus - BOS

Cow's first stomach - RUMEN

Cows - KINE

Coxcomb - FOP

Coypu fur - NUTRIA

Crab claw - CHELA

Crane's kin - BUSTARD

Cranial nerve - VEGUS

Crayfish dish - ETOUFEE

Creative movement of the 60's - OPART

Creattor god of the Incas - VIRACOCHA

Crenshaws - MELONS

Creolized English - GULLAH

Crescent on a fingernail - LUNULA

Crescent-shaped - BICORN

Crescent shaped outline - LUNETTE

Crested bird - HOOPOE

Cretan port - CANEA

Crevasse pinnacle - SERAC

Cricket sound - CHIRR

Crime against the ruler - LESE MAJESTE

Criminal intent - MENSREA

Crisp bread - RUSK

Critical explanation - EXEGESIS

Critical study - EXAMEN

Crocodile kin - GAVIAL

Crocus part - CORM

Cromosome blueprint - GENOME

Crone - BELDAME

Cronic liar - ANANIAS

Cross - ROOD

Cross or crucifix letters - INRI

Cross country skiing - LANGLAUF

Cross threads - WOOF

Cross with a circular loop - ANKH

Crossbow - ARBALEST

Crossbeam - TRAVE

Crosshairs - RETICLE

Crosswise - ATHWART

Croud together - SERRY

Crow family member - DAW

Crow's cousin - ROOK

Crucifix - ROOD

Crude bed - DOS

Crude zinc - SPELTER

Crudely chipped flints - EOLITHS

Crushed sugarcane - BAGASSE

Crustacean - ISOPOD

Cry of the Bacchanals - EVOE

Crypic letter - RUNE

Crystal lined stone - GEODE

Crystaline material - DOLOMITE

Crystaline mineral - EPIDOTE

Crystalline rock - SCHIST

Cub Scout leader - AKELA

Cuban dance - HABANERA

Cubic meter - ARE or STERE

Cuckoo - ANI

Cuckoopint, e.g. - AROID
or ARUM

Cuckoopint & flamingo
lily - ARUMS

Cucumber, e.g. - PEPO

Culex cousin - AEDES

Cultivated land - TILLAGE

Cultural values - ETHOS

Cultured gel or culture
medium - AGAR

Cup - CALIX

Cup bearer to the gods - HEBE

Cupboard - AMBRY

Cupid - EROS or AMOR

Cupids - AMORETTI

Curling broom - BESOM

Curly pasta - ROTINI

Currant-flavored
liqueur - CASSIS

Currency of Afghanistan - PUL

Currency of Albania - LEK

Currency of Algeria - DINAR

Currency of Andorra - PESETA

Currency of Angola - LWEI

Currency of
Austria - SCHILLING

Currency of Belarus - RUBLE

Currency of Bolivia -
CENTAVO or PESO

Currency of Boswana -
PULA or THEBE

Currency of Brazil - REIS

Currency of Bulgaria - LEV
or STOTINKA

Currency of Burma -
PYA or KYAT

Currency of Cairo - POUND

Currency of Cambodia - RIEL

Currency of
Cameroon - FRANC

Currency of Cape
Verde - ESCUDO

Currency of Capetown - RAND

Currency of Chile - PESO

Currency of China - YUAN

Currency of Czecholslovakia -
HALERS or KORUNAS

Currency of
Denmark - KRONER

Currency of Ecuador - SUCRE

Currency of Egypt - PIASTRE

Currancy of Ethiopia - BIRR

Currency of Finland - PENNI

Currency of Georgia - LARI

Currency of Ghana - CEDI

Currency of
Greece - DRACHMA

Currency of Haiti - GOURDE

Currency of Iceland - KRONA

Currency of Iran - RIAL

Currency of Japan - SEN

Currency of Jordan - FILS

Currency of Kuwait - DINAR

Currency of Laos - KIP

Currancy of Lesotho - LOTI

Currency of Libya - RIAL

Currency of Malta - LIRE

Currency of
Mauritania - OUGUIYA

Currency of
Morocco - DIRHAM

Currency of Nepal - RUPEE

Currency of
Nicaragua - CORDOBA

Currency of Nigeria - NAIRA

Currancy of Norway - KRONA

Currency of Panama - BALBOA
or CENTESIMO

Currency of Pakhistan - PAISA

Currency of
Paraguay - GUARAN

Currency of Peru - INTI or SOL

Currency of Poland - ZLOTY

Currency of
Portugal - ESCUDO

Currency of Romania - LEU

Currency of Samoa -
SENE or TALA

Currency of Saudi
Arabia - RIYAL

Currency of Sierra Leone -
RIAL or LEONE

Currency of Sri Lanka - RUPEE

Currency of Sweden - KRONE

Currency of Thailand - BAHT

Currency of Tonga - PAANGA

Currency of Turkey - LIRA

Currency of
Venezuela -BOLIVAR

Currency of Vietnam - DONG

Currency of Western
Samoa - TALA

Currency of Yemen - RIAL

Currency of Yugoslavia - PARA

Curse - ANATHEMA
or WANION

Curtain fabric - NINON,
SCRIM or VOIL

Curtain material - CRETONNE
or SCRIM

Curved molding - OGEE

Curved sword - SCIMITAR

Curved timber - FUTTOCK

Customs - THEWS

Cut made by a saw - KERF

Cuttlefish ink - SEPIA

Cyclades Island - DELOS

Cylindrical - TOROSE

Cylindrical and
tapering - TERETE

Cylindrical larva - REDIA

Cymbeline's daughter - IMOGEN

Cyst - HYDATID

Czar's decree - UKASE

Czarist council - ZEMSTVO

Czech region - MORAVIA

Czech river - ELBE or ODER

DNA component - ADENINE

Dadismpioneer - ARP

Daffodil - NARCISSUS

Dagger - DIRK, PONIARD or STYLET

Dagger, in printing - OBELUS

Dagger with a wavy blade -CREESE

Daisies - ROSTRA

Dakoda dialect - OGLALA

Dakoda Indian - ARIKARA or REE

Dam - WEIR

Dance step - PAS

Dancer's handrail - BARRE

Dandruff - SCALL or SCURF

Dangerous atmosphere - MIAS MA

Dangerous mosquito - AEDES

Danish coin - ORe

Danish King - CNUTE

Danish port - ODENSE

Danube feeder - DRAVA, SAVA or SIRET

Daphni's love - CHLOE

Dark area of the moon - MARE

Dark eyed beauty - HOURI

Dark green mineral - AUGITE

Dark igneous rock - DIABAS

Dark redwood tree - TOON

Darnel - RYE GRASS

Dash - ELAN

Dassie - HYRAX

Daughter of Absalon - TAMAR

Daughter of Agamemnon - ELECTRA

Daughter of Amonasro - AIDA

Daughter of Anakin - LEIA

Daughter of Atlas - HYADES

Daughter of Cadmus - INO

Daughter of Cronus - HERA

Daughter of Dieppe - FILLE

Daughter of Geb – ISIS

Daughter of Helios - CIRCE

Daughter of Hera - HEBE

Daughter of Homer - LISA

Daughter of Hyperion - EOS or SELENE

Daughter of Jacob - DINAH

Daughter of Juan Carlos - ELENA

Daughter of Jupiter - DIANA

Daughter of King David - TAMAR

Daughter of King Juan Carlos - ELENA

Daughter of King Lear -
GONERIL or REGAN

Daughter of King
Minos - ARIADNE

Daughter of King
Pelles - ALAINE

Daughter of Laban - LEAH

Daughter of Leda - HELEN

Daughter of Loki - HEL
or HELA

Daughter of
Mnemosyne - ERATO

Daughter of
Muhammed - FATIMA

Daughter of Oceanus -
DIONNE or TELESTO

Daughter of
Oedipus - ANTIGONE

Daughter of Ops - CERES

Daughter of Pablo
Picaso - PALOMA

Daughter of Poloneus -
LAERTES or OPHILIA

Daughter of Poseidon -
EVADNE or RHODE

Daughter of
Prospero - MIRANDA

Daughter of Rhea - HERA

Daughter of Satan - CERES

Daughter of Saturn - JUNO

Daughter of Tantalus - NIOBE

Daughter of Themis - IRENE

Daughter of Zeus - ATE,
ATHENA, ERATO, HEBE,
HELEN or IRENE

Dawn diety - AURORA

Dawn goddess - EOS

Dawn song - AUBADE

Day of wrath: Lat. - DIES IRAE

Daybreak song - AUBADE

Days of yore - ELD

Dazzling display - ECLAT

Dead Sea kingdom - EDOM

Deaden - OBTUND

Deadly poison - BANE
or URARI

Deadly snake - MAMBA

Dear (Italy) - CARA

Death: pref. - NECRO

Death blow - CORP
DE GRACE

Decadent - EFFETE

Deceive - COZEN or GULL

Decendant - SCION

Deciduous conifer - LARCH

Deck post - BITT

Decorate the edge - ENGRAIL

Decorative metalwork - NIELLO

Decorative ribbon - RIBAND

Decorative tinware - TOLLE

Decortive wall basin - LAVABO

Decree - UKASE

Deductive - APRIORI

Deep blue - ANIL or PERSE

Deep dry gulch - COULEE
Deep Gorge - COULOIR
Deep orange chalcedony - SARD
Deep secrets - ARCANA
Deep sleep - SOPOR
Deer - HART
Deer tail - SCUT
Deer with three pointed
    antlers - SAMBAR
Defeat badly - LARRUP
Delhi stuffed pastry - SAMOSA
Delphinium - LARKSPUR
Demanding
    attention - CLAMANT
Demon - DJINN
Denmark's largest
    island - ZEALAND
Denpasar is its capiital - BALI
Deodar - CEDAR
Depict - LIMN
Depression in a bone - FOVEA
Descendants - SCIONS
Describe - LIMN
Desert garment - ABA
Desert or grassland - BIOME
Desert plant - AGAVE
    or EPHEDRA
Desert rodent - JERBOA
Desicated - SERE
Desiduous conifer - LARCH
Designer's studio - ATELIER
Despot - SATRAP

Destiny goddesses - FATES
Detested person - ANATHEMA
Developing - NASCENT
Devil fish - MANTA
Devotee - VOTARY
Dexterous - HABILE
Diacritical mark -
    MACRON, TILDE
or UMLAUT
Diacritical
    opposite - ANTIPODE
Diagram - SCHEMA
Dictator of ancient
    Rome - SULLA
Didactic sort - PEDAGOG
Dido's love - AENEAS
Die-shaped - CUBOID
Digestive juice - PEPSIN
Digit - DACTYL
Digitalis sourse - FOXGLOVES
Dijon dance - GAJOT
Dijon donkey - ANE
Dilapidated
    tenaments - ROOKERIES
Dill, old style - ANET
Dill seed - ANIS
Dionysus follower - MAENAD
Diplomatic
    protest - DEMARCHE
Direction, in music - SAGUE
Directly - SPANG
Disciples - ACOLYTES

Disciplinarian - MARTINET

Discomfit - ABASH

Discriminate - SACERN

Disease carrying
    mosquito - AEDES

Disgrace - ODIUM

Disgusting - UGSOME

Dish stewed in wine - SALMI

Disparaging
    comment - HUMPH

Dispatch boat - AVISO

Distainful pout - MOUE

Distribution curves - OGIVES

Divine spirit - NUMEN

Diving bird - AUK,
    GANNET, GREBE
LOON, MURRE,
    MURRELET, SCOTER,
    SKUA or SMEW

Diving duck - SCAUP
    or SCOTER

Diving sea bird - PETREL
    or MURRE

Division of a long
    poem - CANTO

Division into
    fractions - SCHISM

Do all assistant - FACTOTEM

Doctor's replacement - LOCUM

Dog family - CANID

Dog in the sky - CANIS

Dog salmon - KETA

Dogstar - SIRIUS

Dogmas - ISM

Dolphin genus - INIA

Domesticated ox - ZEBU

Domination - HEGEMONY

Don Juan's mother - INEZ

Donkey - MOKE

Donut shape - TORUS

Donut shaped - TORIC

Doodad - GEEGAW

Doorkeeper of a lodge - TILER

Doormouse - LEROT

Doorway curtain - PORTIERE

Doosie - ONER

Doric dress - CHLAMYS

Dormant volcano in
    Peru - ELMISTI

Dorsal - NOTAL

Dorsal plate - NOTUM

Dos y dos - QUATRO

Dottering - ANILE

Double - BINAL

Double crystal - MACLE

Double curve - OGEE

Double dagger - DIESIS

Double star in
    Auriga - CAPELLA

Double star in Ursa
    Major - MIZAR

Down under G.I. - ANZAC

Downhill challenge - MOGEL

Downhill run - PISTE

Downhiller's run - SCHUSS

Draft Org. - SSS

Dragon of puppetry - OLLIE

Dragonfly larva - NYMPH

Drain of color - ETIOLATE

Dramatic conflict - AGON

Drapery material - NINON

Draw a picture - LIMN

Drawstring
   handbag - RETICULE

Dreaded mosquito - AEDES

Dream: Fr. - REVE

Dreamer - FANTAST

Dregs - LEES

Dresden duck - ENTE

Dress material - NINON

Dress shape - ALINE

Dried - SERE

Dried plants - HERBERIA

Drink deeply - BIRLE

Drink of
   forgetfulness - NEPENTHE

Drivel - PAP

Dropsy - EDEMA

Dross - SCORIA

Drudge - DOGSBODY

Drudgery - MOIL

Drum set - TIMPANI

Drunkard - TOPER

Dry gully - WADI

Dry lakes - PLAYAS

Dry plaster painting - SECCO

Dry red wine - RIOJA

Drying frame - TENTER

Duck - SMEW

Duck: Ger. - ENTE

Duck genus - ANAS

Duct - VAS

Dugout: Fr. - ABRI

Dugout shelter - ABRI

Duke's domain - DUCHY

Dumplings - GNOCCHI

Dung - ORDURE

Dust particle - MOTE

Dutch cheese - LEYDEN

Dutch city - LEIDEN

Dutch city or commune - EDE

Dutch eathenware - DELFT

Dutch island - AROE

Dutch painting - STEEN

Dutch province - ZEELAND

Dutch river - IJSSEL

Dwarf buffalo - ANOA

Dwarf fish - PYGMEAN

Dying method - BATIC

Dying vat - KIER

Dynamite inventor - NOBEL

Dynasty of French
   Kings - CAPET

Eagle in the night sky - AQUILA

Eagle's home - AERIE

Ear: pre. - OTO

Earache - OTALGIA

Ear bone - INCUS

Ear drum - TYMPANUM

Eared seal - OTARY

Earlier form of a
word - ETYNOM

Early adder - ABACUS

Early Bible - ITALA

Early computer - ENIAC
or UNIVAC

Early English coin - ORA

Early Irish alphabet - OGHAM

Early Jewish ascetic - ESSENE

Early Mexican
inhabitant - OLMEC

Early podium - AMBO

Early radar - ASDIC

Early stage seed - OVULE

Earth goddess - GAEA

Earth: pre. - GEO

Earth quake - SEIS

Earth wolf - AARDWOLF

Earthenware crock - OLLA

Earthenware decorated with
Opaqueglazes - FAIENCE

Earthenware from
Holland - DELFT

Earthenware jar - CRUSE

Earthly - TERRENE

Earth's crust - HORST

Earth's crust layer - SIMA

Earthtone - OCHER

Earthworm and
leech - ANNELIDS

Earthy pigment - OCHER

Earthy substance - SIENNA

Earthy tone - OCHER

East Indian boat - DONI

East Indian gum tree - DHAVA

East Indian heartwood - SAPAN

East Indian herb - SOLA

East Indian sailor - LASCAR

East Indian swine - BABIRUSA

Easter - PASCH

Easter Island - RAPA

Eastern Church
member - UNIATE

Eastern eye makeup - KOHL

Eastern floor covering -TATAMI

Eastern Siberian - YAKUT

Eastern tip - BAKSHEESH

Eastern VIP - AGA

Easy lope - DOGTROT

Eccentric - FEY

Ecclesiastical caps - BIRETTAS

Ecclesiastical council - SYNOD

Ecclesiastical court - ROTA

Ecclesiastical
residence - DEANERY

Edging loop - PICOT

Edible - ESCULENT

Edible clam - QUAHOG

Edible corkscrews - ROTINI

Edible root - PARSNIP

Edible roots - OCAS

Edible rootstock - EDDO

Edible seaweed - ARAME, DULSE, IRISH MOSS or ULVA

Edible starchy root - JICAMA

Edible tuber - OCA, SALEP or TAR0

Edict - FIAT or UKASE

Edit - REDACT

Eelworm - NEMA

Eerie - ELDRITCH

Effeminate - EPICENE

Effluvia - MIASMA

Egg - OOCYTE

Egg, for one – GAMETE

Egg: pref. - OVI

Egg shaped - OVOID

Egg shaped ornaments - OVA

Egg white - GLAIR

Egg-laying mammal - ECHIDNA

Eggplant salad - BABAGHANOUJ

Eggs, fish & rice dish - KEDGEREE

Eggy bread - CHALLAH

Egyptian amulet or beatle - SCARAB

Egyptian Christian - COPT

Egyptian coin - PIASTER

Egyptian corn - DURRA

Egyptian cross - ANKH

Egyptian diety or god - AMENRA, AMON, AMONRA, ATEN, HORUS, OSIRIS, PYAH, SEB or SHU

Egyptian god of evil - SET

Egyptian god of music - BES

Egyptian god of the Underground - OSIRIS

Egyptian god of tombs - ANUBIS

Egyptian god of the universe - AMENRA

Egypian goddess of magic - ISIS

Egyptian king of the dead - OSIRIS

Egyptian pharaoh - RAMSES

Egyptian sacred bull - APIS

Egyptian solar disk - ATEN

Egyptian sun god - AMENRA, ATEN or HORUS

Egyptian symbol of life - ANKH

Egyptian temple site - LUXOR

Egyptian underworld god - OSIRIS

Egyptian underworld queen - ISIS

Egyptian weight - ARDEB or KANTAR

Eight: Fr. - HUIT

Eight: (Italy) - OTTO

Eight: pref. - OCTA

Eight on the mohs
    scale - TOPAZ

Elaborate decoration -
    FROU FROU

Elaborate operetic solo - SCENA

Elaborate tapestry - ARRAS

Elbe feeder - EGER

Eldritch - EERIE

Electric battery
    inventor - VOLTA

Electric cat fish - RAAD

Electric horn - KLAXON

Electric measure - VOLT

Electrical unit - FARAD,
    GAUSS or TESLA

Electrical unit of
    conductance - MHO

Electrified particle - ION

Electron tube - TRIODE

Electronic control
    system -SERVO

Elegently designed - SOIGNE

Element #1 - HYDROGEN

Element #5 - BORON

Element #10 - NEON

Element #16 - SULFUR

Element #20 - CALCIUM

Element #24 - CHROMIUM

Element #25 - MANGANESE

Element #26 - IRON

Element #27 - COBALT

Element #29 - COPPER

Element #30 - ZINC

Element #33 - ARSENIC

Element #34 - SELENIUM

Element #35 - BROMINE

Element#39 - YTTRIUM

Element #45 - RHODIUM

Element #50 - TIN

Element #53 - IODINE

Element #54 - XENON

Element #56 - BARIUM

Element #65 - TERBIUM

Element #68 - ERBIUM

Element #72 - HAFNIUM

Element #75 - RHENIUM

Element #76 - OSMIUM

Element #77 - IRIDIUM

Element #79 - GOLD

Element #80 - MERC

Element #83 - BISMUTH

Element #86 - RADON

Element #99 - EINSTEINIUM

Element #100 - FERMIUM

Element used in
    alloys - YTTRIUM

Elementary particle - BOSON,
    LEPTON or MUON

Elephant goad - ANKUS

Elephant man - MAHOUT

Elephant's tiny kin -HYDRAX

Elevated tract of open
    country - WOLD

Elicit - EDUCE

Emancipate - MANUMIT

Embarrass - DISCOMFIT

Embropmoc sac - AMNION

Embroidery frame - TAMBOUR

Embroidery edging or
    loop - PICOT

Embroidery yarn - CREWEL

Emerald - BERYL

Emetic agent - IPECAC

Empedolcles last stand - AETNA

Emperor after
    Kaligula - CLAUDIUS

Emperor after Galba - OTHO

Emperor after
    Trajan - HADRIAN

Emperor of China - YAO

Empress of Byzantium - IRENE

Emu or rhea - RATITE

Enamalware - TOLE

Encampment - LAAGER

Enchanted - FEY

Encircles - GIRTS

Enclosed areas - VERGES

Enclosed part of a
    blimp - NACELLE

Enclosed passage in a
    church - NARTHEX

Enclosed within
    walls - IMMURE

Encore - BIS

Endangered antelope - ORYX

Endangered buffalo - ANOA

End of small intestine - ILEUM

Endive - ESCAROLE

Endure - DREE

Ends - OMEGAS

England, in poems - ALBION

English bard - SCOP

English cathedral city - ELY

English Channel Island - SARK

English cheese - STILTON

English dishboard - FACIA

English horn - COR

English monk - BEDE

English river - EXE

English seaport - DOVER

Entity's manifestation - AVATAR

Entomb - INTER or INURN

Entrance gallery - LOGGIA

Entrance to Hades - AVERNO

Entreat - OBTEST

Enzyme ending - ASE

Envoy - LEGATE

Enzyme
    stimulent - COFACTOR

Epic poem - ILIAD

Epoch - ERA

Equatorial's opposite - AXIAL

Equilateral
    parallelograms - RHOMBI

Equivocate - PALTER

Ermine - STOAT

Eros' love - PSYCHE

Eskimo craft - UMIAK

Eskimo knife - ULU

Eskimo settlement - ETAH

Esau's grandson - OMAR

Esau's twin - JACOB

Espresso server - BARISTA

Essayist - ELIA

Essential constituent of both
RNA & DNA - GUANINE

Essential oil - ATTAR

Ethiopian prince or title – RAS

Ethiopian money - BIRR

Eucharistic vessel - PYX

Eucharistic
vestment - MANIPLE

Eurasian crows - DAWS

Eurasian deer - ROES

Eurasian duck - SMEW

Eurasian falcons- SAKERS

Eurasian fish - LOACH

Eurasian forest - TAIGA

Eurasian grass - REDTOP

Euroasian mountains - URAL

Eurasian primrose - OXLIP

Euransian
ruminant - ROEDEER

Eurasian sandpiper - REE

Eurasian tree - OLEANSTER

Europe's largest lake -
BALATON or LADOGA

European barracuda - SPEC

European blackbird -
MERL or OUZEL

European canary - SERIN

European card game - OMBRE

European ciema - KINO

European cows - DAWS

European crow - CHOUGH

European doormouse - LEROT

European eagle - ERN

European ermine - STOAT

European finch - SERIN

European flowering
tree - OLEASTER

European gull - MEW

European lake - ONEGA

European mint - HYSSOP

European
plantain - FLEAWORT

European polecat - FERRET

European shore
bird - DOTTEREL

European
songbird - WOODLARK

European thrush - MERLE
or MISTLE

European tree - SORB

European water bird - OUSEL

European weed - GOAT'S
BEARD

European wheat - SPELT

Evening bell or star - VESPER

Evergreen - YEW

Evergreen oak - HOLM

Evergreen of the Pacific
Northwest - MADRONO

Evergreen shrub- ILEX
or TOYON

Evolutionary
theory - COSMISM

Ewe's-milk cheese - PECORINA

Exact opposites - ANTIPODES

Exaggerated pride - HUBRIS

Examine by touch - PALPATE

Excessive flow of
saliva - PTYALISM

Exchange premium - AGIO

Excretes - EGESES

Execate - ABHOR

Exhausted - EFFETE

Exodys figure - AARON

Exodus hero - ARI

Expert - MAVEN

Expert hunter - NIMROD

Exploit - GESTE

Explosive - TONITE

Explosive compound - AMATOL

Explosive gas - FIREDAMP

Explosive
ingredient - TOLUENE

Expressively, in
music - RUBATO

External boundary - AMBIT

Extinct bird - DODO or MOA

Extract - ELUTE

Extremely dry - XERIC

Eye annoyances - MOTES

Eyeball coat - SCLERA

Eye lashes - CILIA

Eyelike spots - OCELLI

Eye makeup - KOHLS

Eye membrane - SCLERA

Eye part - CORNIA, IRIS,
RETINA or UVEA

Eyeball covering - SCLERA

Eyelike spots - OCELLI

Eyes - OCULI

Fabled bird - ROC

Fabric dyeing technique - BATIC

Fabric finish - PLISSE

Facade part - CEDILLA

Facing a glacier - STOSS

Fading away - EVANESCING

Fair hiring initials - EEO

Fairylike creature - PERI

Fairy king - OBERON

Fairy queen - MAB or TITANIA

Fake pearl - OLIVET

Falconry strap - JESS

False argument - SOPHISM

False god - BAAL

False report - CANARD

Falsely blamed - TRADUCED

Famed hostess - MESTA

Fancy cakes - GATEAUX

Fancy marbles - TAWS

Fancy timepiece - HOROLOGE

Far East weight - TAEL

Farewell - VALE

Far flying seabird - PETREL

Farm cart - WAIN

Fast, in music - MOSSO

Fast and exciting, in music AGITATO

Fast vibreto, in music - TREMOLO

Fat - ADIPOSE or LIPO

Fat component - OLEIN

Fatal bacteria - ANTHRAX

Father of Abraham - TERAH

Father of Achiles - PELEUS

Father of Agamemnon - ATREUS

Father of Ahab - OMRI

Father of Ajax - TELAMON

Father of Antigone - OEDIPUS

Father of Aaron - AMRAN

Father of Balder - ODIN

Father of Cainan - ENOS

Father of Cassandra - PRIAM

Father of Charlemagne - PEPIN

Father of Dauphin - ROI

Father of Deimos - ERES

Father of Diomedes - ARES

Father of Electra - AGAMEMNON

Father of Eleazar - AARON

Father of Eliphax - ENOS

Father of Enos - SETH

Father of Esau - ISAAC

Father of Fauvism - MATISSE

Father of Hannibal - AGAMEMNON

Father of Harmonia - ARES

Father of Hector - PRIAM

Father of Horus - OSIRIS

Father of Icarus - DAEDALUS

Father of Isaac - ABRAHAM

Father of Jacob - ISAAC

Father of Japheth - NOAH

Father of John the Baptist - ZACHARIAS

Father of Joseph - JACOB

Father of Juliet - CAPULET

Father of Junipero - TERRA

Father of King Arthur - UTHER

Father of King David - JESSE

Father of King Harald - OLAV

Father of Leah - LABAN

Father of Menelaus - ATREUS

Father of Methuselah - ENOCH

Father of Moab - LOT

Father of Moses - AMRAN

Father of Niobe - TANTALUS

Father of Odysseus - LAERTES

Father of Paris - PRIAM

Father of Phobos - ARES

Father of Rachel - LABAN

Father of Regan - LEER

Father of Reuel - ENOS
Father of Romulus - MARS
Father of Seth - ADAM
Father of Teucer - TELAMON
Father of Theseus - AEGEUS
Father of Thor - ODIN
Father of Zeus - CRONUS
Father of the gods - AMENRA
Father of the Muses - ZEUS
Father of the Titans - URANUS
Fatty - ADIPOSE
Fatty acid - OLEIC or
    STEARATE
Fatty compound - LIPID
Faultfinder of
    Olympus - MOMUS
Faux pas - GAFFE
FDR's dog - FALA
Fe - IRON
Fear of
    foreigners - XENOPHOBIA
Feared mosquito - AEDES
Feast of lots - PURIM
Feathered head
    ornament - AIGRETTE
Febrile condition - AGUE
Felt sunhat - TERAI
Felt-like fabric - BAIZE
Female advisor - EGERIA
Female demon - LAMIA
Female donkey - JENNET
Female fox - VIXEN

Female gamete - OVUM
Female lovers - INAMORATES
Female
    Pharaoh - HATSHEPSUT
Female prophet - SIBYL
Female red deer - HIND
Female ruff - REE or REEVE
Female sandpiper - REE
Female surfer - WAHINE
Female swan - PEN
Female swimmer - NAIAD
Female vampire - LAMI
Female water sprite - UNDINE
Fence pickets - PILING
Fencing dummy - PEL
Fencing feint - APPEL
Fencing foil - EPEE or
    FLEURET
Fermented foam - BARM
Fern-like plant - CYCAD
Fertile earth - MARL
Fertile loam - LOESS
Fertility god - BAAL
Fertilizer compound or
    ingredient - UREA
    or BONEASH
Fertilizer sourse - GUANO
Fertilizer type - MARL
Fettering - GYVING
Feudal estate - FIEFDOM
Feudal land - FIEF

Feudal lord - LIEGE, MESNE or THANE

Feudal serf or worker - ESNE

Feverish - FEBRILE

Fiber - NEP or RAFFIA

Fiber palm - RAFFIA

Fiber plant - ABACA, ALOE, HEMP or THANEX

Fictional ring bearer - FRODO

Field mouse - VOLE

Fiery root - WASABI

Fifth canonical hour - NONES

Fifth pillar of Islam - HAJ

Fig genus - FICUS

Figure eight scale on a globe - ANALEMMA

Figure of speach - TROPE

Film - PATINA

Film fan - CINEAST

Filthy lucre - PELF

Finales - CODAS

Finch - SERIN

Find fault - CAVIL

Fine - AMERSE

Fine cigar - CLARO

Fine cotton - PIMA

Fine grained rock - TRAP

Fine twilled linen - DAMASK

Fine violin - AMATI

Finely ground gypsum - TERRAALBA

Finger or toe - DACTYL

Finger pressure - SHIATSU

Fingernail crescent - LUNULA

Finial - EPI

Finsh seaport - TURKU

Firecracker - PETARD

Fireopal - GIRASOL

Fireplace - INGLE

Fireplace projection or shelf - HOB

First book of prophets - HOSEA

First Chinese capitol - NARA

First computer - ENIAC

First canonical hour - MATIN

First family of Florence - MEDICI

First Hebrew king - SAUL

First King of Egypt - MENES

Firth of Clyde Island - ARRAN

Fish eating bird – LOON

Fish eating duck - SMEW

Fish genus - AMIA

Fish hawk - OSPREY

Fish serving - SASHIMI

Fishing line - SNELL

Fishing net - SEINE

Fistic Muslim - ALI

Flaky pastry - FILO or PHYLLO

Flanders River - YSER

Flask - DEWAR

Flat bread of India - NAN

Flat fish - DAB, PLAICE
or SKATE

Flat nosed antelope - SAIGA

Flat plinth - ORLO

Flavored wine - KIR or NEGUS

Flavorful - SAPID

Flaw - WART

Flax filament - HARL

Flax-like fiber - RAMIE

Flea genus - TUNGA

Fleet of ships - ARGOSY

Flemish capital - GHENT

Flemish River - YSER

Fleshy fruit - PEPO

Fleshy stone fruit - DRUPE

Fleur-de-lis - IRIS

Fleuret - EPEE

Flight of Mohammed - HEGIRA

Flightless bird - RHEA

Flintlock musket - FUSIL

Flint-like rock - CHERT

Flip over - OBVERT

Flock of geese - SKEIN

Flora and fauna - BIOTA

Floral specialist - ROSARIAN

Florence fennel - FINOCCHIO

Florentine palace - PITTI

Florid musical
passage - BRAVURA

Flower arrangement -
RACEME or UMBEL

Flower cluster - AMENT,
CATKIN, RACEME
or UMBEL

Flower of the
southwest - PENOLE

Flower part - CALYX,
NECTARY or SEPAL

Flower polyp - ANEMONE

Flowing moss - PYXIE

Flower spike - AMENT

Flowering tree - CATALPA

Fluid carrier - VENA

Fly - AVIATE

Fly before the wind - SCUD

Fly catcher - PHOEBE

Fly catching bird - PEWEE

Flying flock of geese - SKEIN

Foam - SPUME

Focal point - NODE

Fodder grass - MILLET
or SORGO

Folk medicine plant - BONESET

Follow without
interruption - SEGUE

Follower of Zeno - STOIC

Fondle - COSSET

Food - ALIMENT

Food-coloring plant - SAFFRON

Food fish - BASS, CERO,
HADDOCK, HAKE, IDE,
LING, PERCH, PIKE,
SCUP, SHAD, SMELT,
SNAPPER, SOLE or TUNA

Food of forgetfulness - LOTUS
Food of the gods - AMBROSIA
Food stuf from orchids - SALEP
Fool, of yore - MOME
Foolish - GLAIKIT
Foot bones - TARSI
Footless - APODAL
Footlike part - PES
Footnote abbr. - ETSEQ or IBID
Footnote word - IBIDEM
For both sexes - EPICENE
Forage crop - SOYA
Forage legume - GUAR
Forbidden City - LHASA
Force - DINT
Forcefully - AMAIN
Forcible seizure of
    property - RAPINE
Foreboding
    atmosphere - MIASMA
Foreigner to Honolulu - HAOLE
Foreigner: pref. - XENO
Forerunner of the KGB - OGPU
Forest diety - PA
Forest of evergreens - PINERY
Forested area - SILVA
Foretell - AUGUR or SPAE
Foreword - PROEM
Forgetfulness - LETHE
Fork-tailed flier - KITE
Form of boxing - SAVATE

Form of sugar - HEXXOS
Formal assumption - LEMMA
Formal
    pronouncements - DICTA
Formally, once - ERST
Formative seed - OVULE
Former African
    kingdom - ASHANTI
Former African rulers - DEYS
Former capital of
    Spain - TOLEDO
Former British
    coin - FARTHING
Former capital of Japan - EDO,
    KYOTO or NARA
Former capital of
    Kazakhstan - ALMAATA
Former coin of Iran - KRAN
Former French coin - ECU
Former Hungarian
    coin - PENGO
Former Latvian coins - LATI
Former part of
    USSR - KAZAKHSTAN,
    KYRGYZSTAN,
    TAJIKISTAN or
    UZBEKISTAN
Former Puruvian
    currency - INTL
Former Queen of Jordan - ALIA
Former Queen of Spain - ENA
Former Spanish coin - DOBLA,
    DURO or REAL

Former weight for wool - TOD

Formerly, formerly - ERST
    or WHILOM

Forskers of the
    Faith - APOSTATES

Fort parts - REDOUCTS

Forte - METIER

Fortification - REDAN

Fossil resin - AMBER or COPAL

Foul smelling - OLID

Found in lakes - LACUSTRINE

Founder of
    Babylon - SEMIRAMIS

Founder of Stoicism - ZENO

Four fluid ounces - GILL

Four pence - GROAT

Foursome - TETRAD

Fourteen line poem - RONDEL

Fourth caliph - ALI

Fragrant, of old - OLENT

Fragrant gum - TOLU

Fragrant ointment - NARD

Fragrant oleoresin - ELEMI

Fragrant resin - ELEMI
    or TOLU

Fragrant rootstock - ORRIS

Framework - CADRE
    or SCHEMA

Frankish - SALIC

Fraulein's frock - DIRNDL

Freckle - LENTIGO

Free from slavery - MANUMIT

Freezing - GELID

French apartment
    payments - RENTES

French brandy - ARMAGNAC

French bread - BRIOCHE

French card game - ECARTE

French cathedral city - METZ,
    NIMES or ROUEN

French cavalryman - SPAHI

French city - STLO

French clergyman - ABBE

French coins - ECUS

French comune - CAEN

French cop - FLIC

French corp. - CIE

French department -
    ISERE or ORNE

French earl - COMPE

French eye - OEIL

French goose - OIE

French help - AMOI

French inn - AUBERGE

French lace - VAL

French landscape
    painter - COROT

French lawmaking
    group - SENAT

French leather - CUIR

French military leader - NEY

French noble - COMTE
    or VICOMTE

French patron saint - DENIS

French port - CALAIS

French possessive pronoun - SES

French queen - REINE

French river - AISNE, ISERE, LOIRE, OISE or ORNE

French seaport - BREST

French smell - ODEUR

French soldier - POILU

French soldiers - ARMEE

French soldier's hats - KEPIS

French stew - RATATOUILLE

French story - ETAGE

French textile city LILLE

French vineyard - CRU

French wine region - ALSACE

Frenchman's income - RENTE

Frenchmen - GAULS

Frenzied female - MAENAD

Frequency distributions - OGIVES

Freshwater crustacean - ISOPOD

Freshwater fish - BURBOT, DACE, PLATY or ROACH

Freshwater green algae - DESMID

Freshwater mussel - UNIO

Freshwater polyps - NYDRAE

Friend of Job - ELIHU

Friction match - FUSEE or LOCOFOCO

Friend of Hamlet's - HORATIO

Frilly hat - MOBCAP

Frog genus - RANA

From oil - OLEIC

Froth - SPUME

Froyd - FROZEN YOGURT

Frozen desert - BOMBE

Fruit cakes - SIMNELS

Fruit decay - BLET

Fruit of the maple tree - SAMARA

Fruit of the rowan - SORB

Fruit salt - CITRATE

Fruit type - UVA

Fuji footwear - ZORI

Fulda river feeder - EDER

Full of cracks - RIMOSE

Full of froth - SPUMY

Full of wisdom - SAPIENT

Full skirt - DIRNDL

Fulmar - PETREL

Funeral music - DIRGE

Fungi reproduction - ISOGAMY

Fur trader - FELLMONGER

Furies, in Greek myth - DIRAE or ERINYES

Furry - PILOSE

Fur-trimmed cloak - PELISSE

Future ovum - OOCYTE

Gabled window - DORMER

Gaea, for one - GODDESS

Gaelic - ERSE

Gaelic sea god - LER

Galatea's beloved - ACIS

Gallic goose - AIE

Gambling expert - SCARNE

Game akin to
     Pinochle - BEZIQUE

Game fish - CERO

Game point, in tennis - ADIN

Game ragout - SALMI

Gamets - OVA

Gaming table cover - BAIZE

Gannet goose - SOLAN

Gap - LACUNA

Gaping grin - RICTUS

Garb for Ghandi - DHOTI

Garden pest genus - APHI

Garden rocket - ARUGULA

Garden tool - DIBBLE

Garden trumpet - DATURA

Gargantua creator - RABELAIS

Garland, old style - ANADEM

Garland for the head -
     ANADEM or CHAPLET

Garlic mayonnaise or
     sauce - AIOLI

Gauzy fabric - LENO

Gazelle hound - SALUKI

Geisha's instrument - SAMISEN

Gelded male pigs - GALTS

Gelling agent - AGAR

Gem faces - CULETS

Gemlike stone - SARD

Gemsbok - ORYX

Gemstone - LAPIS

Genetic enzyme - RNASE

Geneva's lake - LEMAN

Genre - SORT

Gentle slope - GLACIS

Genuine - PUKKA

Genuine: Ger. - ECHT

Genus of birds - PITTA

Genus of cattle - BOS

Genus of dogs - CANIS

Genus of frogs - ANURA

Genus of furs - ABIES

Genus of geese - ANSER

Genus of grass - AVENA

Genus of hawks - ACCIPTER

Genus of herbs - GILIA

Genus of heather – ERICA

Genus of lizards - AGAMA

Genus of olives - OLEA

Genus of palms - ARENGA

Genus of
     sagebrush - ARTIMESIA

Genus of sheep - OVIS

Genus of showy
     plants - SCABIOSA

Genus of shrubs - BERBERIS

Genus of species - TAXON

Geological epoch - EOCENE
     or MIOCENE

Geological period - AXOIC
     or NEOCENE

Geological ridge - ESKER

Geometric Buddhist designs - MANDELAS

Geometric curve - PARABOLA

Geometric figure - RHOMBUS

Geometric structure - FRACTAL

Geraint'slady - ENID

German article - DER

German basin - SAAR

German city - HALLE

German coal region - SAAR

German folk songs - LIEDER

German for Germans - DEUTSCH

German fruit bread - STOLLEN

German industrial region - SAAR

German porcelain - MEISSEN

German port - KIEL

German river - EDER, EGER or EMS

German seaport - EMDEN

German wine - RHENISH

Germanic god of thunder - DONAR

Germanic god of war - TIU

Germanic water spirit - NIXIE

Getup and go - BRIO

Giant in Norse mythology - YMIR

Giant with a hundred eyes - ARGUS

Ginger plants - CURCUMAS

Giraffe relative - OKAPI

Girasol - OPAL

Girl Scout emblem - TREFOIL

Give off - EGEST

Glacial deposit - MORAINE

Glacial groove - STRIA

Glacial mass - SERAC

Glacial pinnacle or ridges - ESKER, OSAR or SERAC

Glacial snow - NEVE

Gladly - LIEF

Glass: Fr. - VERRE

Glass component - SILICA

Glassmaker's oven - LEHR

Glass-polishing powder - CERIA

Gliding dance step - CHASSE

Gloomy - STYGIAN

Gloomy and obscure - TENEBROUS

Goat antelope - SEROW

Goat of Asia - SEROW

Goat cheese - CHEVRE or FETA

Goat legged diety - FAUN

Goatlike antelope - SAIGA

God of Agriculture - SATURN

God of commerse or cunning - HERMES

God of discord - LOKI

God of doorways - JANUS

God of fertility - BAAL or DIONYSUS

God of fire - AGNI or LOGI

God of Hades - ORCUS

God of India - KRISHNA

God of lightning - THOR

God of love - CUPIOD,
    EROS or KAMA

God of marriage - HYMAN

God of Memphis - PTAH

God of mischief - LOKI

God of music - APOLLO

God of old Memphis - PTAH

God of passion - EROS

God of pleasure - BES

God of ridicule - MOMUS

God of sleep - HYPNOS

God of Spain - DIOS

God of Strife - TYR

God the ancients - DAEMON

God of the east wind - EURUS

God of the heavens - ZEUS

God of the
    Incas - VIRACOCHA

God of the lower world - DIS

God of the north
    wind - BOREAS

God of Thebes - AMON

God of the sea - AEGIR, LER,
    NEPTUNE or POSEIDEN

God of the sun - ATEN,
    HELIOS or SOL

Godof the underworld -
    DIS or PLUTO

God of the universe - AMENRA

God of the winds - AEOLUS

God of wine - DIONYSUS

God of thunder - DONAR,
    INDRA or THOR

God of war - ARES,
    TIU or TYR

God of war, magic &
    poetry - ODIN

God of wisdom - THOTH

God's blood - ICHOR

Goddess of abundance - OPS

Goddess of agriculture -
    CERES or DEMETER

Goddess of beauty - VENUS

Goddess of chance - TYCHE

Goddess of child
    bearing - HERA

Goddess of childbirth -
    DIANA or HERA

Goddess of criminal folly - ATE

Goddess of dawn -
    AURORA or EOS

Goddess of destiny - FATES,
    FORTUNA, NORN
    or URD

Goddess of discord -
    ATE or ERIS

Goddess of divine
    retribution - NEMESIS

Goddess of earth - GAEA

Goddess of fate - NORN

Goddess of fertility - ASTARTE or ISIS

Goddess of folly - ATE

Goddess of fortune - TYCHE

Goddess of fruit trees - POMONA

Goddess of hades - HECATE

Goddess of healing - EIR

Goddess of hope - SPES

Goddess of justice - ASTRAEA

Goddess of love - APHRODITE, ASTART or VENUS

Goddess of love poetry - ERATO

Goddess of magic - ISIS

Goddess of marriage - JUNO

Goddess of mischief - ERIN

Goddess of nature - ISIS

Goddess of night - NOX

Goddess of Norse myth - NURN

Goddess of peace - IRENE or PAX

Goddess of plenty - OPS

Goddess of recklessness - ATE

Goddess of sorcery - HECATE

Goddess of strife - DISCORDIA or ERIS

Goddess of the earth - GAEA or RHEA

Goddess of the harvest - CERES, DEMETER or OPS

Goddess of the hearth - HESTIA or VESTA

Goddess of the hunt - ARTEMIS or DIANA

Goddess of the moon - ARTEMIS, DIANA, HECATE or SELENE

Goddess of the Nile - ISIS

Goddess of the rainbow - IRIS

Goddess of the seasons - HORAE

Goddess of the underworld - HECATE

Goddess of vengance - NEMESIS

Goddess of victory - NIKE

Goddess of war - ATHENA, ENYO or SELLONA

Goddess who loved Odysseus - CIRCE

Goddess of wisdom - ATHENA

Goddess of witchcraft - HECATE

Goddess of Youth - HEBE

Goddess with an owl - ATHENA

Goddess with cow horns - ISIS

Gods of ancient Rome - DEI

Gold braid - ORRIS

Gold coin of ancient Rome - SOLIDUS

Gold coin of old - DUCAT

Gold: Sp. - ORO

Gold/Silver alloy - ELECTRUM

Golden - AURIC

Golden tin alloy - ORMOLU

Golf ball covering - BALATA

Golf term - DORMIE

Gong - TAMTAM

Goose - BRANT

Goosefoot plant - ORACH

Goose genus - ANSER

Gorge - ARROYO

Gormet delight - VIAND

Gormet mushroom - ENOKI

Gothic arch - OGIVE

Gourd-like plant - CUCURBIT

Government by a
few - OLIGARCHY

Govt. org. - USIA

Graceful girl - SYLPH

Grafting shoot - SCION

Grain awn - ARISTA

Grain beard - AWN

Grain blight - ERGOT

Grain bristles - ARISTAE

Grain diety - SERES

Grain sorghum - KAFIR

Granada governess - DUENNA

Granada greeting - HOLA

Grand - HOMERIC

Grand dame - DOYEN

Grand slam - VOLE

Grandchild of Japanese
Immigrants - SANSEI

Grandfather of
Abraham - NAHOR

Grandfather of Omar - ESAU

Grandfather of Saul - NER

Grandma Moses first
name - ANNA

Grandmother to Caesar - AVIA

Grandson of Abraham - JACOB

Grandson of Jacob - ERI

Grandson of
Methuselah - NOAH

Granitelike rock - GNEISS

Grape, e.g. - UVA

Grapefruit hybrid - UGLI

Grapefruit kin - POMELO

Graph line - YAXIS

Grass or sedge stem - CULM

Grassland - LEA

Grassland area - PAMPA

Grasslike plant - SEDGE

Grassy area - SWARD

Grassy plain - LLANO

Gravelly ridges - OSAR

Gravid - PREGNANT

Gray haired - HOARY

Gray horse - DUN

Gray mineral - TRONA

Grayish green - RESEDA

Grayish blend of colors - LOVAT

Grayish brown
duck - GADWALL

Graylags - GEESE

Greaseproof paper - GLASSINE

Great barrier island - OTEA

Great helmsman
follower - MAOIST

Great: Lat. - MAGNA

Great lakes whitefish - CISCO

Great mosque site - ALEPPO

Greater Omenta - CAULS

Grecian Theater - ODEA

Greedy - ESURIENT or
RAPACIOUS

Greek - ARGIVE or HELLENE

Greek adviser - NESTOR

Greek aurora - EOS

Greek cafe - TAVERNERA

Greek cheese - FETA

Greek city/state - POLIS

Greek colonade - STOA

Greek colony - IONIA

Greek community - DEME

Greek concert site - ODEA

Greek concubines - HETAERAE

Greek contest - AGON

Greek cross - TAU

Greek demigod - SATYR

Greek dessert - BAKLAVA

Greek diety - HERMES

Greek drink - RETSINA

Greek earth goddess - HECATE

Greek flask - OLPE

Greek goat god - PAN

Greek goddess - ATHENA,
HERA or ORNYX

Greek goddess of the
moon - SELENE

Greek harp - TRIGON

Greek heaven - URANUS

Greek horseshoe - OMEGA

Greek island - CRETE, DELOS
KITHERA, SAMOS or TINOS

Greek lasagna - MOUSSAKA

Greek letter - ALPHA (1),
BETA(2), CHI(22),
DELTA(4), EPSILON(5),
ETA(7), GAMMA(3),
IOTA(9), KAPPA(10),
LAMBDA(11), MU(12),
NU(13), OMEGA(24),
OMICRON(15), PHI(21),
PI(16), PSI(23), SIGMA(18),
RHO(17), TAU(19),
THETA(8), UPSILON(20),
XI(14) or ZETA(6).

Greek legislature - BOULE

Greek lyric poem - EPODE

Greek lyric poet - SAPPHO

Greek marketplace - AGORA

Greek monster - LAMIA

Greek monument - SELA

Greek mount - ATHOS

Greek P - RHO

Greek peak - OSSA

Greek penny - LEPTA

Greek philospher DIOGENES, TIMON or ZENO

Greek Physician - GALEN

Greek portico - STOA

Greek resistance movement- ELAS

Greek/Roman god - APOLLO

Greek sculptor - PHIDIAS

Greek sorceress - MEDEA

Greek T - IOTA

Greek temple - NAOS

Greek under ground river - LETHE

Greek war god - ARES

Greek warrior - AJAX

Greek weeper - NIOBE

Greek weight units - OBOLI

Greek wind god - AEOLUS

Greek wine - RETSINA

Greek wine flask - OLPE

Greek woods god - PAN

Green - VERDANT or VIRID

Green fly - APHID

Green gem - BERYL or PERIDOT

Green, in heraldy - VERT

Green parrots - KEAS

Green turtles - CHELONIA

Greenbrier - SMILAX

Greenhorn - NAIF

Greenish cheese - SAPSAGO

Greenish sloths - STIKINE

Gribble - ISOPOD

Grimace - MOUE

Groom: var. - OSTLER

Groove - STRIA

Group fund - TONTINE

Group of badgers - CETE

Group of eight - OCTAD or OCTIVE

Group of five - PENTAD

Group of four - TETRAD

Group of frogs - ARMY

Group of geese - GAGGLE or SKEIN

Group of larks - BEVY

Group of nine - NONET or ENNEAD

Group of one hundred - SENATE

Group of pheasants - NIDE

Group of poems - EPOS

Group of quail - BEVY

Group of seven - HEPTAD or SEPTET

Group of six - HEXAD

Group of three - TRIAD or TRINE

Group of toads - KNOT

Group of turtles - BALE

Group of twenty - SCORE

Group of two - DYAD

Grow together - ACCRETE

Growing around
    rocks - SAXATILE

Growing old - SENESCENT

Growl - GNAR

Guardian spirits - LARES

Guest bungalow - CASITA

Guidonian note - ELA

Guilded - AUREATE

Guinea pig - CAVY

Guitar cousin - SAMISEN

Guitar device - CAPO

Guitar solo - RIFF

Gulch - COULEE

Gulf of Aden vessel - DHOW

Gullet - MAW

Gullible one - NAIF

Gulliver's first name - LEMUEL

Gully - NULLAH

Gum Arabic tree - ACACIA

Gum base - CHICKLE

Gum resin - ELEMI

Gum-producing plant - GUAR

Gunundrum's husband
    or victim - ATLI

Gunwale pin - THOLE

Guru's community or
    retreat - ASHRAM

Gutta-Percha
    alternative - BALATA

Guttersnipe - GAMIN

Gypsy - CALO or ROMANY

Gypsy males - ROMS

Gyro compass
    inventor - SPERRY

Habit - WONT

Hacienda room - SALA

Haggis ingredient - OATS

Hair covering - MANTILLA

Hair protein - KERATIN

Hairlike structure - PILUS

Hairy - HIRSUTE or PILOSE

Hairy ox - YAK

Half - MOIETY

Half a cone - NAPP

Half a decade - LUSTRUM

Half a Zwei - EINS

Half brother of Athena - ARES

Half-goat man - FAUN
    or SATYR

Half eagle, half lion
    creature - GRIFFIN

Half note - MINIM

Hallux - TOE

Halogen compound - HALIDE

Halogen salt - IODATE

Hamite - AGAO

Hamlet - DORP or THORP

Hamlet's home - ELSINORE

Ham's relative - CBER

Hand died fabric - BATIK

Hand operated mill - QUERN

Hand tied fly - HERL

Hand woven rugs - RYAS

Handel opera - SEMELE

Handrail post - NEWEL

Hands: Sp. - MANO

Hang fire - PEND

Hanging basket
    plant - VERBENA

Hanoi dress - AODAI

Happiness - EUDAEMONIA

Hard, crisp bread - RUSK

Hard, crumbly cheese - ASIAGO

Hard money - SPECIE

Hard liquor - ARAK
    or ARRACK

Hard resin - COPAL

Hard rubber - EBONITE

Hardy wheat - SPELT

Hare constelation - LEPUS

Harem - SERAGLIO,
    SERAI or ZENANA

Harem room - ODA

Harness part - HAME

Harness ring - TERRET

Harpsicor - CEMBALO

Harridan - SHREW

Harshness - ASPERITY

Hartebeest - TORA

Harvest blubbler - FLENSE

Hat ornament - TORSADE

Hatred - ANIMUS

Haul with tackle - BOUSE
    or BOWSE

Hautboy - OBOE

Having a ragged edge - EROSE

Having five sharps - INB

Having handles - ANSATE

Having no key - ATONAL

Having wings - ALAR

Hawaiian acacia - JOA

Hawaiian beverage - KAVA

Hawaiian bird - KIWI or NENE

Hawaiian carving - TIKI

Hawaiian chant - MELE

Hawaiian cloth - TAPA

Hawaiian coffee - KONA

Hawaiian cooking pit - IMU

Hawaiian goose - NENE

Hawaiian grass - HILO

Hawaiian hawk - IOS

Hawaiian island - KAUAI,
    LANAI or OAHU

Hawaiian non-native - HAOLE

Hawaiian song - MELE

Hawaiian thrush - OMAO
    or SHAMA

Hawaiian tree - KOA

Hawaiian tuber - TARO

Hawaiian tuna - AHI

Hawaian VIP - KAHUNA

Hawaiian wind - KONA

Hawk cage - MEW

Hawk-headed god - HORUS

Hawk parrot - HIA

Hay wagon - WAIN

Headache remedy - APC

Head band - BANDEAU

Head wreath - ANADEM

Headland - NESS

Healthful - SALUTARY

Healthy: Fr. - SAIN

Healing herb - COMFREY

Heart chamber - ATRIA

Hearth - INGLE

Heat resistant
    material - CERMET

Heated debate - POTHER

Heather - LING

Heather genus - ERICA

Heaven: comb.form or prefix
URANO

Heavenly - SUPERNAL

Heavenly altar - ARA

Heaviest metal - OSMIUM

Heavy barge - HOY

Heavy drapery
    fabric - MOREEN

Heavy mallet - MAUL

Heavy material - LODEN

Heavy metric weight - TONNE

Heavy particle - BARYON

Heavy reading - TOME

Heavy silk fabric - SAMITE

Heavy twillied
    fabric - PRUNELLA

Hebdomad - WEEK

Hebrew ascetic - ESSENE

Hebrew dry measure - OMER

Hebrew eve - EREB

Hebrew dry measure - EPHAH

Hebrew fathers - ABBAS

Hebrew holiday - PURIM

Hebrew judge - ELI

Hebrew leader: var. - ALEF

Hebrew letter - ALEPH (1),
    BETH (2) AYIN (16),
    DALETH (4), GIMEL
    (3), HEH (5), HETH (8),
    KAPH (11), LAMED (12),
    MEM (13), NUN (14), PEH
    (17), QOPH(19), RESH(20),
    SADHE(18), SAMEKH(15),
    SHIN(21), SIN(22),
    TAV (23), TETH(9),
    TSADE(18), WAW(6),
    YOD(10), or ZAYIN (7)

Hebrew letter: var. - ALEF

Hebrew lyre - ASOR

Hebrew measure - EPHAH,
    KOR or OMER

Hebrew monastic
    brotherhood - ESSENAS

Hebrew month - ADAR (6),
    AV (11), ELUL (12),
    HESHVAN (2), YAR (8),
    KISLEV (3), NISAN (7),
    OMER (5), QOPH(12),
    SHEBAT (5), SIVAN (9),
    TAMMUZ(10), TEVET
    (4) or TISHRI (1)

Hebrew patroarch - ABRAHAM

Hebrew priest - ELI

Hebrew prophet - AMOS, ELISHA, EZEKIEL, HOSEA, ISAIAH, JEREMIAH, MICAH or NAHUM

Hebrew school - YESHIVA

Hebrew ten - ESER

Hewbrew toast - LCHAIM

Hebrew underworld - SHEOL

Hebrew weight - OMER or REBA

Hebrew zither - ASOR

Hebrides Island - IONA or SKYE

Heir - SCION

Helen of Troy's mother - LEDA

Heliotrope - BLOODSTONE

Hellenic: pref. - GRECO

Hellenic letter - PHI or ETA

Helmet - CASQUE

Helmet with a visor - BASINET

Helmet shaped - GALEATE

Helmet wreath - ORLE

Hemp fibre for caulking - OAKUM

Hemp for rope - SISAL

Heraldic - ARMORIAL

Heraldic band border or filets - ORLE

Heraldic cross - SALTIRE

Heraldic dragon - WYVERN

Heraldic fur - PEAN or VAIR

Heraldic design - SEME

Heraldic silver - ARGENT

Herald's tunic - TABARDS

Heraldry wreath - TORSE

Herb flavored tea - TISANE

Herbal beverage - INFUSION or TISANE

Herbal drink - SAGE TEA

Herculon's fiber - OLEFIN

Here: Sp. - ACA

Heretofore - ERENOW

Hermit - ERMITE

Heroic champion - PALADIN

Heroic tale - EPOS

Heroin - SCAG

Heroine of "The Last Days of Pompeii - IONE

Heron colony - SIEGE

Herring - SPRAT

Herring kin - SHAD

Herringlike fish - MENHADEN or MOONEYE

Hic-Hoc link - HAEC

Hidden - PERDU

High altitude probe - SONDE

High backed bench - EXEDRA

High dudgeon - IRE

High energy snack - GORP

High explosive - TONITE

High grade cotton - PIMA

High plateau - PUNA

High protein stuff - MISO

High society - BON TON

Highland dagger - DIRK

Highland hillside - BRAE

Highland plant - GORSE

Highland tongue - ERSE

Highly seasoned ragu - SALMI

Highly seasoned
stew - BURGOO

Hillock - KNOLL

Hillside Dugout or
shelter - ABRI

Him in Italy - LUI

Himalayan antelope - SEROW

Himalayan Buddhist
language - PALI

Himalayan cedars - DEODARS

Himalayan monkhood - ATIS

Himalayan River - GANGES

Himalayan wild goat - TAHR

Hindu ascetic - FAKIR,
SADHU or YOGI

Hindu creator - BRAHMA

Hindu diety - DEVA, RAMA,
SIVA or VISHNU

Hindu disipline - YOGA

Hindu doctorine - TANTRA

Hindu garment - SARI

Hindu gateway - TORAN

Hindu gentleman - BABU

Hindu god - DEVA, MARA,
RAMA or SIVA

Hindu god of desire - KAMA

Hindu god of destruction -
SHEVA or SIVA

Hindu god of fire - AGNI

Hindu god of love - KAMA

Hindu goddess - DEVA,
DEVI, KALI
or VAC

Hindu gods - DEVAS

Hindu holy man - SADHU

Hindu honorific - SWAMI

Hindu incarnation - AVATAR

Hindu law giver – MANU

Hindu loincloth - DHOTI

Hindu master - SWAMI

Hindu maxim - SUTRA

Hindu music - RAGA

Hindu mystic - YOGI

Hindu peasant - RYOT

Hindu people ORIYA

Hindu philosophy - VEDANTA

Hindu poet - RISHI

Hindu prince or ruler - RAJA

Hindu queen - ASURA
or RANEE

Hindu rain god - INDRA

Hindu retreat - ASHRAM

Hindu sacred text or
scripture - VEDA

Hindu sage - RISHI

Hindu scripture - VEDA

Hindu slave girl - DASI

Hindu spirit - AHURA

Hindu teacher - GURU or SWAMI

Hindu title of respect - SHRI or SRI

Hindu truths - SUTRA

Hindu weight - SER

Hindu writings - TANTRA

Hinged tongue - PAWL

Hip bones - COXAE or ILIA

Hip joint - COXA

Historical record - ACTA

Histrionic - STAGY

Hives - UREDO

Hodgepodge - FERRANGO, MELANGE, PASTICHE or OLIO

Hogfish - WRASSE

Hokkaido City - SAPPORO

Hokkaido native people - AINU

Hokkaido port - OTARU

Hold forth - OPINE

Holiday - FETE

Holiday time - EVE

Holing device - TREPAN

Hollow rocks - GEODES

Holly or Holm oak or genus - ILEX

Hollywood trickery - CGI

Holy places - SANCTA

Holy Roman emperor - OTTO or OTTOII

Holy water basin - STOUP

Home of Odysseus - ITHACA

Home of the Muses - HELICON

Home of the Norse gods - ASGARD

Home of the sirens - CAPRI

HOMES - GREAT LAKES (Huron, Ontario, Michigan, Erie, Superior)

Homo sapiens - HOMINID

Hondurian River - ULUA

Honey badger - RATEL

Honorary deg. - LLD

Honshu city - KYOTO

Honshu mat - TATAMI

Honshu seaport - KOBE, NAGOYA or OSAKA

Hoofed mammal - UNGALATE

Hooked anatomical part - UNCUS

Hooded clock - CAPOTE

Hooded jacket - ANORAK

Hoopster - CAGER

Hopi doll - KACHINA

Hops oven - OAST

Hops stems - BINES

Horizontal threads - WEFT

Hormone - ACTH

Horned antelope - BONGO

Horned goddess - ISIS

Horned shaped bone or structure - CORNU

Horned viper - ASP or
    CERASTES
Hornless - MULEY
Horny - CORNEOUS
Horny: pref. CERATO
Horse bit - SNAFFLE
Horse-donkey
    offspring - HINNY
Horse foot part - PASTERN
Horse handler - OSTLER
Horsehue - DUN
Horse pill - BOLUS
Horse shoe part - CALK
Horsemint genus - MONARDA
Hot compress - STUPE
Hot milk curdled with
    ale - POSSET
Hot wind - SAMIEL
Hot wine drink - GLOGG
    or NEGUS
Household - MENAGE
Household gods - LARES
    or PENATES
Household spirit - LAR
Hovering falcon - KESTREL
Howling - ULULANT
Hub - NAVE
Hubris - PRIDE
Hudson tributary - MOHAWK
Hulled grain - GROATS
Humman CPU's - SENSORIA
Hummus ingredient - TAHINI

Humpback's kin - SEI
Humped bovine - ZEBU
Hungarian coin - ENGO
Hungarian language - MAGYAR
Hungarian language
    e.g. - UGRAIN
Hungarian river - EGER
Hungarian sheep dog - PULI
Hungarian wine - TOKAY
Hung-wu's dynasty - MING
Hunter's cap - MONTERO
Hunting call - TANTARA
Huntress of myth - ATALANTA
    or ARTEMIS
Husband of Amiens - MARI
Husband of Bathsheba - URIAH
Husband of
    Desdemona - OTHELLO
Husband of Fatima - ALI
Husband of Frigg - ODIN
Husband of Gundrun - ATLI
Husband of
    Helen - MENELAUS
Husband of Hidalgo - ESPOSO
Husband of Isis - OSIRIS
Husband of Jezabel - AHAB
Husband of Judith - ESAU
Husband of Octavia - NERO
Husband of Ops - SATURN
Husband of
    Persephone - HADES

Husband of
    Pocahontas - ROLPHE
Husband of Pompeia - CAESAR
Husband of Rebekah - ISAAC
Husband of Ruth - BOAZ
Husband of Sarah - ABRAHAM
Husband of SITA - RAMA
Husband of Titania - OBERON
Hyalite - OPAL
Hybrid citrus - UGLI
Hybrid meat - CATTALO
Hybrid primrose - OXLIP
Hydroxyl compound - ENOL
Hymn of praise - PAEAN
Hymn of
    Thanksgiving - TEDEUM
Iberian sheep - MERINO
Icecream creation - BOMBE
Icelandic coin - EYRIR
Icelandic work - EDDA
Ice mass or pinnacle - SERAC
Icy - GELID
Icy pinnacles - OSAR
Idle - FAINEANT
Igneous rock - BASALT
    or OBSIDIAN
Iguana relative - ANOLE
Ike's command - ETO
Ilicitly distilled
    whiskey - POTEEN
Ilium - TROY
Ill gotten gains - PELF

Image: pre. - ICONO
Imaginary moster - CHIMERA
Imaginary substance - ETHER
Imitation - ERSATZ
Imitation of gold - ORMOLU
Immature
    cucumber - GHERKIN
Implied - TACIT
Imported cheese - HAVARTI
Imported porcelain - IMARI
Impressive display - PANOPLY·
Improve - AMELIORATE
Impudent - MALAPERT
Impulse conductor - AXON
Impute - ASCRIBE
In hiding - DOGGO
In name only - TITULAR
In the same place: Lat. -
    IBIB or IBIDEM
Inability to read - ALEXIA
Inability to smell - ANOSMIA
Inactive state - TORPOR
Incan capital - CUZCO
Incarnation of Vishnu -
    AVATAR, KRISHNA or
    RAMA
Incised carving - INTAGLIO
Incisive - MORDANT
Inclination from
    vertical - HADE
Inconsistent - ANOMALOUS
Indehiscent fruit - ACHENE

Indian - CREE, OTOE or UTE

Indian address - SAHIB

Indian beans - CATALPAS

Indian bigwig - NAWAB

Indian bread - NAN or NANN

Indian butter - GHEE

Indian cave temple
  sote - ELLORA

Indian chief - SACHEM

Incian coin - ANNA

Indian diety - KRISHNA

Indian dish - DAL

Indian dog - DHOLE

Indian drum - MRINDANGAM
  or TABLA

Indian evergreen - NEEM
  or SANDALWOOD

Indian fabric - MADRAS

Indian fig tree - PEEPUL
  or PIPAL

Indian flour - ATTA

Indian grass - KANS

Indian groom - SYCE

Indian instruments - TABLAS

Indian kettle - TABLA

Indian language - ORIYA

Indian lentil dish - DAL

Indian lute - SAROD, SITAR
  or TAMBURA

Indian nurse - AMAH

Indian musical form - RAGA

Indian nanny - AMAH

Indian Officers Club - LATHI

Indian ox - GAUR or ZEBU

Indian pastry - SAMOSA

Indian peasant - RYOT

Indian police club - LATHI

Indian port - CALCUTTA

Indian prince - MAHARAJA
  or RANI

Indian queen - RANEE

Indian rug - DHURRIE

Indian sage - MAHATMA

Indian sailor - LASCAR

Indian seaport - MADRAS

Indian shrub - SOLA

Indian soldier - SEPOY

Indian sovereign - MAHARANI

Indian spice - CARDAMON

Indian state or tea - ASSAM

Indian stork - ARGALA

Indian title - NAWAB

Indian turban - PATA

Indian VIP - SIDAR

Indian water vessel - LOTA

Indian weight - SER or TOLA

Indiana's flower - PEONY

Indic language - URDU

Indiginous Japanese AINU

Indigo dye or plant - ANIL

Individual clone
  member - RAMET

Indo-European - ARYAN

Indo-Malayan evergreens - BETELS

Indonesian island - BALI, BORNEO, CERAM, SUMATRA, SUMBA or TIMOR

Indonesian island group - ANU

Indonesian ox - ANOA

Indonesian sailboat - PROA

Indonesian soybean cake - TEMPEH

Indonesian volcano - KRAKATAU

Inedible orange - OSAGE

Indoor pool - NATATORIUM

Inert gas - ARGON or ZENON

Inert gaseous element - KRYPTON

Infant - NEONATE

Infantry campsite - ETAPE

Infantry officer's half pike - SPONTOON

Infernal abyss - TARTARUS

Infidel in Islam - KAFIR

Inflammmatory swelling - BLAIN

Ingenuous - NAIF

In honor of, or in the manner of - ALA

Ink ingredient - EOSIN

Inland sea - ARAL

Inlay material - NIELLO

Inlet - RIA

Inn, in the east - CARAVANSARY

Inner Hebrides island - IONA

Inner part of a Greek temple - NAOS

Inner self - ANIMA

Innkeeper - BONIFACE

Innocent - NAIF

Inscribed pillar - STELE

Insect adult stage - IMAGO

Insect appendage or feeler - PALP

Insect repellent - CITRONELLA

Insect stage - IMAGO or PUPA

Insectivorous bird - VIREO

Insense spice - STACTE

Insense stick - JOSS

Insertion mark - CARET

Insight - APERCU

Insincere person - POSEUR

Insincere speech - CANT

Insolublle protein - KERATIN

Insulating material - PERLITE

Intermediate, in law - MESNE

Intermission - CAESURA or ENTRACTE

Interobang - QUESTIONMARK

Intersection point - NODE

Interstices - AREOLAE

Intestinal divisions - ILIA

Intro - PROEM

Intuit knife - ULU

Intuitive apprehension of spiritual

truth - CORRIGENDA

Invaders of Kent - JUTES

Invaders of Rome - VANDELS

Inward - ENTAD

Ionian island - CORFU, ZAKINTHOS or ZANT

Ionian Sea gulf - ARTA

Iota - WHIT

Iowa commune - AMANA

IQ test developer - BINET

Iranian coin - RIAL

Iranian faith - BAHAI

Irational number - SURD

Ireland's De Valera - EAMON

Irish county - LAOIS or SLIGO

Iris part - UVEA

Irish lad - BOYO

Irish lake - LOUGH

Irish money - PUNT

Irish moonshine - POTEEN

Irish river - SHANNON

Irish Sea god - LER

Irish seaport - SLIGO or TRALEE

Irish toast - SLAINTE

Iron - FE

Iron ore - HERMATITE, OCHER or SIDERITE

Ironic - WRY

Iron rich mountain range - MESABI

Iroquois Indian - SENECA

Iroquoian language - ERIE or WYANDOT

Irregular edge - DECKLE

Irregularly notched - EROSE

Isaac's mother - SARAH

Isinglass - MICA

Islam follower - SUNNI

Islam holy month - RAMADAN

Islamic call to prayer - AZAN

Islamic decrees - FATWAS

Islamic devil - WHAITAN

Islamic diety - ALLAH

Islamic divorse - TALAK

Islamic doctor - ULEMA

Islamic holy war - JIHAD

Islamic infidel - KAFIR

Islamic leader or ruler - CALIPH, EMIR or IMAM

Islamic patriarch - SHEIK

Islamic salutation - SALAAM

Islamic scholars - IMAMS

Islamic spirit - DJINN

Islamic spiritual leader - CALIPH

Islamic temple - MOSQUE

Islamic title - EMIR

Islamic tower - MINARET

Island - AIT

Island country in the
Pacific - PALAU

Island goose - NENE

Island in Galway - ARAM

Island in the Antilles - SABA

Island in the Saronic - SALAMIS

Island in the Taiwan
straight - AMOY

Island off Donegal - ARAN

Island off
Greenland - ELLESMERE

Island off Scotland - IONA

Island resort IBIZA

Islands near New
Guinea - AROE

Islet - AITor HOLM

Isolated hill - BUTTE

Isolated mountain - MASSIF

Isotope of Thorium - IONIUM

Israeli airline - ELAL

Israeli city - ACRE

Israeli coin - AGORA

Israeli dance - HORA

Israeli native - SABRA

Israeli port - ACRE

Israeli port city - EILAT
or ELATH

Israeli seaport - ACRE

Italian brandy - GRAPPA
or SREGA

Italian cathedral - DUOMO

Italian cheese - ASIAGO
or DOLCELATTE

Italian city - ASTI

Italian colony, once - ERITREA

Italian
commune - ATR, AOSTA,
ASOLO, CASERTA,
or ESTE

Italian dessert - TIRAMISU

Italian dumplings - GNOCHI

Italian flat bread - FOCACCIA

Italian friends - AMICI

Italian ice cream - CASSATA
or GELATO

Italian industrial
center - PADUA

Italian innkeeper - OSTE
or PADRONE

Italian instrument - ARPA

Italian isle - ISOLA

Italian magistrate - PODESTA

Italian marble city - MASSA

Italian noble family - ORSINI

Italian nobleman - CONTE

Italian
noblewoman - MARCHESA

Italian port - ANCONA,
GENOA, SALERNO
or TRIETE

Italian range - APENNINES

Italian resort - LIDO

Italian seaport - ANCONA,
    BARI, NAPOLI
    or SALERNO

Italian staircase - SCALA

Italian stringed
    instrument - ARPA

Italian river - ARNO

Italian title of respect -SIGNOR

Italian violin - AMATI

Italian white wine - SOAVE

Italy's largest lake - GARDA

Itchy - PRURIENT

Itchy problem - TINEA

Ivied stand - PERGOLA

Jack-in-the-pulpit plant - ARUM

Jackal-headed god - ANUBIS

Jacob's brother - ESAU

Jacob's father - ISAAC

Jacob's father-in-law - LABAN

Jacob's son - ASHER,
    LEVI or REUBEN

Jacob's twin - ESAU

Jacob's wife - LEAH

Jagged - EROSE

Jamaican citrus - UGLI

Jamaican dish - ACKEE

Jamaican music - SKA

Jamaican rum - TAFIA

Japan's first capital - NARA

Japanese aborigine or
    native - AINU

Japanese American -
    ISSEI or NISEI
or SANAI

Japanese art form - ORIGAMI

Japanese apricot - UME

Japanese ax – ONO

Japanese bathtub - FURO

Japanese bedroll - FUTON

Japanese box - INRO

Japanese brew - KIRIN

Japanese caldera - ASO

Japanese carp - KOI

Japanese cartoons - ANIME

Japanese carved ivory items
NETSUKES

Japanese city - OTARU

Japanese
    commander - SHOGUN

Japanese divine being - KAMI

Japanese dog - AKITA

Japanese drama or drum - NOH

Japanese dressing
    gown - YUKATA

Japanese elder - GENRO

Japanese emperor - AKIHITO

Japanese fencing - KENDO

Japanese
    feudalnobleman - DAIMYO

Japanese fish delicacy - FUGU

Japanese food fish - TAI

Japanese gateway - TORII

Japanese home divider - SHOJI

Japanese honorific - SAN

Japanes horse radish - WASABI

Japanese imigrant - ISSEI

Japanese ink - SUMI

Japanese instrument - SAMISEN

Japanese isinglass - AGAR

Japanese island - OKI

Japanese knife - GINSU

Japanes legislature - DIET

Japanese martial art -
    AIKIDO or KENDO

Japanese mat - TATAMI

Japanese metalware - TOLE

Japanese money - RIN

Japanese mushroom - ENOKI
    or SHIITAKE

Japanese nobleman - DAIMYO

Japanese noodle - SOBA
    or UDON

Japanese noodle soup - RAMEN

Japanese paper art - ORIGAMI

Japanese paper
    folding - KIRIGAMI

Japanese parliament - DIET

Japanese pearl diver - AMAS

Japanese people - SINU

Japanese pill box - INRO

Japanese plum - LOQUOT

Japanese poem - HAIKU
    or TANKA

Japanese porcelain - IMARI

Japanese porgy - TAI

Japanese portal - TORII

Japanese pottery - IMARI
    or RAKU

Japanese primitve - AINU

Japanese radish - WASABI

Japanese receptacle - INRO

Japanese salad ingredient - UDO

Japanese sandal - ZORI

Japanese sash - OBI

Japanese seaport - KOBE,
    OSAKA, OTARU
    or SASEBO

Japanese seaweed - NORI

Japanese script - KANA

Japanese ship - MARU

Japanese shrine gateway - TORII

Japanese sliding door - SHOJI

Japanese soup - MISO

Japanese statesman - ITO

Japanese stringed
    instument - KOTO

Japanese style arbor - PERGOLA

Japanese tourist center - NARA

Japanese vegetables - UDOS

Japanese verse - HAIKU

Japanese volcano - ASO

Japances waist pouch - INRO

Japanese wooden clog - GETA

Japanese working dog - AKITA

Japanese wrestling - JUJISU

Japanese writing - KANA
    or KANJI

Japanese zither - KOTO

Japan's first capital - NARA

Jar - OLLA

Jargon - CANT

Jason's wife - MEDIA

Java seaport - SEMARANG

Javanese carriages - SADOS

Javanese ruler - RAJA

Jawbone - MAXILLA

Jehovah - ELOHIM

Jelly for germs - AGAR

Jersey genus - BOS

Jester's cap - COXCOMB

Jewel - BIJOU

Jewelery stone - JET

Jewish festival - HANUKKAH

Jewish harvest
    festival - SUKKOTH

Jewish holiday - PURIM

Jewish Jehovah - ELOHIM

Jewish month - ADAR (6),
    AV(11), ELUL(12),
    HESHVAN(2), IYAR(8),
    KISLEV(3), NISAN(7),
    SHEVAT(5), SIVAN(9),
    TAMUZ(10), TEVET(4)
    or TISHRI(1)

Jewish mystic of old - ESSENE

Jewish mystics - HASIDIM

Jewish noodle pudding - KUGEL

Jewish occult
    phiosophy - CABALA

Jewish religious
    cap - YARMULKE

Jewish sage - HILLEL

Jewish shawl - TALLITH

Jewish teacher REBBE

Jews not in Israel - DIAPORA

Jezebel's husband - AHAB

Jiao - MAO

Jipajapa hat - PANAMA

Johnny cakes - PONES

Joie de vivre - ELAN

Joker - WAG

Jordan queen - NOOR

Jot - ATOM or WHIT

Joule fraction - ERG

Judah's son - ONAN

Judeo-Spanish
    language - LADINO

Judges bench - BANC

Judge's chamber - CAMERA

Judicial proceedings - ACTA

Juliet's family name - CAPULET

July birthstone - CORNELIAN

Jump on skates - LUTZ

Jungfrau, e.g. - ALP

Jungian self - ANIME

Jungle cat - CIVET

Jungle cuckoo - ANI

Jungle ivy - LIANNA

Juniper tree - CADE

Junk copper - NARC

Jupiter - JOVE
Jury pool - VENIRE
Justification for
    existing - RAISON
D'ETRA
KGB forerunner - OGPU
Kapok tree - CEIBA
Karate school - DOJO
Karate teacher - SENSEI
Kazakhstan range - ALTAI
Keellike structure - CARINA
Keepers of sacred
    fire - VESTALS
Kenyan oxan - ZEBU
Kerfufful - ADO
Kernel's coat - TESTA
Kettle drum - NAKER
Kettle drums - PIMPANI
Key - AIT
Keyboard
    instrument - CELESTA
Ketboard layout - QWERTY
Kid around - JAPE
Kidney bean - HARICOT
Kidney enzyme - RENIN
Kidney related - RENAL
Killer of a god - DEICIDE
Kimono sash - OBI
Kind of acid - OLEIC
Kind of algebra - LINEER
Kind of antenna - DIPOLE
Kind of bean - SIEVA

Kind of bulrush - TULE
Kind of butterfly - SATYR
Kind of canto - BEL
Kind of cap - COIF
Kind of charm - TOADSTONE
Kind of cherry - GEAN
Kind of engine - CARNOT
Kind of fibre - BAST
Kind of gazelle - DORCAS
Kind of hut - NISSEN
Kind of jay - SCRUB
Kind of lily - SEGO
Kind of moth - LUNA
Kind of Mushroom - MOREL
Kind of orange - SEVILLE
Kind of palm - SAGO
Kind of terrier - CAIRN
Kind of thread - LISLE
Kind of tide - AGGER
King mackerel - CERO
King of Crete - MINOS
King of Denmark - CANUTE
King of Egypt - FUAUD
King of France - CAPET,
    LEROI or ROI
King of Israel - JEHU or OMRI
King of Judea - AMON,
    ASA or HEROD
King of legend - MIDAS
King of Phrygia - MIDAS
King of Pylos - NESTOR

King of Scotland - BALIOL
King of the fairies - OBERON
King of the Visigoths - ALARIC
King of the Huns - ATLI
King of Thebes - CREON
King of Troy - PRIAM
King of Tyre - HIRAM
Kingdom east of
    Babylonia - ELAM
Kingdom in the
    Himalayas - BHUTAN
Kingdom of Croesus - LYDIA
Kingdom of Tereus - THRACE
Kingly - BASILIC
Kings Peak range - UINTA
Kirghiz Mtn range - ALAI
Kirsch, for one - SCHNAPS
Kishke covering - DERMA
Kissed - OSCULATED
Kitchen slicer - MANDOLINE
Knave - VARLET
Kneeling bench for
    prayer - PRIEDIEU
Knife, of old - SNEE
Knight's tunic - TABARD
Knit fabric -TRICOT
Knobby - NODAL
Knot at the nape - CHIGNON
Knot in wool - BURL
Knowledge gained through
Meditation - JNANA

Knowledge of spiritual
    truth - GNOSIS
Koeon - RIDDLE
Korean apricot - ANSU
Koran chapter - SURA
Korea/China separator -
    YELLOW SEA
Korean soldier - ROK
Kyushu volcano - ASO
Lab gel - AGAR
Lab heaters - ETNAS
Lab straw - PIPETTE
Lab tube - PIPET
Labratory tube - BURET
Lace end - AGLET
Lace maker's thread - GIMP
Lachrymose - TEARFUL
Lacquer - JAPAN
Lacquered metalware - TOLE
Lacquer resin - ELEM
Lacy frills - PICOTS
Lacy openwork - TRACERY
Ladder like - SCALAR
Ladder step - RUNDLE
    or STAVE
Lady friend in Italy - AMICA
Ladylove - INAMORATA
Lady oracle - SIBYL
Lady's maid in Indian - AYAH
Lake: Fr. - LAC
Lake in Ethiopia - TANA
Lake in Ireland - ERNE

Lake in Italy - COMO
or GARDA

Lake in Scotland - KATRINE

Lake near Rome - ALBANO

Lake of Geneva - LAMAN

Lake or pond - MERE

Lamb or kid - YEANLING

Lamb stew - HARICOT

Lambs: Lat. - AGNI

Land of hope - RURITANIA

Lament - ELEGY

Lament loudly - ULULATE

Laments loudly - KEENS

Land locked
country - UGANDA

Language Jesus
spoke - ARAMAIC

Language of India - TAMIL

Language of Iran - FARSI

Language of
Provence - OCCITAN

Language of South
China - KOBO

Language of Sri Lanka - TAMIL

Language of the
Gypsies - ROMANY

Lanos - WOOLY

Lapland nomad - SAMI

Lapwing - PEEWIT

Large African
stork - MARABOU

Large antelope - BONGO,
GEMBOK

or ORYX

Large awk - MURRE

Large basket - PANNIER

Large Brazilian
parrot - HYACINTH

or MACAW

Large cacti - SAGUROS

Large center piece - EPERGNE

Large clam - PISMO

Large eyed primate - LORIS

Large duck - PEKIN

Large fern - BRACKEN

Large fish - CERO

Large food fish - MEGRA

Large green moth - LUNA

Large headed match - FUSEE

Large Lemur - INDRI

Large moth - LUNA

Large nocturnal animal - PACA

Large parrot - KEA

Large pig - DUROC

Large pill - BOLUS

Large raptor - GOS HAWK

Large scale flight - DIASPORA

Large red hog - DUROC

Large sea bird - SKUA
or SOLAN

Large statues - COLOSSI

Large tuna - ALBACORE

Large umbrella - GAMP

Large wine
    bottle - METHUSELAH
Large whale - LEVIATHAN
Large wooden goblet - MAZER
Largess - ALMS
Largest asteroid - CERES
Largest domesticated
    cattle - GAURS
Largest lake in central
    Europe - BALATON
Largest Lake in
    Europe - LADOGA
Last book of the Torah - DEUT
Last month - ULTIMO
Last of the Minor
    Prophets - MALACHI
Last six lines of a
    sonnet - SESTET
Last supper room - CENACLE
Late sleeper - SLUGABED
Latin American Christmas
    Festival - PASADA
Latin being - ESSE
Latin case - DATIVE
Latine north wind - BOREAS
Latin I word - EST
Latin farewell - VALE
Latin law - LEX
Latin Mass - MISSA
Latin poet - OVID
Latino grocery - BODEGA
Latvian port - RIGA

Latino beliefs - FES
Laugh in contempt - FLEER
Laughing - RIANT
Laughing
    jackass - KOOKABURRA
Laurel wreath - CORONAL
Lawn bowling - BOCCE
Lawyer's group - ABA
Laxative from aloe - ALOIN
Layer - LAMINA
Layer of skin - DERMA
Layered rock - GNEISS
Layers of tissue - TELAE
Layman at the
    monastery - OBLATE
Lazy - OTIOSE
Lead ore or sourse - GALENA
Lead-tin alloy - TERNE
Leaf pore - STOMA
Leaflike part - BRACT
Leaf-stem angle - AXIL
Leafstock - PETIOLE
Leander's love - HERO
Leap - CAPRIOLE
Leaping rodent - JERBOA
Learned scholar - SAVANT
Lear's daughter - REGAN
Leather flask - OLPE
Leather whip - TAWS
Leather wine bottle - BOTA
Leatherwood - TITI

Lebanese malitia - DRUSE

Lebanese port - Beirut

Lecherous man - ROUE

Lector - OSTIARY

Lecture hall - LYCEUM

Lecturer - DOCENT

Lectern - AMBO or PODIUM

Leeward Island - NEVIS

Left hand page - VERSO

Left handed - SINISTRAL

Leftover food - ORT

Leg covering - PUTTEE

Leg of lamb or mutton - GIGOT

Legal copy - ESTREAT

Legal matter - RES

Legal right - DROIT

Legendary soul seller - FAUST

Legendary tales - MYTHI

Legislators - SOLONS

Leguminous plant of
    India - DAL

Lei man - HAOLE

Leisurely stroll - PASEO

Leporid - HARE

Lethargy - HEBETUDE
    or TOPOR

Let stand - STET

Letter embellishment - SERIF

Lettuce alternative - ESCAROLE

Libertine - ROUE

Library cubicle - CARREL

Lice and ticks - EPIZOA

Lie - TARRADIDDLE

Light beige - ECRU

Light carriage - GIG

Light cotton - ETAMINE

Light four-wheeled
    carriage - PHAETON

Light granite rock - SIAL

Light helmet - ARMET

Light measure - PHOT

Light particle - PHOTON

Light trianngular scarf - FISH

Light unit - PHOT

Light turban - PUGREE

Light yellow cheese - TILSIT

Lighthouse - PHAROS

Lightweight cotton - ETAMINE

Lightweight cotton
    cloth - JACONET

Lightweight fabric - ETAMINE,
    NINON, PLISSE or VOILE

Lightweight
    material - FOULARD

Like a goose - ANSERINE

Like a soothsayer - VATIC

Like a wolf - LUPINE

Like an old woman - ANILE

Like some victories - PYRRHIC

Lily: Fr. - LIS

Lily family plant - CAMAS

Lily like plant - HOSTA
    orYUCCA

Lily plant - ALOE, CALLA, HOSTA or MARIPOSA

Limbless genus - APODA

Lime tree - TEIL

Limestone rock formation - KARST

Lingo - ARGOT or PATOIS

Link - NEXUS

Link together - CONCATENATE

Linking verb - COPULA

List extender - ETC

List of errors - CORRIGENDA

List of lapses - ERRATA

Listen - HIST

Literary collection - ANA or ANALETS

Literary conflict - AGON

Literary connection - SEGUE

Literary devise - TROPE

Litter of pigs - FARROW

Little bits of land - AITS

Little cupids - AMORETTI

Little gray birds - VIREOS

Liturgical language - SYRIAC

Liturgical vestment - AMICE

Lively - TARE

Lively, in music - ANIM

Lively dance - GIGUE

Lively old dance - GALOP

Lively wit - ESPRIT

Liverleaf - HEPATICA

Living in still waters - LENTIC

Lizard - AGAMA, ANOLE or SAURIAN

Lizardlike - SAURIAN

Llama relative - VICUNA

Loamy deposit - LOESS

Loamy fertilizer - MARL

Lobster claw - CHELA

Lobsters & crabs - DECAPODS

Local theater - NABE

Local trees - SILVAN

Location of ancient Samos - IONIA

Location of the Great Mosque - HERAT

Locking lever - DETENT

Locust bean - CAROB

Lodge doorkeeper - TILER

Lohengrin's love - ELSA

Log-birling contest - ROLEO

Loincloth - DHOTI

Long bodied cat - EYRA

Long leaved lettuce - COS

Long legged bird - AVOCET

Long necked squash - CUSHAW

Long poem - EPOEE

Long stole - TIPPET

Long tailed African monkey - GUENON

Long tailed finch - TOWHEE

Long tailed lizard - AGAMA

Long tailed monkey - TITI

Long tunic - CAFTAN

Long winded - PROLIX

Long wooden bench - SETTLE

Longest river - NILE

Loom attachment - DOBBY

Loom bar - ERASER

Loom reed - SLEY

Looped handle - ANSA

Loose cloak - RELISSE

Loose rock debris- SCREE

Loose tunic - CAFTAN

Lop eared hog - DUROC

Lord's lands - FIEFS or
DEMESNE

Loss-of-hair
condition - ALOPECIA

Loss of sense of
smell - ANOSMIA

Loss of speach - APHASIA

Loss of volition - ABULIA

Loud firecrackers - PETARDS

Loudness measure - PHON

Loudness units - BELS

Louisiana tribe - CADDO

Louvre Pyramid designer - PEI

Love: Sp. AMOR

Love of fine art - VIRTU

Love poem for
singing - MADRIGAL

Lover of Aeneas - DIDO

Lover of Aphrodite - ARES

Lover of Daphnis - CHLOE

Lover of Eros - PSYCHE

Lover of Isolde - TRISTAN

Lover of Narcissus - ECHO

Lover of Radames - AIDA

Low stool - TABORET

Lower - NETHER

Lower class, in London - NONU

Lower Niger River
people - EBOS

Lowest deck on a ship - ORLOP

Lowly freeman - CEORL

Lozenge - TROCHE or PASTIL

Luau baking pits - IMUS

Lucerne - ALFALFA

Lugubrious - MOURNFUL

Luke's father - DARTH

Lulaby - BERCEUSE

Lulu - ONER

Luminous eminations - AURAE

Lunar plain - MARE

Lunar valley - RILLE

Luncheon, in London - TIFFIN

Lustus fabric - HONAN

Lustrus velvet - PANNE

Lute of India - SARODE
or SITAR

Luzon port - MANILA

Lyons River - SAONE

Lyric poem - EPODE

Lysergic acid sourse - ERGOT

M1 - GARAND

M. Hulot creator - TATI

Macadamize - PAVE

Macao money - AVO

Macaw - ARA or ARARA

Macbeth witch - HECATE

Mace bearer - BEADLE

Macedonian mall - AGORA

Mackerel's kin - CERO

Madagascar primate -
   INDRI or LEMUR

Mafioso's code of
   silence - OMERTA

Magic amulet - MOJO

Magic image - SIGIL

Magic showplace - ORENA

Magical goddess - CIRCE

Magical symbol - SIGIL

Magnetic
   accelerators - BETATRONS

Magnetic alloy - ALNICO

Magnetic induction unit -
   HAUSS or TESLA

Magnetic mineral
   magnetite - LODESTONE

Mah-jong suit - BAM

Maiden loved by
   Hercules - IOLE

Maiden turned into a
   spider - ARACHNE

Maine seaport - BATH

Majestic shield - AEGIS or EGIS

Major or Minor - CANIS

Make a mosaic - TESSELATE

Make better - AMELIORATE

Make cloth gathers - SHIRR

Make inconspicuous - EFFACE

Make slender - ATTENUATE

Make
   undrinkable - DENATURE

Make unnecessary - OBVIATE

Makeshift
   conveyance - TRAVOIS

Malay boat - PROA

Malay coin - TRA

Malay gibbon - LAR

Malay ismus - KRA

Malayan dagger - CREESE
   or KRIS

Malayan outrigger -
   PROA or PRAU

Malayan palms - SAGOS

Malaysian knife - PARANG

Malasian seaport - MALACCA

Malasian state - PERAK
   or SARAWAK

Male badger - BOAR

Male ballet dancer - DANSEUR

Male cat - GIB

Male demon - INCUBUS

Male eagle or hawk - TIERCEL

Male gypsy - ROM

Male hawk - TERCEL
   or TIERCEL

Male reddeer - HARTS or SPAYS

Male swan - COB
Maligne - TRADUCE
Malt kiln - OAST
Malt liquor yeast - BARM
Mammal's coat - PELALGE
Man of prominence - NABOB
Manatee's cousin - DUGONG
Mandarin residence - YAMEN
Mandela org. - ANC
Maneuverable, nautically - YARE
Manorial land - DEMESNE
Manumit - FREE FROM
    SLAVERY
Manuscript gap - LACUNA
Manuscript marks - OBELI
Maori canoe - WAKA
Map in a map - INSET
Maple genus - ACER
Marabou - STORK
Marat's assassin - CORDAY
Marble mount of
    Greece - PENTELICUS
Marshy - PALUDIC
Mariana Island - GUAM
    or ROTA
Marine mollusk - SEAHARE
Marine snail - WHELK
Mark of insertion - CARET
Mark used in part singing - PRE
Market town - BOURG
Mars moon - DEMOS
    or PHOBOS

Marsh bird - CRAKE, RAIL,
    REEVE, SNIPE or SORA
Marsh grass - SEDGE
Marsh hawk - HARRIER
Marsh hen - COOT
Marsh plant - CATKIN,
    REED or TULE
Martinique volcano - PELEE
Masada defender - ESSENE
Masked
    buffoon - HARLEQUIN
Masquerade ball - RIDOTTO
Masonary block or
    stone - ASHLAR
Masonic doorkeeper - TILER
Mass calender - ORDO
Massacre - POGROM
Massage deeply - ROLPH
Massenet opera - THAIS
Massonet opera - THAIS
Matador - TORERO
Material used to make
    glass - FRIT
Matter Matter - MUON
Mature insect - IMAGO
Maturing egg cell - OOTID
Maui retreat - HANA
Maui tree - KOAQ
Maven - SAVANT
Maxims - DICTA
Mayan gibbon - LAR
Mayan Indian - NAM

Meadow mouse - VOLE

Means of connection - NEXUS

Measure of electric
    charge - COULOMB

Measure of loudness - SONE

Meat avoider - VEGAN

Meat dross - GRISTTLE

Meat pie - PASTY

Mecca shrine - KAABA

Mecca visitors - HAJIS

Mechanical device - PAWL

Medical staffs - CADUCEI

Medicated compress - STUPE

Medicinal - IATRIC

Medicinal brew - TISANE

Medicinal herb or
    plant - ARNICA,
    BONESET, JALAP,
    SAGE or SENNA

Medicinal shrub - CASSIA
    or IPECAC

Medicinal tuber - SALEP

Medieval brass
    horn - CLARION

Medieval capital of
    Flanders - LILLE

Medieval catapult - ONAGER

Medieval chest - ARCA

Medieval devil - MEPHISTO

Medieval form of
    trombone - SACKBUT

Medieval French
    coins - OBOLES

Medieval fluid - HANSA

Medieval helmet - ARMET
    or BASINET

Medieval instruments - REBECS

Medieval money - ORA

Medieval musical
    pieces - MADRIGALS

Medieval poem - LAI

Medieval Scottish
    soldier - KERN

Medieval Sicilian coin - TARI

Medieval sword - ESTOC

Medieval tale - GEST

Medieval weapon - POLEAXE

Mediteranian region - LEVANT

Mediteranian vessel - CAIQUE,
    FELLUCA or ZEBEC

Mediteranian wind - MISTRAL
    or SIROCCO

Medium-sweet
    sherry - OLOROSO

Melodic - ARIOSE

Melodic flourish - CADENZA

Melodies: Sp. - AIRES

Melodious composition or
    passage - ARIOSO

Melville character - PELEG

Melville opus - OMOO
    or TYPEE

Member of a
    convent - CENOBITE

Member of a Jewish sect - ESSENE

Member of a ruling clique - OLIGARTH

Member of the lowest Hindu caste - SUDRA

Membrane of grasses - PALEA

Membranes - SEPTA

Membranous covering - VELAMEN

Membranous tissue - TELA

Memorial stone - STELE

Memory - ROTE

Memory pathway - ENGRAM

Memphis god - PTAH

Menial worker - DOGSBODY

Mercenary - VENAL

Merchant guild - HANSA

Merchantman - ARGOSY

Mercurous cloride - CALOMEL

Mercury ore - CINNABAR

Mercury, to an Alchemist - AZOTH

Merganser - SMEW

Merry - JOCOSE or RIANT

Mesopotamian earth god - AGAN

Messy munchie - SMORE

Metal alloy - ALNICO

Metal basket - CRESSET

Metal coffee cup holder - ZARF

Metyal engraving tool - BURIN

Metal marble - STEELIE

Metal mixture - MATTE

Metal mold - PIG

Metal shaper - SWAGE

Metal used in alloys - BISMUTH

Metal waste - DROSS

Metalic element - NIOBIUM or RHENIUM

Metamorphic rock - GNEISS or SCHIST

Metaphysical concepts - MONISMS

Meteoric fireballs - BOLIDES

Meteorite remains - TEKTITE

Metonymy - TROPE

Metric feet - IAMBS

Metric measure - ARE or STERE

Metric unit of area - ARE

Metric unit of mass - GRAM

Metric unit of volumn - STERE

Metrical foot - ANAPEST, DACTYL or TROCHEE

Metrical unit - IAMBUS

Metrical unit of two feet - DIPODY

Mexicali munchie - TOSTADA

Mexican annuals - CHIAS

Mexican Indian - ZAPOTEC

Mexican Indians - OTOMI

Mexican January - ENERO

Mexican language - NEHUATL

Mexican mountain - ORIZABA

Mexican policeman - RURALES

Mexican raccoon - COATI

Mexican resort - OAXARA

Mexican salamander - AXOLTI

Mexican sandel - HUARACHE

Mezzanine - ENTESOL

Miasma - ODOR

Mica, in thin sheets - ISINGLAS

Microwave generator - MASER

Midmorning prayer - TERSE

Middle East
    beverage - ARRACK

Mideast appetizer - FALAFEL

Mideast marketplace - SOUK

Mideast Muslim
    militants - HAMAS

Mideast religion - BAHAI

Mid eastern porters - HAMALS

Middle ear bone - MALLEUS

Middle East chief - AMEER

Middy - CADET

Midianite king - REBA

Midieval chest - ARCA

Midieval fortress - ESTE

Midieval helmet - ARMET

Midnight assembly of
    Witches - SABBAT

Midnight stroll - PASEO

Mignonette - RESEDA

Migrating Herring - ALEWIFE

Mild breeze - ZEPHYR

Mild cigar - CLARO

Military cap - KEPI or SHAKO

Military dictator - CAUDILLO

Military post office – APO

Military storehouse - ETAPE

Milk cheese - EDAM

Millionth of a meter - MICRON

Mills waterwheel - NORIA

Milne' donkey - EEYORE

Mind: Lat. MENS

Mine entrance - ADIT

Mine excavation - STOPE

Mine: Fr. - AMOI

Mine prop - SPRAG

Mineral pigment - OCHER

Mineral residue - CALX

Mineral salt - ALUM

Mineral used as a gem - BERYL

Mini monkey - TITI

Mining nail - SPAD

Mining tool - TREPAN

Minnesota range - MESABI

Minor actor - SUPE

Minor parish official - BEADLE

Minor profit - AMOS

Minstrel's song - LAY

Mint family member - CHIA

Mint family plant - SALVIA

Mint product - SPECIE

Minute amounts
    (Scottish) - HAETS

Minute aquatic organism - ROTIFER

Mirror backing - TAIN

Miscellany - VARIA

Mischievious girl - GAMINE

Mischievious prank - DIDO

Mishmash - OLIO

Misleading fabrication -CANARD

Mississippi sourse - ITASCA

Missouri feeder - KANSAS, KNIFE or OSAGE

Missouri tribe - ARIKARA

Mist – BRUNE

Mite - ACARUS or ACARID

Moccasin - PAC

Mock - JAPE

Model of the solar system - ORRERY

Moderate in tempo - ANDANTE

Molasses - TREACLE

Molder - ROT

Molly coddle - COSSET

Molting - ECDYSIS

Mom & Pop store group - SBA

Money box, of old - ARCA

Mongolian mountain rang - ALTAI

Mongoose kin - GANET

Monitary unit of Angola - LWEI

Monitary unit of Honduras - LEMPIRA

Money for patronage - PAP

Money in Equador - SUCRE

Money premium - AGIO

Mongol tent - YURT

Mongolian range - ALTAI

Mongolian warrior - TATAR

Mongolian wild sheep - ARGALI

Mongoose - MEERKAT

Monkey bread tree - BAOBAB

Monk's book - PSALTER

Monk's cheese - OKA

Monk's haircut - TONSURE

Monks hood - ACONITE or COWL

Montana peak - BIG ELK

Monteverdi opera - ORFEO

Moon fish - OPAH

Moon goddess - DIANA, LUNA or SELENE

Moon of Jupiter - CALISTO, ELARA, EUROPA, GAYTMEDE, LEDA or TITAN

Moon of Mars - DEIMOS

Moon of Neptune - TRITON or NEREID

Moon of Saturn - ATLAS, DIONE, HELENE, HYPERION, IAPETUS, JANUS, PHOEBE, RHEA, TETHYS or TITAN

Moon of Uranus - ARIEL, ARIES, OBERON or TITANIA

Moonstone - OPA

Moon valley - RILLE

Moor - HEATH

Moor shrub - GORSE

Moorish palace - ALHAMBRA

More, in music - PIU

Mormon: abbr. - LDS

Morph lead in - ENDO

Morrocan port - AGADIR, CEUTA, SAFI or TABGIERS

Morrocan tree - ARAR

Morsel of meat - NOISETTI

Mortice insert or mate - TENON

Mosaic piece - SMALTO or TESSERA

Moselle feeder - SAAR

Moses brother - AARON

Moses mount - NEBO

Moslem judge - CADI

Moslem noble - AMIR

Mosque priest - IMAM

Mosquito genus - AEDES

Moth - LUNA

Mother of a holy Hampshire - CREDSOW

Mother of Achilles - THETIS

Mother of Aeneas - VENUS

Mother of Aphrodite - DIONE

Mother of Apollo - LETO

Mother of Ares - ENYO or HERA

Mother of Artimus - LETO

Mother of Brunhilde - ERDA

Mother of Castor - LEDA

Mother of Ceres - OPS

Mother of cities - KIEV

Mother of Clytemnestra - LEDA

Mother of Constantine - HELENA

Mother of Cronus - GAEA

Mother of Demeter - RHEA

Mother of Dionysus - SEMELE

Mother of Don Juan - ENA or INEZ

Mother of Galatea - DORIS

Mother of Gallahad - ELAINE

Mother of Hades - RHEA

Mother of Hector - HECUBA

Mother of Hebe - HERA

Mother of Helen - LEDA

Mother of Heleos - THEA

Mother of Hephaestus - HERA

Mother of Hera - RHEA

Mother of Hermes - MAIA

Mother of Horus - ISIS

Mother of Isaac - SARAH

Mother of Ishmael - HAGAR

Mother of Jove - OPS

Mother of Juda or Levi - LEAH

Mother of Jupiter - OPS

Mother of King
    Minos - EUROPA

Mother of Levi - LEAH

Mother of Memnon - EOS

Mother of Maia - PLELONE

Mother of Miletus - ARIA

Mother of Oedipus - JOCASTA

Mother of Paris - HECUBA

Mother of pearl - NACRE

Mother of pearl
    sourse - ABALONE

Mother of Peer Gynt - ASE

Mother of Perseus - DANAE

Mother of Pollux - LEDA

Mother of Poseidon - RHEA

Mother of Promeseus - ASIA

Mother of Proserpine - CERES

Mother of Rajiv - INDIRA

Mother of Reuben - LEAH

Mother of Romulus - RHEA

Mother of Scarlett - ELLEN

Mother of Seth - EVE

Mother of
    Solomon - BATHSHEBA

Mother of Superman - LARA

Mother of the Titans - GAEA

Mother of Uranus - GAIA

Mother of the Valkyries - ERDA

Mother of Venus - DIONE

Mother of Zephyrus - EOS

Mother of Zeus - RHEA

Motherless calf - DOGIE

Mother's kin - ENATE

Motionless - STASIS

Motor cycle passenger
    seat - PILLION

Mottled soil - GLEY

Moulding ridge - ARRIS

Mountain ashes - ROWANS

Mountain
    chain - CORDILLERA

Mountain crest - ARETE

Mountain goat - IBEX
    or TAKIN

Mountain in Geenisis - HOREB

Mountain in
    Martinique - PELEE

Mountain in Thessaly - OSSA

Mountain Lake - TARN

Mountain laurel - KALMIA

Mountain nymph - ECHO
    or OREAD

Mountain of Crete - IDA

Mountain pass - COL

Mountain Pass in India - GHAT

Mountain pool - TARN

Mountain ridge or spur -
    ARETE, OSAR or TOR

Mountain side debris - SCREE

Mountain spinach - ORACH

Mountain system of
    Asia - ALTAI

Mountain top fortress in
Israel - MASADA

Mountains of Utah - LASAL

Mounted sentry - VEDETTE

Mournful,
musically - DOLOROSO

Mourning song - DIRGE

Mouselike mammal - SHREW

Mouth part - UVULA

Mouth: Sp. - BOCA

Mouths - ORA

Movement slower than
andante - ADAGIO

Mrs. Shakespear - ANNE

Mud fish - AMIA

Mud hut - JACAL

Mug wump - SLAP

Mulberry bark - TAPA

Mulled wine - NEGUS

Multicolored - PIED

Murmer - SUSURRATE

Muscat native - OMANI

Muscular weakness - ATONY

Muse of astonomy - URANIA

Muse of comedy - THALIA

Muse of epic
poetry - CALLIOPE

Muse of history - CLIO

Muse of lyic poetry - EUTERPE

Muse of memory - MNEME

Muse of music - EUTERPE

Muse of poetry - ERATO

Muse of sacred
poetry - POLYHYMNIA

Muse of song &
dance - TERPSICHORE

Muse of
tragety - MELPOMENE

Muses - RUMINATES

Museum animal
display - DIORAMA

Museum guide - DOCENT

Mushroom - AGARIC

Mushroom cap - PILEUS

Mushroom stem - STIPE

Mushroom variety - ENOKI

Music for nine - NONET

Music halls - ODEA

Music of Indian - RAGA

Musical composition or
study - ARIOSO,
CANTATA, ETUDE
or RONDO

Musical cord - TRIAD

Musical direction - ADUE,
ARIOSO, ASSAI, LENTO,
POCO, PRESTO,
SOPRA or TACET

Musical ending - CODA

Musical florish - GLISSANDO

Musical forms - FUGUES

Musical gourd - MARACA

Musical hold - TENUTO

Musical instrument - OUD

Musical interval - OCTAVE

Musical line - TIMA

Musical medley - OLIO

Musical notation - REST or
    SECCO   Musical note
    combinations - TRIOLES

Musical passages - ANDANTE
    or ARIOSO

Musical postscript - CODA

Musical repeat signs -
    SEGNI or SEGNOS

Musical tempo - ANDANTINO

Musicly, "Be silent" - TACET

Musicly, from
    thebeginning - DACAPO

Musicly, not too
    much - NONTROPPO

Musicly, with the bow - ARCO

Muslim ascetic - DERVISH

Muslim belief - SHIISM

Muslim branch - SUNNI

Muslim caliph - ALI

Muslim call to prayer -
    ADAN or AZAN

Muslim cap - TAJ

Muslim crusade - JIHAD

Muslim decree - FATWAS
    or IRADE

Muslim factotum - IMAM

Muslim greeting - SALAAM

Muslim holiday - EED

Muslim holy man - FAKIR

Muslim judge or
    magistrate - CADI
or HAKIM

Muslim months - RABI

Muslim mystics - SUFIS

Muslim pilgrim - HADJI

Muslim pilgrimage - HADJ

Muslim porter - HAMAL

Muslim prayer leader - IMAM

Muslim priest - IMAM

Muslim prince - AMEER

Muslim religious
    student - SOFTA

Muslim scholers - ULEMA

Muslim shrine - KAABA

Muslim soldier - GHAZI

Muslim spirit - DJIN or DJINNI

Muslim teacher - IMAM
    or MULLAH

Muslim title - AGA or AGHA

Muslim veil - PURDAH
    or YASHMAK

Muslim weight - ROTL

Muslim woman's gown - IZAR

Musk sourse - CIVIT

Mustard plants - COLES

Mustardy condiment - WASABI

Mute swan - OLOR

Myrtle tree - ALLSPICE

Mysterious stuff - ARCANA

Mystic letter - RUNE

Mythical bird - ROC

Mythical dieties - FAUNS

Mythical giant - ANTAEUS

Mythical giantess - URDAR

Mythical goat-man - FAUN

Mythical or obscure - RUNIC

Mythical Greek
    king - TANTALUS

Mythical horseman - SATYR

Mythical huntress - ATALANTA

Mythical monster -
    CHIMERA or ORC

Mythical queen of
    Carthage - DIDO

Mythical son of
    Helen - XUTHUS

Mythical swan - LEDA

Mythical sorceress - MEDEA

Mythological nymph or
    swimmer - NAIA

Mythical weaver - ARACHNE

Mythological weeper - NIOBE

NC school - ELON

Nabokov novel - ADA
    or LOLITA

Nail with a hole - SPAD

Naive girl - INGENUE

Naive person - NAIF

Name - YCLEPT

Name for many a
    theatre - LYCEUM

Name of God - YAHWEH

Nape - NUCHA

Nape covering
    style - CHIGNON

Napoleon's Marshall - NEY

Narcotic shrub - KAT or KHAT

Narrative poem - EPOS or IDYL

Narrative tale - CONTE

Narrow channels - STRIAE

Narrow fillet - ORLE

Narrow furrow, groove or
    ridge - ARETE or STRIA

Narrow inlet - RIA

Narrow minded - ILLIBERAL

Nasal dividers or
    membranes - SEPTA

Nasal passages - NARES

Nasty rumor - CANARD

Native - INDIGENE

Native African tree - BAOBAB

Native Alaskan
    language - TLINGIT

Native American
    rations - PEMMICAN

Native Egyptian - COPT

Native Israeli - SABRA

Native Nigerian - IBO

Native of Patna - BIHARI

Native of the Steppes - TATAR

Natives of Oulu - FINNS

Natterjack - TOAD

Natural gas
    constituent - ETHAN

Nausea inducing agent - EMETIC

Nautical beginning - AERO

Nautical chain or rope - TYE

Nautical pin - THOLE

Nautical tackles - SWIGS

Navajo dwelling - HOGAN

Navigational system - LORAN or SHORAN

Near east inn - SERAI

Neck of mutton - SCRAG

Neck ruffle - JABOT or RUCHE

Neclace spacer - RONDEL

Nectar-feeding parrot - LORY

Needle case - ETUI

Negative charged ion or particle - ANION

Negligee - PEIGNOIR

Neighbor of Ethiopia - ERITRIA

Nelumbo-lotus - LILY

Neon fish - TETRA

Neopolitan secret society - MORRA or REMORRA

Nepalese peak - ANNAPERNA

Nephrite - JADE

Nero's successor - GALBA

Nerve branches - RAMI

Nerve cell - NEURON or RECEPTOR

Nerve cell extension, fibre or part - AXON

Nerve network - PLEXUS or RETE

Nerve parts - AXONS

Nest - NIDUS or VESPIARY

Nest building fish - GOURAM

Nest of pheasants - NIDE

Nestling - EYAS

Netherland's commune - EDE

Netherlands River - ISSEL

Netlike cap - SNOOD

Netted hat lining - CAUL

Networks of nerves - RETIA

Neural fiber part or transmitter - AXON

Neural junction - SYNAPSE

Neural network - RETE or RETIA

Neural transmitter - AXON

Never theless - WITHAL

Nevus - BIRTHMARK

New born lamb - EAN

New Guinea port - LAE

New Jersey range - RAMAPCO

New Mexico sky city - ACOMA

New Testament book - TITUS

New world monkey - SAI

New world parrot - MACAW

New Zealand bird - OII

NewZealand Island - NIUE

New Zealand parrot - KAKA, KAKAPO or KEA

New Zealand reptile - TUATARA

New Zealand tree - RIMU

New Zealand tribe - ATI

Newspaper page - OPED

Newt - EFT

Next-to-last syllable - PENULT

Niamey's land -NIGER

Nicker - NEIGH

Nigerian - IBO

Nigerian ruler - OBA

Nigeria's largest city - LAGOS

Nigerian wood - OBECHE

Night blooming cactus - CEREUS

Night in France - NUIT

Nightclub - BOITE

Nightmare world - DYSTOPIA

Nile valley region - NUBIA

Nimbus - HALO

Nine am service - TERSE

Nine: pref. - ENNEA

Nine-sider - NONAGON

Nineveh diety - NISROCH

Ninth day before the Ides - NONES

Nirvana attainer - ARHAT

Nisei's child - SANSEI

Nit-picker - PEDANT

Nitrogen compound - AMIDE, AMINE or AZID

Nitrogen once - AZOTE

Noah's son - HAM or SHEM

Nobby - NODAL

Noble gas - AGON or XEION

Nocturnal primate - LORIS or TARSIER

Noisome - FEDIT

Noisy fight - FRAY

Nonessential amino acid - SERINE

None clerics - LAICS

None foldable money - SPECIE

Nordic rugs - RYAS

Norman Neighbors - BRETONS

Norse chieftan - ROLLO

Norse dieties - VANIR

Norse giant - YMER or YMIR

Norse god - AESIR, LOKI, ODIN or TYR

Norse god of fate - NORN

Norse god of fire - LOGI

Norse god of peace or good weather - FREY

Norse god of the sea - AEGIR

Norse god of war - ODIN, TIU or TYR

Norse goddess of fate - NORNS

Norse goddess of death - HEL

Norse goddess of destiny - NORN

Norse goddess of love - FREYA

Norse gods - AESIR

Norse literary collection - EDDA

Norse mythological hero - EGIL

Norse pantheon - AESIR

Norse sea god - AEGIR

Norse underwolrd queen - HEL

North African
Antelope - ADDAX

North African lizard - ADDA

North African
mountains - ATLAS

North African
seaport - ALGIERS

North American
dogwood - OSIER

North American forest - TAIGA

North Dakota
native - MANDAN

North Sea feeder - DEE,
ELBE, ES, MEUSE,
ODOR or YSER

North Sea islands - FRISIAN

North Sea monster - KRAKEN

North seaport - AMDEN

North wind or northeast - BORA

Northeast wind - BORA

Northern bird - AUK

Northern constellation - LYRA

Northern forest - TAIGA

Nose & throat
problem - CARARRH

Nose feature - ALARE

Nostril - NARES

Not supported by
fact - APRIORI

Notch made by a saw - KERF

Notched - EROSE

Notched as a leaf - CRENATE

Not cleric - LAIC

Notable exploit - GEST

Nothing in Tantes - BIEN

Not kosher - TREF

Not spoken - TACIT

Not too much,
musically - NONTROPPO

Notch in wood - KERF

Noted fur trader - ASTOR

Noted weeper - NIOBE

Nothing - NIHIL

Notorious - ARRANT

Notty spot - NODUS

Nourishment - ALIMENT

November meteor
show - LEONIDS

Now: Sp. AHORA

Noxious - NOISOME

Noxious atmosphere or
gases - MIASMA

Noxious weed - TARE

NT book - HEB

Nuclear reactor in PA - TMI

Nucleus element or
particle - PION

Number system base - RADIX

Numeric start - OCTO

Nun's cap - COIF

Nurse sharks - GATAS

Nursemaid in India -
     AMAH or AYAH

Nutgeg's kin - ARIL

Nutria - COYPU

NYC museum - MOMA

NYC subway line - IRT

Nyctalopia - NIGHT
     BLINDNESS

Nymph - OREAD

Nymph of Greek
     mythology - CALLISTO

Nymph of the woods - DRYAD

Nymph turned into a laurel
     tree - DAPHNE

Nymph who loved
     Apollo - DAPHNE

Nymph who loved
     Narcissus - ECHO

Oar holder - THOLE

Oatmeal color - ECRU

Oatmeal
     concoction - POLENTA

Objects d'art - VIRTU

Oblong vestment - AMICE

Observation - ESPIAL

Observation balloon - SONDE

Occasional - ORRA

Occult doctorine - CABALA

Ocean-current vortexes - GYRES

Ocean sunfish - MOLA

Oceanid - NYMPH

Ocular receiver - RETINA

Oder triburary - WARTA

Odin by another
     name - WOTAN

Odin's home - ASGARD

Odorless, colorless gas - ARGON

Odysseus' dog - ARGUS

"Oedipus" composer - ONESCO

Of a people, pref. - ETHNO

Of a royal court - AULIC

Of an ancient alphabet - RUNIC

Of an epoch - ERAL

Of bears - URSINE

Of blood poisoning - TOXEMIC

Of dreams - ONEIRIC

Of five - PENTA

Of gold - AURIC

Of inferior social
     statuss - DECLASSE

Of lizards - SAURIAN

Of lyric poems - ODIC

Of sheep - OVINE

Of the breastbone - STERNAL

Of the cheekbone - MALAR

Of the dawn - AUROREAN
     or EOAN

Of the ear - OTIC or AURAL

Of the farm - AGRI

Of the intestines - ILEAC

Of the liver - HEPATIC

Of the morning - MATUTINAL

Of the soft palate - VELAR
Of the third order – TERTIARY
Of the tongue - GLOSSAL
Officer's badge - COCKADE
Official announcement - RESCRIPT
Official emissary - LEGATE
Official proceedings - ACTA
Official seal - CACHET
Official serving Caesar - AEDILE
Offspring - SCION
Oil free art - TEMPARA
Oil from orange flowers - NEROLI
Oil jar - CRUSE
Oily acid salt - OLEATE
Oily fish - MENHADEN
Oily liquid - OLEIN
Oily resin - ELEMI
Oily secretion - SEBUM
Ointment - NARD
Oise feeder - AISNE
Okinawa port - NAHA
Oklahoma Indian - ARAPAHO CHOCTAW
Old adage - SAW
Old alms box - ARCA
Old alphabet script - OGHAM
Old British coin - GROAT
Old card game - OMBER
Old Chinese kingdom - SHU

Old Chinese money - TAEL
Old city in Iran - SUSA
Old Egypian headdress Emblem - URAEUS
Old English bard - SCOP
Old English coin - GROAT or HAPPY
Old English gold piece - RYAL
Old English letters - EDHS
Old European coin - ECU
Old fool - MOME
Old French coin - ECU, SOU or OBOLE
Old French dance - GAVOTTE
Old Gaelic alphabet - OGHAM
Old Germanic coin - TALER or THALER
Old Germans - TEUTONS
Old gold coin - DUCAT
Old gold coin of Spain - PISTOLE
Old Greek city - ARGOS
Old Greek coins - OBOLI
Old Greek medicine man - GALEN
Old hag - BELDAM
Old Hebrew bushel - EPHA
Old Indian coin - ANNT
Old Irish alphabet - OGHAM
Old Italian coin - SOLDO
Old Jewish village - SHTETLS
Old manuscript sybols - OBELI

Old Italian coins - SCUDI or SOLDI

Old manuscript marks - OBELI

Old Nick - BEELZEBUB

Old Norse character Inscription or poem - RUNE

Old Norse poetry collection - EDDA

Old ointment - NARD

Old person - WIGHT

Old Peruvian currency - INTI

Old Portuguese coin - REI

Old Portuguese currency - ESCUDO

Old quilted garmet - ACTON

Old Roman port - OSTIA

Old sayings - SAWS

Old scratch - SATAN

Old shield - TARGE

Old Spanish coin - DINAR, DURO or REAL

Old stringed instrument - REBEC

Old style poetry - EPODE

Old sweetheart - LEMAN

Old territory in Morocco - IFNI

Old Testament judge - DEBORAH

Old Testament prophet - MICAH

Old Testament scribe - EZRA

Old thrusting sword - ESTOC

Old time dill - ANET

Old Turkish city - EDESSA

Old Turkish coin - ASPER

Old U.S. coin - DESME

Old, ugly woman - BELDAME

Old violin - CREMONA or REBEC

Old wagon - WAIN

Old womanish - ANILE

Old world badger - RATEL

Old world buffalo - ANOA

Old world bunting - ORTOLAN

Old world deer - ROE

Old world doormouuse - LEROT

Old world duck - SMEW

Old world finch - LINNET or SERIN

Old world fruit tree - SORB

Old world grain - RAGI

Old world lily - ASPHODEL

Old world lizard - AGAMA or SEPS

Old world monkey - VERVERT

Old world palm - ARECA

Old world plover - PEEWIT

Old world sandpiper - TEREK

Old world thrush - CHAT

Old world tree - SORB

Olefin - ALKENE

Olive genus - OLEA

Olive-green bird - VIREO

Olivine - PERIDOT

Olla podrida - STEW

Olympic cupbearer - HEBE

Omer, to a ephah - TENTH

Omnium gatherum - OLIO

On ones back - SUPINE

One after another - SERIATIM

One ampere per volt - SIEMENS

One-horse carriage - CARIOLE

One hundred dinars - RIAL

One hundred make a
    dracma - LEPTA

One hundred square
    meters - ARE

One-millionth of a
    meter - MICRO

One name model - IMAN

One name singer - SADE

One name supermodel - EMME

One of the Archangels - URIEL

One of the Fates - ATROPOS,
    CLOTHO or LACHESIS

One of the Furies - ALECTO,
    MEGAERA or
    TISIPHONE

One of the Hebrides -
    SKYE or IONA

One of the Maji GASPAR

One of the Muses - EUTERPE

One of the Pleiades - STEROPE

One of the wise men - CASPAR

One piece bathing
    suit - MAILLOT

One-quarter pint - GILL

One-seat carriage - STANHOPE

One-seeded fruits - AKENES
    or DRUPES

One square meter - CENTARE

One thousand
    calories - THERM

One thousand
    escudos - CONTO

One thousand fils - DINAR

One with a light
    bodybuild - ECTMORPH

Ones specialty - METIER

Oniony roll - BIALY

On the right - DEXTRAL

Oolong or Assam - TEA

Open air arcade - LOGGIA

Open air swimming pool - LIDO

Open shelter or openwork
    Trellis - RAMADA

Opera glasses - LORGNETTE

Opera passages - ARIOSOS

Operatic composition - SCENA

Operatic heroine - MIMI

Operatic passage - ARIOSO

Oppose - REPUGN

Opposite if kosher - TREF

Optical area - UVEA

Optomistic - ROSEATE

Oracle - SIBYL

Oracular - VATIC

Oral statement - PAROL

Orange like fruit - GENIPAP

Orbit point - APSIS

Orchestral gong - TAMTAM

Orchid product - SALEP
or TUBER

Ordinary worker - PROLE

Ore of Copper - AZURITE

Ore of iron - SIDERITE

Organ effect - TREMOLO

Organic basis of bone - OSSEIN

Organic compound - ACETAL,
AMIDE, AMINE, ENOL,
ESTER, HEXANE,
IMIDO or PHENOL

Organic fats - LIPIDS

Organized slaughter - POGROM

Oriental inn - SERAI

Oriental lynx - CARACAL

Oriental maid - AMAH

Oriental sailor - LASCAR

Oriental sash - OBI

Oriental tea - CHA

Oriental
warehouse - GODOWN

Orifices - ORA

Orinoco feeder - CARONI

Orinoco tributary - ARO

Orion's left foot - RIGEL

Oriole, e.g. - OSENE

Ornamental carp - KOI

Ornamental case - ETUI

Ornamental
candlestick - FLAMEAU

Ornamental Chinese
tree - GINKGO

Ornamental loop - PICOT

Ornamental plant -
CANNA or PILEA

Ornamental purse - ETUI

Ornamental shrub - JAPONICA,
OLEASTER or SPIREA

Ornamental stud - AGLET

Ornamental tree - CASSIA

Ostiary - LECTOR

Ostrich cousin – RHEA

Orthodox branch of
Islam - SUNNI

Ostrich cousin - RHEA

Ostrich relaltive - TINAMOU

Ostrich or emu - RATITE

O T Book - AMOS, DEUT,
ECCLES, ESTH, EXOD,
EZRA, ESTHER, HOSEA,
EZEK, GEN, HAB,
HAGGAI, ISA, JONAH,
LAM, LEV, MI CAH,
NEH, NEHUM, NUM,
OBAD, OBADIAH, PBAD,
PSA, PSALMS or RUTH

Othello's friend - IAGO

Other: Sp. - OTRA

Other: Lat. - ALIA

Other nations to
Israelis - GOYIM

Otic - AURAL

Ottoma - POUF

Outback instrument - DIGERIDOO

Outcast - PARIAH

Outer boundary - AMBIT

Outer coat of a seed - TESTA

Outer: Pref. - ECTO

Out lying community - EXURB

Oven for drying hops - OAST

Overhead cable car - TELPHER

Ox of India - ZEBU

Oxygen compound - OXIDE

Oxygen dependent creature - AEROBE

Oyster farm: Fr. - PARC

Pacific canoe - BANCA

Pacific island - SAMAR

Pacific plant - TARO

Pacific island country - NAURU

Pack leader – AKELA

Page size of a book - OCTAVO

Pagoda - TAA

Pain unit - DOL

Paint a word picture - LIMN

Painter of ballet dancers - DEGAS

Painter's undercoat - GESSO

Painting genre - OPART

Painting on dry plaster - SECCO

Painting technique - IMPASTO

Pair - DYAD

Paisa – 1/100th of a rupee

Pakistan bread - NANS

Pakistan language - ERDU

Pakistan River - INDUS

Pakistan rupee - PRE

Palace in Florence - PITTI

Palace in Istambul - TOPKAPI

Palace in Vatican City - LATERAN

Palatable - SAPID

Pale dry sherry – FINO

Pale yellow - ECRU

Palm cuckatoo - ARA

Palm starch - SAGO

Palm thatch - NIPA

Palm tree - ARECA

Pamper - COSSET

Panamanian coin - CESTESIMO

Pangolin - ANTEATER

Panhandle - CADGE

Papal embassador - NUNCIO

Papal body - CURIA

Papal cape - FANON or ORALE

Papal court - CURIA

Papal garment, veil or Vestment - ORALE

Papal hat - BIRETTE or MITRE

Papal scarf - ORALE

Papal silver coins - PAOLI

Papal tribunal - ROTA

Papaya - PAPAW

Papaya enzyme - PAPAIN
Paper measure - QUIRE
Paper size - DEMY
Papyrus plant - SEDGE
Parade of bullfighters - PASEO
Paradise - ELYSIUM
Paradise dweller - HOURI
Parasidic plant - DODDER
Parched - SERE
Parent of Titan - SATURN
Pariah - LEPER
Paris palace - ELYSEE
Paris' mother - HECUBA
Parisian seasons - ETES
Parish official - BEADLE
Parka - ANORAK
Parkinson's disease
    drug - LDOPA
Parquet circle - PARTERRE
Parr - SAMLET
Parrot - ECHO, KEA or LORY
Parson bird - TUI
Part of A. D. - ANNO
Part of D.O.S. - SYST.
Part of N.B. - BENE
Part of Q.E.D. - ERAT
Part of RSVP - SIL
Part of TNT - TOLUENE
Part of a T.A.E. - ALVA
Part of a chair - SPLAT
Part of a Krone - ORE

Part of a lariat - HONDO
Part of a meter - IAMB
Part of a nerve cell - AXONE
Part of a neuron - AXON
Part of a ships bow - HAWSE
Part of a sonata - RONDO
Part of a spur - ROWEL
Partial: pref. - SEMI
Particles in
  ·   electrolysis - ANIONS
Particles in
    suspension - COLLOIDS
Partner of Charybdis - SCYLLA
Partner of Lares - PENATES
Party to - INON
Passages in the body - ITERS
Passe - DEMODE
Passover - PESACH
Passover feast - SEDER
Pasta variety - ROTINI
Pasta wheat - DURAM
Paste gem - STRASS
Paste made from seseme
    seed - TAGINI
Pasternak heroine - LARQA
Pastoral diety - FAUN
Pastoral poem - IDYLL
Pasturage grass - FESCUE
Patched - PIEBALD
Patience - SOLITAIR
Patriotic group - SAR
Patron saint of artists - ELOI

Patron saint of girls - AGNES

Patron saint of Paris - DENIS

Patron saint of lawyers - IVES

Patronage - AEGIS

Paving block or stone - SETT

Payment to expedite service - BAKSHEESH

Peaceful - IRENIC

Peace pipe - CALUMET

Peaseful - IRENIC

Peach or apricot - DRUPE

Peacock constellation - PAVO

Peacock feather eyes - OCELL I

Peaked cap - KEPI

Pear-shaped fiddle - REBEC

Pear-shaped gem - BOULE

Pear variety - COMISE

Pearl diver - AMA

Pearly muscle - UNIO

Peasant - RYOT

Peasant skirt - DIRNDL

Peculiar: Pre. - IDIO

Pedestal base - PLINTH

Pedestal part - DADO

Peep show - RAREE

PeerGynt's composer - GRIEG

PeerGynt's creator - IBSEN

PeerGynt's dancer or princess - ANITRA

PeerGynt's mother - ASE

Pellet-size pasta - FARFEL

Pelvic bones - ILIA or SACRA

Pennant - FANON

Penquinlike bird - AUK

Pens and needles - STYLI

People of Borneo - DYAKS

People of Eastern Siberia - YAKUT

People of social standing - NOBS

Perceived by the ear - AURAL

Percussion istrument - CELESTA

Perennial herb - ACANTHUS or ARNICA

Perfect expression - MOTJUSTE

Perfidious - PUNIC

Perfume - CENSE

Perfume bottle - FLACON

Perfume ingredient - AMBERGRIS, ORRIS OR ROSEOIL

Perfume oil - NEROL

Perfumer's liquid - ACETAL

Perrywinkle genus - VANCA

Persian despot or governors - SATRAP

Persian elves or fairies - PERIS

Perssian profet - ZOROASTER

Persian sun god - MITHRAS

Persian wheel - NORIA

Persians - MEDES

Person with a loud voice - STENTOR

Personal instability - ANOMIE

Perspire - EGEST

Pertaining to deserts -EREMIC

Pertaining to dreams - ONEIRIC   Pertaining to hair - PILAR

Pertaining to knowledge - LORAL

Pertaining to the ear - OTIC

Pertinent - ADREM

Peruke - PERIWIG

Peruvian beast - ALPACA

Peruvian city - ICA

Peruvian coin - SOL

Pet peeve - BETA NOIRE

Petrarch's beloved - LAURA

Petty objection - CAVIL

Petty ruler or tyrant - SATRAP

Pharaoh - RED ANT

Pharaonic tomb - MASTABAH

Pheasant brood - NIDE

Pheasant ragu - SALMI

Philippine banana tree - ABACA

Philippine fibre - ABACA

Philippine fruit - PINA

Philippine island - CEBU, LEYTE, MINDANOA, PANAY or SAMAR

Philippine native - ATI

Philippine palm - NIPA

Philippine people - MOROS

Phiilippine plant - ABACA

Philippine seaport - CEBU, ILOILO, LUZON or MANILLA

Philippine termite - ANAI

Philippine tree - IBA

Philippine volcano - TAAL

Philistine city - GATH

Philistine god - DAGON

Philodendron, e.g. - AROID

Phoenician city - SIDON or TYRE

Phoenician diety - BAAL

Phoenician god or goddess - ASTARTE or BAAL

Phoenician port - TYRE

Phoney - POSEUR

Photographic, as memory - EIDETIC

Pianist's challenge - ARPEGGIO

Piano relative - CELESTA

Pickled food - SOUSE

Pictograph - GLYPH

Picture - LIMN

Picture puzzle - REBUS

Pidgeon's nose - CERE

Pie filling - NESSELRODE

Piedmont province - TORENO

Pig: Sp. - GORDO

Piglet - SHOAT

Pigment - OCHER

Pilasters - ANTAE

Pilchard - SARDINE

Pile of hay - MOW
Pile of stones - CAIRN
Pileus - CAUL
Pilgrim to Mecca - MOSLEM
Pillage - RAPINE
Pillow cover - SHAM
Pine tar derivaive - RETENE
Pineapple: Sp. - PINA
Pineapple fiber - ISTLE
Pinguid - OILY
Pintail duck - SMEE
Pions & kaons - MESONS
Pipe - HOOKAH
Pipe residue - DOTTLE
Pipe sealant - LUTE
Piranhas - CARIBES
Pita fiber - ISTLE
Pitcher - EWER or OLLA
Pitcher of beer - GROWLER
Pith helmet - TOPEE or TOPI
Pity - PATHOS
Place: Fr. - LIEU
Place of extreme
    torment - GHENNA
Plain weave fabric -
    BATISTE or REPP
Plains Indians - KIOWA
Plains tribe - DAKOTA
Planetary reflectioms - ABEDOS
Planetary shadow - UMBRA
Plankton form - DIATOM

Plant & animal life - BIOTA
Plant aperture - STOMA
Plant chewed in Arabia - QAT
Plant fluids - SERA
Plant fungus - DRYROT
Plant genus - ALOE
Plant louse - APHID or APHIS
Plant malady - EDEMA
Plant of hot regions - AGAVE
Plant of the arum or lily
    family - AROID
Plant pest - APHID or PHIS
Plant pore - STOMA
Plant root - RADIX
Plant rust - UREDO
Plant substance - TRAMA
Plant with a fragrant
    rootstock - ORRIS
Plant with colorful
    flowers - GENTIAN
Plant with human-like
    root - MANDRAKE
Plant with sword-shaped leaves -
    AGAVE or GLADIOLA
Plant with yellow flowers - AVE
Plantain lily - HOSTA
Plaster of Paris - GESSO
Plastics ingredient - UREA
Plate armour - CUIRASS
Plating alloy - TERNE
Playful leap - CAPRIOLE
Playing marble - NIB

Pleasingly plump - ZAFTIG

Pleasure seeker - HEDONIC

Pleated lace edging - RUCHE

Plenty, once - ENOW

Plexus - RETE

Pliable branch - WITHY

Plinth - ORLO or SOCLE

Plot - CABAL

Plow sole - SLADE

Plumb brandy - MIRABELLE

Plumbago - GRAPHITE

Plume of feathers - AIGRETTE

Plumed hat - SHAKO

Plunder - RAPINE or REAVE

Plunderer - RAPPAREE

Plunger for churning
    butter - DASHER

Pluto - DIS

Pluvious - RAINY

Poem division - CANTO

Poem's final stanza - ENVOI

Poem with 17 syllables - HAIKU

Poet's pause - CAESURA

Poetic feet - PAEONS

Poetic foot - IAMB

Poetic lament - ELEGY

Poetic patchwork - CENTO

Poetic postscript - ENVOI

Poetic Rhythm - METER

Poetic stanza - FESTINA

Poetry collection - EPOS

Poet's feet - ANAPESTS

Poet's Ireland - ERIN

Poet's muse - ERATO

Poi root - TARO

Poi sourse EDDO

Poinsettia, for one - SPURGE

Point of origin - SITUS

Pointed arch - OGIVE

Pointed window - LANCET

Pointless - OTIOSE

Poison - BANE

Poison oak or shrub - SUMAC

Poison snake - ADDER

Poison tree - UPAS

Poisonous evergreen
    shrub - OLEANDER

Poisonous evergreens - YEWS

Poisonous mosquito - AEDES

Poisonous
    mushroom - AMANITA

Poisonous plant - HEMLOCK
    or HENBANE

Poisonous snake - TAIPAN

Polar wear - ANORAK

Polder - LOWLAND
    RECLAIMED
FROM THE SEA

Polish dance - MAZZURKA

Polish lancer - UHLAN
    or ULAN

Political
    falsehood - ROORBACK

Political refugee - EMIGRE

Politically
neutral - MUGWUMP

Pollen bearer or
produce - ANTHER

Polynesian beverage - KAVA

Polynesian idol - TIKI

Polynesian skirt - PAREU

Polynesian wrap - LAVALAVA

Pompous - OROTUNG

Pond - MERE

Pond dross - SCUM

Pond plant - ALGA

Ponds - SEDGE

Pool table cover - BAIZE

Poor imitation - ERSATZ

Pope's emissary - LEGASE

Pope's fanon ORALE

Popeye's creator Segar - ELZIE

Poplar tree - ALAMO or ABELE

Porous limestone - TUFA

Port in Germany - KIEL

Port in Mexico - TAMPICO

Port in Portugal - TORO

Port near Belfast - LARNE

Port near Haifa - ACRE

Port of Brazil - BELEM

Port of Crete - CANE

Port of Israel - ACRE,
EILAT or HAIFA

Port of Italy - BARI

Port of old Rome - OSTIA

Port of Spain - BILBOA
or CADIZ

Port of Tunisia - SFAX

Port of Yeman - ADEN

Port on the Firth of Clyde AYR

Port on the Gulf of
Lion - MARSEILLES

Port on the Seine - ROUEN

Port on the Norweigen
Sea - BERGEN

Porte cochere - COVERED
DRIVEWAY

Portable supply
cabinet - TABORET

Portents - OMENS or
PRESAGES

Portico of old Grease - STOA

Portray - LIMN

Portuguese cape - ROCA

Portuguese colony in
India - GOA

Portuguese seaport - SETUBAL

Portuguese
statesman - GRANDEE

Portuguese wine - MADEIRA

Positive particle - CATION

Poster paint - TEMPERA

Posterior - CAUDAL

Pot - OLLA

Pot herb - ORACH

Potassium compound - NITER

Potato dumpling - GNOCCI

Potato pancake - LATKE

Potato pastry - KNISH

Potpourri - OLIO

Pouch - BURSE

Pout - MOUE

Pourboire - TIP

Powder from caster oil
plant - RICIN

Powdered diamonds - BORT

Powdered, in heraldry - SEME

Powdered volcanic rock - TRASS

Power org. - TV

Powerful - PUISSANT

Powerful explosive - AMATOL

Practice fly ball - FUNGO

Prank - DIDO

Pray in Latin - ORA

Prayer - ORISON

Prayer bench - PRIEDEAU

Praying figure in art - ORANT

Pre-Aztec Indian - TOLTEC

Preamble or preface - PROEM

Predatory bird - KITE or SKUA

Predatory sea bird - JAEGER

Prefix for both - AMBI

Prefix for seven - HEPTA

Prefix meaning "bone" - OSTEO

Prefix meaning "peculiar" - IDIO

Pregnant - ENCIENTE

Prehistoric ax - CELT

Prehistoric stone tool - EOLITH

Prehistoric tomb - CIST

Pre-Mayan people - OLMEC

Prepare into pellets - PRILL

Presidential pooch - FALA

Press to commit
perjury - SUBORN

Prestige - CACHET

Pretender - POSEUR

Prickley pear - NOPAL

Prickly plant - TEASEL

Prickley shrub - Briar or GORSE

Priest of Babylon - EZRA

Priestly dress - EPHOD

Priestly vestment - FANO

Priest's cloak - COPO

Priest's robe - ALB

Priestess of Bacchus - MAENAD

Prima ballarina - ETOILE

Primary Roman
hill - POLATINE

Prime minister before
Gladstone - DISRAELI

Primitive wheat - SPELT

Primrose relative - OXLIP

Prince Valiant's wife - ALETA

Princess Leia's last
name - ORGANA

Princess of myth - IOLE

Principal ore of lead - GALENA

Principle - TENET

Printer's direction -
CARET or STET

Printer's
    emblem - COLOPHONE
Printer's mark - CARET
    or DELE
Printer's measure - EM or PICA
Printing ink ingredient - ELEMI
Printing mistakes - ERRATA
Printing term - STET
Prized clam - QUAHOG
Proceedings - ACTA
Process of mountain
    formation - ORDGENY
Professional retirees - EMERITI
Profet - AUGUR
Profound sleep - SOPOR
Profusion - ARIOT
Progressive emaciation - TABES
Promatory - NESS
Promenade - PASEO
Promise of
    marriage - AFFIANCE
Promising up-and-
    comer - PHENOM
Promoting pease - IRENIC
Pronouncements - DICTA
Pronunciation
    dots - DIAERESIS
Property seller - ALIENOR
Prophet of Delphi - ORACLE
Prophetess of Israel - DEBORAH
Proscribe - BAN
Prosperity - WEAL

Prospero's servant - ARIEL
Prospero's slave - CALIBAN
Prostitue - TRULL
Protection - AEGIS
Protection: var. - EGIS
Potest angrily - INVEIGH
Protozoan - AMOEBA
Provencal song - SERENA
Provencal verse - SESTINA
Province of China - SHENSI
Prufrock's creator - ELIOT
Prussian lancer - UHLAN
Psychological threshold - LIMEN
Public lecture hall - LYCEUM
Public place for
    walking - PASEO
Public sentiment - ETHOS
Public warehouse - ETAPE
Publishing # - ISBN
Puccini heroine - MIMI
Puckered fabric finsih - PLISSE
Pueblo ceremonial
    chamber - KIVA
Pueblo dweller - ZUNI
Pueblo Indian - PIRO
Pueblo Iindian village - ACOMA
Pueblo people - TIWA
Puerto Rican seaport - PONCE
Puff adder - HOGNOSE
Pulitzer novelist - AGEE
Pulpit - AMBO

Pulverize - TRITURATE

Pumpkin or squash - PEPO

Pundit - SWAMI

Punish - MULET

Punish by fine - AMERSE

Punishment stick - FERULE

Punjabi beleiver - SIKH

Punkie - GNAT

Pupa graduate - IMAGO

Purple seaweed - NORI

Purpose - NONCE

Purposeful - TELIC

Put forward as fact - POSIT

Put on clothes - DIGHT

Puzzle - REBUS

Pyramus' lover - THISBE

Pyrenees Republic - ANDORRA

Q.E.D word - ERAT

Quadriceps locales - LEGS

Quality of taste - SAPOR

Quarter acre of land - ROOD

Quarter of a
    denarius - SESTERSE

Quarter-pint - GILL

Queen of Carthage - DIDO

Queen of France - REINE

Queen of Hades - HECATE

Queen of heaven - HERA

Queen of Italy - ELENA

Queen of Jordan - NOOR

Queen of Norway - SONJA

Queen of Persia - ESTHER

Queen of Spain - ENA

Queen of Sparta - LEDA

Queen of Thebes - NIOBE

Queen of the fairies - TITANIA

Queue - BRAID

Quibble - CAVIL

Quick drying paint - TEMPERA

Quick glance or
    impression - APERCU

Quickly - PRESTO

Quip - EPIGRAM or SALLY

Quisling - TRAITOR

Quivering - ASPEN

Qumram inhabitant - ESSENE

Quorum in a
    synagog - MINYAN

RNA component - URACIL

Rabbit - CONEY

Rabbit-eared bandicoot - BILBY

Rabbit ears - DIPOLE

Rabbit fur - CONY or LAPIN

Rabbit kin - AGOUTI

Rabbit's tail - SCUT

Raccoon kin - COATI

Raccoon like mammal - PANDA

Rachel's father - LABAN

Radame's beloved - AIDA

Radioactivity unit - CURIE

Radon, originally - NITON

Raga rythem-maker - TABLA

Rain god - CHAAC

Rain forest cat - JAGUAR

Rain forest vine - LIANE

Rainbow goddess - IRIS

Rainbow trout - STEELIE

Rajah's wife - RANI

Rake - ROUE

Rams-horn horn - SHOFER

Range of Kyrgyzstan - ALAI

Range ridge - ARETE

Rank in taste - RAMMISH

Rapacious seabird - SKUA

Rare-earth element - TERBIUM

Ravine - BARRANCA
or NULLAH

Rayed flower - ASTER
or OXEYE

Razor-billed auk - MURRE

Razor-billed birds - AUKS

Reach in amount - RUN TO

Readily - LIEF

Reading desk – AMBO

Real - PUKKA

Reason to say "oy vey" - TSURIS

Recess in a church - APSE

Recital halls - ODIA

Recluse - ANCHORET
or EREMITE

Recorded proceedings - ACTA

Recoverable cargo cast
adrift - LAGAN

Recurring musical
phrases - LEITMOTIV

Rectangular paving stone - SETT

Rectangular pier or
pilaster - ANTA

Red - CERISE

Red bood cell
component - HEME

Red cedar - SAVIN

Red chalcedony - CARNELIAN

Red deer - HART

Red dye - EOSIN

Red dye plant - MADDER

Red giant star - MINA

Red pig - DUROC

Red pigment - OCHER

Red quartz - JASPER

Red rockfish - TAMBOR

Red sea port - JIDDA or SUEZ

Red soil - LATERITE

Redactor - EDITOR

Reddish brown - RUSSETY

Reddish-brown
gemstone - SARD

Reddish deer - ROES

Reddish hartebeest - TORA

Reddish orange - JACINTH

Reddish rash - ROSEOLA

Redolent compound - ESTER

Reedy pond - SLUE

Refractive unit - DIOPTER

Refuge - EMIGRE

Refuges - ASYLA

Refuse - OFFAL

Regan's dad - LEAR

Regarding - ANENT

Region of Egypt and
    Sudan - NUBIA

Region of France - ALSACE

Region of old
    France - DANELAW

Region of South
    America - PATAGONIA

Region of Spain - CASTILE

Region south of the
    Sahara - SAHEL

Region that includes
    Ephesus - IONIA

Regional life - BIOTA

Related maternally - ENATE

Related on the father's
    side - AGNATE

Relating to grandparents - AVAL

Relating to lungs - LOBAR

Relating to summer - ESTIVAL

Relating to the
    cheekbone - MALAR

Release a claim to - REMISE

Release Mechanism - DETENT

Relevant - APROPOS

Relevant in law - ADREM

Relict - WIDOW

Religious booklet - ORDO

Religious convert - PROSELYTE

Religious flight - REGIRA

Religious recluse - EREMITE

Religious residence - PRIORY

Religious retreat - ASHRAM

Relinquish - DEMIT

Reliquary - ARCA

Remaining out of sight - PERDU

Remarkable - UNCO

Remarkable person - PHENOM

Remission - REMITTAL

Remove in printing - DELE

Renaissance
    instrument - REBEC

Repetition - ROTE

Representative - TYPAL

Reproductive cells - GAMETES

Reptile covering - SCUTE

Research baloon - SONDE

Resin - ANIME

Resin used in
    varnish – SANDARAC

Resonant of voice - OROTUND

Respected one - DOYEN

Restrain - BATE or TRAMMEL

Retardanto - SLOWER

Retinal cells - RODS

Retired - AMERITUS

Retired professors - EMERITI

Reused wool - MUNGO

Rhine feeder - AARE, MOSEL,
    MOSELLE or RUHR

Rhone feeder - ISERE or SAONE

Rhythmic pattern of a stanza - METER

Rib - COSTA

Ribbed cloth - TRICOT

Ribbed fabric - FAILLE or REP

Rice dish - KEDGEREE or RISOTTO

Rice like pasta - ORZO

Rich fertilizer - GUANO

Rich ice cream - TORTONI

Rich king - CROESUS

Rich: Sp. - RICO

Rich tapestry - ARRAS

Rich-voiced - OROTUND

Rich yeast bread - STOLLEN

Riches - PELF

Riddle - KOAN

Ridge - ARETE

Ridge with a cliff - CUESTA

Ridges - WEALS

Riding crop or whip - QUIRT

Rigel's constellation - ORION

Right hand page - RECTO

Rigid disciplinarian - MARTINET

Ring of color - AREOLA

Ring shape - ANNULAR

Ring stone - SARD

Ring-tailed lemur - MAKI

Ring worm - TINEA

Rio Grande feeder - PECOS

Rio native - CARIOCA

Ripple pattern on a stamp - MOIRE

Risque - SCABROUS

Ritual washbasin - LAVABO

Rival of Sparta and Athens - ARGOS

River at Runnymede - THAMES

River deposit - ALLUVIUM

River in Africa - NIGER or UELE

River in Alaska - YUKON

River in Albania - DRIN

River in Albuqueque - RIO GRANDE

River in Amiens - SOMME

River in Ann Arbor - HURON

River in Arezzo - ARNO

River in Argentina - PARANA

River in Arizona - GILA

River in Arles - RHONE

River in Asia - AMUR, OXUS or YALU

River in Australia - NAMOI

River in Austria - ENNS

River in Avignon - RHONE

River in Baghdad - TIGRIS

River in Bath - AVON

River in Belarus - NEMAN

River in Belgium - LYS, LESSE, OISE or YSER

River in Berlin - HAVEL
or SPREE

River in Bolivia - BENI or RIO

River in Bonn - RHINE

River in Boston - CHARLES

River in
Botswana - OKAVANGO

River in Brazil - PARA
or PARNAIBA

River in Breslau - ODER

River in British
Columbia - FRASER
or SKEENA

River in Burma - IRRAWADDY

River in Caen - ORNE

River in Canada - LIARD

River in Cardiff - TAFF

River in Carlsbad - PECOS

River in Carolina - NEUSE
or PEEDEE

River in Chanilly - OISE

River in Chile - LOA

River in China - AMUR, HAN,
HSI, HUANG, ILI or WEI

River in Cologne - RHINE

River in Columbia -
CAUCA or META

River in Cornwall - TAMAR

River in Cuxhaven - ELBE

River in Dallas - TRINITY

River in Devon - EXE

River in Dresden - ELBE

River in East Asia - AMUR

River in England - AIRE,
AVON, EXE, OUS,
OUSE, SARRY or SEINE

River in Essen - RHUR

River in Ethiopia - OMO

River in Europe - EGER

River in Flanders - YSER

River in Florence - ARNO

River in Flores - REO

River in France - LOIRE, LYS,
OISE, ORNE, SAONE,
SELLE or YSER

River in Frankfurt - ODER

River in Geneva - RHONE

River in Germany - EDER,
ELBE, EMS, ILLE,
ISAR, RHONE, RUHR,
SAAR or WESER

River in Ghana - VOLTA

River in Glasgow - CLYDE

River in Grenoble - ISERE

River in Hades - LETHE

River in Hamburg - ELBE

River in Hartes - EURE

River in Holland –
IJSSEL or LEK

River in Hungary - EGER

River in Iberia - MINHO

River in Illinois - KASKASKIA

River in Indiana - MAUMEE
or WABASH

River in Interlaken - AARE

River in Ireland - ERNE
or SHANNON

River in Italy - ARNO,
NERA or RUBICON

River in Kansas - OSAGE

River in Karnak - NILE

River in Kashmir - INDUS

River in Kazakhstan -
URAL or CHU

River in Kenya - TANA

River in Khabarovsk - AMUR

River in Khartoum - NILE

River in Koln - RHINE

River in Korea - KAN or YALU

River in Krakow - VISTULA

River in Kubla Kahn - ALPH

River in Leeds - AIRE

River in Leningrad - SEVA

River in Lisbon - TAGUS

River in Louisville - OHIO

River in Lyon - RHONE
or SAONE

River in Maine - SACO

River in Mali - NIGER

River in Manchester - MERSEY

River in Manchuria -
AMUR or YALU

River in Memphis - NILE

River in Mongolia - ARIVER

River in Montana - MARIAS
or TETON

River in Munich - ISAR

River in Nantes - LOIRE

River in Nebraska - PLATTE

River in New
Brunswick - RARITAN

River in Newcastle - TYNE

River in New Jersey - PASSAIC

River in New York - AUSABLE,
GENESEE or TIOGA

River in Normandy - ORNE

River in North
Carolina - PEEDEE

River in North Dakota -
GOOSE or SHEYENNE

River in North Korea - YALU

River in Nottingham - TRENT

River in Ohio - SCIOTO

River in Opole - ODER

River in Orel - OKA

River in Orenburg - URAL

River in Orleans - LOIRE

River in Orsk - URAL

River in Pakistan - INDUS

River in Paris - SEINE

River in Pennsylvania - TIOGA

River in Perth - TAY

River in Peru - SANTA

River in Pittsburg - OHIO

River in Poland - NEISSE
or ODER

River in Richmond - JAMES

River in Roanne - LOIRE

River in Rochester - GENESEE

River in Romania - OLT
or MURES

River in Rome - TIBER

River in Rostov - DON

River in Russia - DON, LENA,
NEVA, OKA, SERET,
URAL or VOLGA

River in Rutgers - RARITAN

River in Rybinsk - VOLGA

River in Saragossa - EBRO

River in Saxony - WESER

River in Scotland - AFTON,
CLYDE, DEVON or TAY

River in Siberia - LENA
or AMUR

River in Silesia - ODER

River in Soissons - AISNE

River in Solothurn - AARE

River in South Africa -
LIMPOPO or VAAL

River in South
Carolina - SANTEE

River in Spain - EBRO

River in Staffordshire - TRENT

River in Stettin - ODER

River in St. Petersburg - NEVA

River in
Stratford - HOUSATONIC

River in Suffern - RAMAPO

River in SW Asia - ARAS

River in Sweden - TORNE

River in Terre Haute - WABASH

River in Texas - SABINE

River in Thailand - NAN

River in Thun - AAR

River in Tibet - INDUS

River in Timbuktu - NIGER

River in the Congo - UELE

River in the Punjab - RAVI

River in Toledo - MAUMEE

River in Tours - LOIRE

River in Turkey - ARAS

River in Tuscany - ARNO

River in Ukraine - DONETS,
ONESTR or STYR

River in Venezuela -
APURE, ARO
or ORINOCO

River in Wroclaw - ODER

River in Verdun - MEUSE

River in Virginia - OTTER

River in Warsaw - VISTULA

River in
Washington - SPOKANE

River in West Virginia - OHIO

River in Yakutsk - LENA

River in York - OUSE

River in Yorkshire - AIRE,
OUSE or URE

River in Zaire - EULE

River in Xanadu - ALPH

River into Issyk-kul - CHOW

River into Lake Utah - PROVO

River into the Severn - AVON

River into the Snake - GROS VENTRE

River into the Oise - AISNE

River into the Wash - OUSE

River islets - AITS or RIAS

River near Lethe - STYX

River near Nottingham - TRENT

River near Rutgers - RARITAN

River near Monterey - SALINAS

River nymph - NAIAD or NAIS

River of Aragon - EBRO

River of Argentina - PARANA

River of Brandenburg - ODER

River of England - OUSE

River of Flanders - YSER

River of Florence - ARNO

River of forgetfulness - LETHE

River of France - AUBE

River of Frankfurt - ODER

River of Grand Forks - RED

River of Hades - LETHE

River of Hesse - EDER

River of Indiana - WABASH

River of Ireland - ERNE

River of Leeds - AIRE

River of Oblivion - LETHE

River of Portugal & Spain – TAGUS

River of Provance - RHONE

River of Sweden - UME

River of Xanadu - ALPH

River rat - COYPU or NUTIA

River through Alaska - YUKON

River through Bejing - HAI

River through Logono - EBRO

River through Hesse - FULDA

River through Lower Saxony - EMS

River through Northern Ireland - ERNE

River through Opole - ODER

River through Pakistan - INDUS

River through Perth Amboy - RARITAN

River through Pittsburg - OHIO

River through Rouen - SEINE

River through Switzerland - RHINE

River through the Savoy Alps - ISERE

River through Toledo - MAUMEE

River through Tours - LOIRE

River through Wales - SEVERN

River to Donegal Bay - ERNE

River to Korea Bay - YALU

River to Lake Baikal - SELENGA

River to Lake Geneva - RHONE

River to Lake Ontario - OSWEGO

River to Siegen - EDER

River to the Amazon -
    JAPURA or NEGRO

River to the Adriatic - ADIGE

River to the Arabian
    sea - INDUS

River to the Arctic
    Ocean - LENA

River to the Balltic - ODER

River to the Black sea -
    DANUBE or DNEPR

River to the Caspian Sea -
    KURA, URAL or VOLGA

River to the
    Chesapeake - POTOMAC

River to the Colorado - GILA

River to the Congo - UBANGI

River to the Danube - DRAVE,
    ENNS or ISAR

River to the Dniester - SECRET

River to the Ebro - ARAGON

River to the Elbe - EGER
    or OSTE

River to the English
    Channel - EXE
or SOMME

River to the Euphrates - TIGRIS

River to the Fulda - EDER
    or WESER

River to the
    Gironde - GARONNE

River to the Gulf of
    Finland - NEVA

River to the Gulf of
    Lions - RHONE

River to the
    Hudson - MOHAWK

River to the Irish Sea - DEE

River to the Laptev Sea - LENA

River to the Ligurian
    Sea - ARNO

River to the
    Mediteranian - EBRO

River to the Mississippi - OHIO,
    ST.CROIX or YAZOO

River to the Missouri - KANSAS,
    OSAGE or PLATTE

River to the Moselle - SAAR

River to the North Sea - ELBE,
    EMS, GREAT, MEUSE,
    ODER, OUSE, RHINE
    TEES, TYNE, WESER
or YSER

River to the Odor - OPPA
    or WARTA

River to the Ohio - MIAMI
    or WABASH

River to the Oise - AIRE,
    AISNE or CAM

River to the Orinoco -
    AARO or CARONI

River to the Ouse -
    AIRE or CAM

River to the Severn -
    AVON or WYE

River to the Rennes - ILLE

River to the Rhine -
    AARE, MOSEL
or RUHR

River to the Rhone -
    ISERE or SAONE

River to the Rio
    Grande - PECOS

River to the Sea of
    Okhotsk - AMUR

River to the Seine - AUBE,
    EURE, MARNE or WYE

River to the Severn - AVON

River to the South China
    Sea - MEKONG

River to the
    St.Lawrence - OTTAWA

River to the Ubangi - UELE

River to the Volga - KAMA,
    OKA or SAMARA

River to the Yangtze - HAN

River to the Yellow Sea - YALU

Riverbank plant - SEDGE

Riverleaf - HEPATICA

RNA component - URACIL

RNA constituent - ADENINE

Robery by a gang - DACOITY

Robin relative - VEERY

Rock boring tool - TREPAN

Rock braking tool - GAD

Rock garden plant - SEDUM

Rock mineral - FELDSPAR

Rock plant - LICHEN

Rock salt - HALITE

Rock shelter - ABRI

Rocky barren plateau - FJELD

Rocky peak or crag - TOR

Rochy ridge - ARETE

Rodent - AGOUTI

Roll of coins - ROULEAU

Romaine - COS

Roman body armour - LORICA

Roman bronze - AES

Roman Catholic
    tribunal - ROTA

Roman coin - AES or
    SESTERCE

Roman commander - AGRIPPA

Roman commoner - PLEB

Roman courtyard - ATRIA

Roman dictator - SULLA

Roman emporer - OTHO,
    NERVA or TRAJAN

Roman emperor after
    Galba - OTHO

Roman emperor after
    Trajan - HADRIAN

Roman festival - FERIA

Roman galley - BIREME
    or TRIREME

Roman god - AMOR,
    DIS or LAR

Roman god of festivity &
    Revelry - COMUS

Roman god of the
sea - NEPTUNE

Roman god, to a poet - JOVE

Roman goddess - BONA,
DEA or PAX

Roman goddess of
horses - EPONA

Roman goddess of
war - BELLONA

Roman gods - DEI

Roman guardian spirits - GENII

Roman hades - ORCUS

Roman hero - AENEAS

Roman historian - LIVY

Roman household gods -
LARES or PENATES

Roman judge or
magistrate - EDILE
or PRAETOR

Roman market place - FORA

Roman moon goddess - LUNA

Roman official - EDILE

Roman philosopher - SENECA

Roman poet - CATO or OVID

Roman politician or
censor - CATO

Roman road - ITER

Roman robe - STOLA

Roman ruler - OTHO

Roman sea god - NEPTUNE

Roman senate - CURIA

Roman squares - FORA

Roman statesman - CATO

Roman token - TESSERA

Roman tunic - STOLA

Romanian coin - BANI or LEU

Romanian round
dance - HORAH

Romanov emperor - TSAR

Rome's port - OSTIA

Romeo's
surname - MONTAGUE

Roofing material - TERNE

Rookie - TYRO

Rooms in a harem - ODAS

Rooster - CHANTICLEER

Root - RADIX

Root used in perfume - ORRIS

Root vegetable - CELERIAC
or SALSIFY

Rootrot - EDEMA

Rope fibre - ABACA, BAST,
COIR or OAKEM

Rope plant - AGAVE

Rorqual - SEI WHALE

Rose bay - OLEANDER

Rose colored dye - EOSIN

Ross island volcano - EREBUS

Roster - ROTA

Rotary enginer
name - WANKEL

Rough earthenware - RAKU

Round mass - BOLUS

Round windows - OCULI

Rounded molding - OVOLO
Royal crown - DIADEM
Royal treasury - FISC
Rubber trees - ULES
Ruby - CARMINE
Rubylike jemstone - SPINEL
Rudimentary seed - OVULE
Ruffles on shirts - JABOTS
Ruined city in Jordan - PETRA
Ruins of Thebes - LUXOR
Ruler of Tunis - DEY
Ruling clique
    member - OLIGARCH
Rum cake - BABA
Rumanian coin - LEY
Rumba-like dance - BEGUINE
Rumor - ONDIT
Rump - NATES
Run away from debt - LEVANT
Run quickly - HARE
Rural - BUCOLIC
Rural diety - FAUN
Russian alphabet - CYRILLIC
Russian assembly - DUMA
Russian ballet - KIROV
Russian brew - KVASS
Russian city - OREL
Russian commune - MIR
Russian comrade - TOVARISH
Russian convention - RADA
Russian cooperative - ARTEL

Russian crepe - BLINI
Russian dog breed - BORZOI
Russian farm - ARTEL
Russian forest - TAIGA
Russian hemp - RINE
Russian inland sea - ARAL
Russian lake - ONEGA
Russian legislative body - DUMA
Russian measure of
    distance - VERST
Russian pancake - BLINI
Russian parliament - DUMA
Russian peasant - KULAK
    or MOUJIK
Russian prison - GULAG
Russian range - ALAI or URAL
Russian retreat - DACHA
Russian river - OKA or URAL
Russian saint - OLGA
Russian sea - AZOV
Russian summer home or
    villa - DACHA
Russian village - MIR
Russian wolfhound - BORZOI
Rustling sound - SUSURRUS
Rye fungus - ERGOT
Rye grass - DARNEL
Sabbath bread - CHALLAH
Sacrament vessel - PYX
Sacramental oil - CHRISM
Sacred Bookks of
    Hinduism - VEDA

Sacred Buddhist
Mountain - OMEI

Sacred bull of Egypt - APIS

Sacred chest - ARCA

Sacred chorale - MOTET

Sacred Egyptian bird - IBIS

Sacred Egyptian bull - APIS

Sacred Hindu writings - VEDA

Sacred poem - PSALM

Sacred: Pref. - HAGIO

Sacred river of Kubla
Khan - ALPH

Sacred song - MOTET

Sacred story set to
music - ORATORIO

Sacred text - TORA

Sacred tree of India - BO

Sacrifice - IMMOLATE

Sad song - DIRGE

Saddle part - CANTLE

Safecracker - YEGG

Saga - GEST

Sage - AGNOSTIC, RAMONA,
SALVIA or SAVANT

Sagebrush genus - ARTEMISIA

Saharan nomad - TUAREG

Saharan wind - SIROCCO

Sailing vessel - XEBEC

Sailor's saint - ELMO

Salad cheese - FETA

Salad style - NICOISE

Salad veggie - ESCAROLE

Salamander - EFT or NEWT

Salinger heroine - ESME

Sally - QUIP

Salmon that has spawned - KELT

Salt - NACL or OLEATE

Salt containing gold - AURATE
or AUREATE

Salt: Fr. - SEL

Salt tree - ATLE

Saltpeter - NITER

Salve - UNGUENT

Samhita - VEDA

Samoan capital & sea
port - APIA

Samoan coin - TALA

Samoan currency - SENE

Samoan island - UPOLU

Samoan port - APIA

Samoan skirt - LAVALAVA

Samuel's teacher - ELI

Samurai code - BUSHIDO

Sand-laden wind - SIMOOM

Sandarac tree - ARAR

Sandpiper - REEVE

Sandpiper's
cousin - RHALAROPE

Sandy ridge - ESKER

Sarandac tree - ARAR

Satelite of Jupiter - ELARA,
EUROPA or LEDA

Satelite of Mars - DEIMOS
or PHOBOS

Satalite of Neptune -
    TRITON or HEREID

Satelite of Saturn - DIONE,
    HELENE, RHEA or TYR

Satelite of Uranus - ARIEL,
    OBERON, MIRANDA,
    TITANIA or UMBRIEL

Satiate - CLOY

Saudi Arabian coin - RIYAL

Savage - LUPINE

Sawbones saw - TREPHINE

Saxony River - WESER

Saxony seaport - EMDEN

Scale on the underside of
    a snake - SCUTE

Scandinavian coin - ORE

Scandinavian god of strife - TYR

Scandinavian rugs - RYAS

Scan-line pattern - RASTER

Scar - CICATRIX or POCK

Scenic walk - PASEO

Schmaltz - BATHOS

Scholar - PEDANT

Scholarly - ERUDITE

Scholarly book - TOME

Scholarly paper - TREATISE

Schonbrunn palace
    site - VIENNA

School of
    Buddhism - MAHAYANA

School of whales - GAM or POD

Scope - AMBIT

Score after deuce - ADIN

Scorpion, E.G. - ARACHNID

Scottish boat - SKAFFIE

Scottish
    broadsword - CLAYMORE

Scottish chieftan - THANE

Scottish church - KIRK

Scottish dagger - DIRK,
    SKEAN or SNEE

Scottish dowry - TOCHER

Scottish hawke - GOS

Scottish highlander - GAEL

Scottish hillside - BRAE

Scottish island - ARRAN,
    IONA or SKYE

Scottish port - AYR

Scottish resort - OBAN

Scottish spa - TROON

Scottish tenant farm - CROFT

Scottish tree - ARN

Scottiosh uncles - EMES

Scoundrel - LOSEL

Scourge - KNOUT

Scree - TALUS

Scriptual
    manuscripts - CODICES

Scriptures reader - LECTOR

Scup - PORGIE

Scythe handle - SNATH

Sea bird - PETREL

Sea cow - DUGONG

Sea cucumber - TREPANG

Sea duck - SCOTER

Sea eagle - ERNE

Sea east of the Caspian - ARAL

Sea god - NEPTUNE

Sea goose - GANNET

Sea holly - ERYNGO

Sea in Russia - AZOV

Sea lettuce - ULVA

Sea monster - LEVIATHAN

Sea nymph - NEREIDES
    or OCEANID

Sea off Corfu - IONIAN

Sea otter - KALAN

Seagulls - MEWS

Seaport in Belgium - GHENT

Sea polyp - ANEMONE

Seaport in Brittany - BREST

Seaport in India - MADRAS

Sea port in Jordan - AQABA

Sea port in West
    Glamorgan - SWANSEA

Seaport of Ghana - TEMA

Sea port of Italy - GENOA
    or RIMINI

Sea port on Hokkaido - OTARU

Sea port on the Bay of
    Biscay - LAROCHELLE
    or SANTANDER

Seaplane inventor
    Glenn - CURTISS

Sea urchins - ECHINI

Seal - SIGIL

Sealing substance - LUTE

Seaside shrub - GORSE

Seasonal laborer - BRACERO

Seasoning paste - MISO

Seaweed extract or
    product - AGAR
or POTASH

Second crop of hay - ROWEN

Secret - ARCANUM

Secret stuff - ARCANA

Sect of Islam - SHIA

Secular - LAIC

Secular priest - ORATORIAN

Seed appendage - ARIL

Seed coat or cover - TESTA

Seed plant - SESEME

Seed scars - HILA

Seedlet - OVULE

Seine - NET

Seine feeder - AUBE, EURE,
    MARNE, OISE or SAONE

Self destructive
    instinct - THANATOS

Self evident truth - AXION

Self: pref. - AUT

Semi-aquatic rodent -
    CAPY BARA

Semicircular bench - EXEDRA

Semiconductor
    additives - DOPANTS

Semimetalic element - BORON

Semiprecious gem - BALAS

Senate of old Rome - CURIA

Senile sort - DOTARD

Senior member - DOYEN

Sense of touch - TACTUAL

Sentimentaal: Fr. - GARDE

Seoul soldier - ROK

Seraglio - HAREM or ZENANA

Seraglio unit - ODA

Serbian folk dance - KOLO

'Serf - THRALL

Serf, of old - ESNE

Serpent - PHIDIAN

Servant slave - THRALL

Serving tray - SALVER

Sesame plant - BENNE or TIL

Sesame seed paste - TAHINI

Seth's brother - ABEL

Seth's son - ENOS

Setting for
    Hamlet - ELSINMORE

Seven: Sp. - SIETE

Severn tributary - AVON
    or WYE

Seville attraction - ALCAZAR

Sewing machine
    inventor - HOWE

Sexless word - EPICENE

Shad like fish - ALEWIVES

Shaddock fruit - POMELO

Shade of brown - SEPIA

Shaded walk - ALAMEDA

Shaggy rug - RYA

Shakespear's foot - IAMB

Shakespearean king - ALONZO

Shakespearean sprite - ARIEL

Shalom - PEACE

Sham: Pref. - PSEUDO

Shank - CRUS

Shanks - CRURA

Sharp crest - ARETE

Sharp ridge - ARRIS

Shasta - DAISY

Sheath - THECA

Shed, as skin - SLOUGH

Sheepfold - COTE or REE

Sheepish - OVINE

Sheepskin leather - ROAN

Sheer fabric - NINON

Sheet - PONE

Sheik's garmet - ABA

Shellback - SAILOR

Shell-less marine
    snail - NUDIBRANCH

Shelter for birds - COTE

Sherry of Spain - XERES

Shield bearing or border - ORLE

Shield boss - UMBO

Shield of Zeus - AEGIS

Shield with a coat of
    arms - ESCUTCHEON

Shiite leader - AYATOLLAH

Shinbone - TIBIA

Shinto temple gateway - TORII

Ship-shaped clocks - NEFS

Ship's boat - PINNACE

Ship's deck - ORLOP

Shipworm - BORER
or TEREDO

Shiva - PERIOD OF
MORNING

Shivering - AGUEY

Shoe Part or strip - WELT

Shooter marble - RAREE

Shore bird - AVOCET,
CURLEW, DOTTREL,
ERNE, PLOVER, RAIL,
SORA or TERN

Short billed rail - CRAKE

Short billed wading
bird - PLOVER

Short cape - MANTELEY

Short, erect tail - SCUT

Short fibre - NOIL

Short legged horse - COB

Short lived things - EPHEMERA

Short operatic solo - ARIETTA

Short prose tale - NOVELLA

Short song - ARIETTA

Short story - CONTE

Short synopsis - APERCU

Shortage - DEARTH

Shorten - TRUNCATE

Short tailed lemur - INDRI

Short tailed rodent - VOLE

Shoshonean - KOSO

Shoulder blades - SCAPULAE

Showy African plant - COLEUS

Showy display - ECLAT

Showy flower - CANNA

Showy trinket or
ornament - GAUD

Showy plant - CANNA

Shredded tobacco - SHAG

Shrew - HARRIDAN,
TERMAGANT
or VIRAGO

Shrew's genus - SOREX

Shrewish woman - HARPY
or VIRAGO

Shrill noise - STRIDOR

Shrine at Mecca - KAABA

Shrub - SUMAC

Shrubbery trellis - ESPELIER

Shrubby thicket - CHAPARRAL

Siamese coin - TICAL

Siamese coins - ATTS

Siamese fighting fish - BETTA

Siamese temple - WAT

Siberiea flower - URAL

Siberian forest - TAIGA

Siberiean River - AMUR

Sicilian fortified
wine - MARSALA

Sicilian Mountain - ETNA

Sicilian resort - ENNA

Sicilian sea port - SYRACUSE

Siddhartha author - HESSE

Side pedals - ALAE
Sidereal altar - ARA
Sign of royalty - DIADEM
Signal flare - FUSEE
Sikkim antelope - SEROW
Silent in music - TACET
Silk cotton - CEIBA
Silk dye - EOSIN
Silk fabric - FAILLE,
    HONAN, SAMITE
    SURAH or TULLE
Silk like fabric - RAMIE
Silk scarf - FOULARD
Silk tree - MIMOSA
Silken - SERIC
Silkworm - ERIA
Silkworm moth - CECROPIA
Silky fabric - HONAN
    or PONGEE
Silly poetry - DOGGEREL
Silver - ARGENT
Silver in heraldry or silvery
    white - ARGENT
Silver peso - DURO
Silver refiner - CUPEL
Silvery white - ARGENT
Simple organism - MONAD
Simple planetarium - ORRERY
Simple wind
    instrument - TONETTE
Sinew -THEW

Single-celled
    microorganism - MONAD
Single named
    supermodel - IMAM
Single-seeded fruit - DRUPE
Sinus cavity - ANTRUM
Sioux Indians - OTOS
Sister: Lat. SOROR
Sister of Aaron - MIRIAM
Sister of Apollo - ARTEMIS
Sister of Ares - ERIS
Sister of Antigonnes - ISMEME
Sister of Caliope or Clio -
    ERATO or THALIA
Sister of Cordelias - REGAN
Sister of Erato - CLIO
    or URANIA
Sister of Goneril - REGAN
Sister of Helios - EOS
    or SELENE
Sister of Laetes - OPHELIA
Sister of Margaux - MARIEL
Sister of Melpomene - ERATO
Sister of Mertes - OHPILEA
Sister of Moses - MIRIAM
Sister of Napoleon - SOEUR
Sister of Nephthys - ISIS
Sister of Osiris - ISIS
Sister of Orestes - ELECTRA
Sister of Paris - SOEUR
Sister of Pollus - HELEN
Sister of Polyhymnia - ERATO

Sister of Rachael - LEAH
Sister of Snow
    White - ROSERED
Sister of Terpsichore - ERATO
Sister of Thalia - ERATO
Sister of Tante - MERE
Sister of Urania - ERATO
Sister of Venus - SERENA
Sitar accompaniment - TABLA
Site of ancient Greek
    games - VAMEA
Sitting in art - SEDENT
Situated at the tip - APICAL
Situated below - NETHER
Six: Sp. - SIES
Six-line poem - SESTET
Six penny piece - TANNER
Size of paper - DEMY
Skein of yarn - CLEW
Ski run - PISTE
Skillful - HABILE
Skin colorer - MELANIN
Skin defect - WEN
Skin disease - TINEA
Skin: pre. - DERMA
Skin spot - NEVUS
Skin woe - TINEA
Skirt insert - GODET or GORE
Skirt slit - PLACKET
Scull bone - INION
Skullcap - COIF

Skull point - INION
Sky: Fr. - CIEL
Sky altar - ARA
Sky whale - CETUS
Slag - DROSS or SCORIA
Slave - MOIL
Slayer of Castor - IDAS
Sleek dog - SALUKA
Sleep: Comb.form - NARCO
Sleepy - TORPID
Sleeveless robe - ABA
Slender and pointed - STYLOID
Slender bristle - ARISTA
Slender cat - REX
Slender dagger - PONIARD
Slender graceful
    woman - SYLPH
Slender pointed
    weapon - STYLET
Slender stem - PETIOLE
Slight trace - SOUPCO
Sloe-flavored
    liqueur - PRUNELLE
Slothful - OTIOSE
Slow dances - HABANERAS
Slow musical
    movement - LARGO
Slow passage in music - ADAGIO
Slow primate - LORIS
Slow stroll - PASEO
Slowing, in
    music - LENTANDO

Slowish - ANDANTE

Slowly, musically - LENTO

Slowly, to Bach - ADAGIO

Sluggish - TORPID

Slur over a syllable - ELIDE

Small amount - DRIB,
    MODICUM or SOUPCON

Small antelope - ORIBI

Small ape - GIBBON

Small barracudas - SPETS

Small bird - PEWEE
    or TOMTIT

Small bone - OCCICLE

Small buffalo - ANOA

Small case - ETUI

Small capped
    mushroom - ENOKI

Small computer
    program - APPLET

Small deer - ROES

Small diving bird - DABCHICK
    or MURRELET

Small drum - TABLA or TABOR

Small eel - GRIG

Small Eurasian duck - SMEW

Small Eurasian
    ruminant - ROEDER

Small evergreen tree - CITRON

Small falcon - KESTREL
    or MERLIN

Small finch - LINNET
    or SERIN

Small fish - SMELT or SPRAT

Small flag - FANION

Small Florida
    orange - SATSUMA

Small freshwater fish - DACE

Small fruit - ACHENE

Small goose - BRANT

Small green bird - VIREO

Small gull - MEW

Small hand drum - TABLA

Small hawk - KITE

Small heron - BITTERN

Small herring - SPRAT

Small hill - KOPJE

Small insect - MIDGE

Small insect-eating bird - VIREO

Small lake or pond - MERE

Small lamp - ETNA

Small laquer box - INRO

Small liquid measure - MINIM

Small marine animal - SALP

Small merganser - SMEW

Small monkey - TITI

Small napsack - MUSETTE

Small old world lizard - AGAMA

Small open boat - SHALLOP

Small orange - SATSUMA

Small ox - ANOA

Small parrot - LORIKEET

Small perfume bottle - FLACON

Small razor-billed bird -AUKET

Small rodent - LEROT or VOLE

Small Russian
 turnovers - PIROSHKI

Small sailing craft - PINNACE

Small salamander - NEWT

Small salmon - COHO

Small sandpiper - STINT

Small seabird - PETREL

Small shed - COTE

Small slender
 dagger - PONIARD

Small song bird - PIPIT,
 VIREO or WREN

Small space - AREOLA

Small struffed triangular
 turnover - SAMOSA

Small sturgeon - STERLET

Small stream - RUNNEL

Small table - GUERIDON

Small tailess mammal - PIKA

Small toucan - ARACARI

Small town - PODUNK

Small whale - SEI

Small wild ox - ANOA

Small woods - COPSE

Smallest bit - JOT

Smelly - OLID

Smog - MIASMA

Smoked salmon - NOVA

Smoking pipe - CALABASH

Smooth transition - SEGUE

Smoothly, in music - LEGATO

Snack - NOSH

Snake - MAMBA

Snake hair women - FURIES

Snake: Pref. - OPHI

Snipe's kin - GODWIT

Snow leopard - OUNCE

Snow field - NEVE

Snow white dog - SAMOYED

So much, musically - TANTO

Soak - IMBRUE

Soaks - RETS

Soap ingredient - OLEATE

Soap plant - AMOLE

Soap stone - TALC

Soap substitute - AMOLE

Soapberry tree - AKEE

Social climber - PARVENU

Social outcast - PARIAH

Sod - SWARD

Sodium carbonate - TRONA

Sodium cloride - NACL

Sodium hydroxide - NAOH

Soft metallic element - CESIUM

Soft palate - VELUM

Soft part of the palate - UVULA

Soft roe - MILT

Soft sheer fabric - BATISTE

Soft thin silk cloth - PONGEE

Soft velvet - PENNE

Softly in music - PIANO

Solar diety or disc- ATEN

Solar lunar equalizer - EPACT

Solar plexus - RETE

Solar system model - ORRERY

Soldier from down
   under - ANZAC

Solfeggio - SCALE

Solidified lava - BASALT

Solvent substance - ACETAL

Some collegians - ELIS

Some musical
   passages - TUTTIS

Some triangles - SCALENE

Something to eat - VIAND

Somewhat, in music - POCO

Somme city - AMIENS

Sommelier - CUPBEARER

Son of Aaron - ELEAZAR

Son of Abraham - ISAAC
   or ISHMAEL

Son of Adam - SETH

Son of Agamemnon - ORESTES

Son of Agrippina - NERO

Son of Aphrodite -
   AENEAS, EROS
or PRIAPUS

Son of Apollo - ION

Son of Arba - ANAK

Son of Ares - EROS

Son of Bathsheba - SOLOMON

Son of Bilhah - DAN

Son of Cain - ENOCH

Son of Cronos - PLUTO
   or ZEUS

Son of Daedalus - ICARUS

Son of David - ABOLOM

Son of Dionysus - PRIAPUS

Son of EBER - PELEG

Son of Eliphaz - OMAR

Son of Frigg - BALDER

Son of Gad - ERI

Son of
   Germanicus - CALIGULA

Son of Ham - CANAAN

Son of Hecaba - PARIS

Son of Hera - ARES

Son of Hirohito - AKIHITO

Son of Indira - RAJIV

Son of Isaac - EDOM,
   ESAU or JACOB

Son of Jacob - ASHER,
   BENJAMIN, DAN,
   LEVI or SIMEON

Son of Japheth - TIBAL

Son of Jehiel - NER

Son of Joktan - OBAL

Son of Joseph - EPHRAIM

Son of Judah - ONAN

Son of Kish - SAUL

Son of Lapetus - ATLAS

Son of Leah - LEVI or SIMEON

Son of Loki - NARE

Son of Lot - MOAB

Son of Noah - HAM, JAPHETH or SHEM

Son of Odin - BALDER, BRAGI, THOR or TYR

Son of Osiris - HORUS

Son of Polonius - LAERTES

Son of Poseidon - ORION or TRITON

Son of Priam - PARIS

Son of Prince Valiant - ARN

Son of Rachel - BENJAMIN

Son of Rebekah - ESAU

Son of Rhea - PLUTO

Son of Salah - EBER

Son of Sarah - ISAAC

Son of Seth - ARAM or ENOS

Son of Shem - ELAM

Son of Shiza - ADINA

Son of Telamon - AJAX

Son of Uranus - TITAN

Son of Uther - ARTHUR

Son of Venus - AMOR

Son of Zebulun - SERED

Son of Zeus - APOLLO, ARES or HERCULES

Sonata movement - RONDO

Song of praise - PAEAN

Songbird - OSCINE or VIREO

Songlike - ARIOSE

Songs - LAYS

Song thrush - MAVIS

Sonnet finale or part - SESTET

Sonora native - YAQUI

Soothing tea - CHAMOMILE

Soothsayer - AUGER, SEER or SIBYL

Sorceress in Greek myth - CIRCE

Sorceress of Colchis - MEDEA

Sorrowful poem - ELEGY

Sort of blue - CERULEAN

Soul - ANIMA or PNEUMA

Sound characteristic - TIMBRE

Sound: Prefix - SONO

Sound of rippling water - PURL

Sound quality - TIMBRE

Soup pasta - ORZO

Soup served cold - SCHAV

Sour mash - ALEGAR

Sour tasting - ACERB

Sourness - VERJUICE

Source of agar - REDALGAE

Source of bast fibre - RAMIE

Source of Blue Nile - TANA

Source of caviar - STERLET

Source of hemp - ABACA

Sourse of royal purple - MUREX

Sourse of the Mississippi - ITASCA

South African flower - IXIA

South African fox - ASSE

South African grassland - VELDT

South African iris - IXIA

South African monkey - VERVET

South African stockade - KRAAL

South American bear - OSO

South American dolphin - DORADOR

South American finch - RED SISKIN

South American fish - ACARA

South American Indians - AUCAS or ONAS

South American mammal - VICUNA

South American monkey - SAI or TITI

South American plain - LLANO

South American plateau region - ALTIPLANO

South American raptor - HARPY EAGLE

South American rodent - CAVY, COYPU or PACA

South American sloths - AIS

South American tuber - OCA

South Dakota Indian - OGLALA

South east wind - EURUS

South Indian language - TAMIL

South Korean soldier - ROC or ROK

South of France - MIDI

South Korean port - PUSAN

South Pacific area - OCEANIA

South Pacific boat - PRAU

South sea island - JAVA

South west wind - AFER

Southern constellation - ARA, APUS, ARGO or MENSA

Southern Mexican - OXACAN

Southwestern beans - FRIJOLES

Southwestern plant - CHIA

Southwestern promenade - PASEO

Southwestern salamander - AXOLOTL

Soverign - SKIV

Soviet cooperative - ARTEL

Soybean-based paste - MISO

Space between leaf veins - AREOLA

Space between two teeth - DIASTEMA

Spadefoot, for one - TOAD

Spanish Almighty - DIOS

Spanish aunt - TIA

Spanish bears - OSO

Spanish conifer - PINO

Spanish dance - JOTA

Spanish dances - SARABANDS

Spanish dish - PAELLA

Spanish enclave in Morocco - CEUTA

Spanish eyes - OJOS

Spanish grocery - BODEGA

Spanish gypsy - GITANO

Spanish hall - SALA

Spanish health - SANO

Spanish hors d'oeuvres - TAPAS

Spanish house - CASA

Spanish inn - POSADA

Spanish king - RAY

Spanish kiss - BESO

Spanish lady - DONA

Spanish mackerel - PINTADO

Spanish muralist - SERT

Spanish naval base - VIGO

Spanish nobleman - GRANDEE

Spanish port - ALMEREA

Spanish princess - ELENA

Spanish queen - ENA or REINA

Spanish rice - ORROZ

Spanish Road - CAMINO

Spanish sausage - CHORIZO

Spanish scarf - MANTILLA

Spanish seaport - CADIZ

Spanish she-bear- OSA

Spanish sherry - OLOROSO

Spanish silver - PLATA

Spanish silver dollar - DURO

Spanish six - SEIS

Spanish snacks - TAPAS

Spanish stew - PAELLA

Spanish sword - ESPADA

Spanish tar - BREA

Spanish town - AVILA

Spanish town mayor - ALCALDE

Spanish uncle - TIO

Spanish wine - MALAGA or RIOJA

Spanish wine bag - BOTA

Sparkly rock - GNEISS

Sparoid fish - SAR

Sparton queen - LEDA

Sparton serf or slave - HELOT

Spauning area - REDD

Speach beginnings - EXODIA

Speaker's platform - BEMA or PODIA

Spear - ASSEGAI

Specialized idiom or Vocabulary - ARGOT

Specialties - METIERS

Species - GENERA

Speck - MOTE

Specs with a handle - LORGNETTE

Speedy Amtrak train - ACELA

Speer with a long blade - ASSAGAI

Spend thrift - WASTREL

Sphere of operation - AMBIT

Spice girl - POSH

Spice girl Halliwell - GERI

Spice used in incense - STACTE

Spiced tea - CHAI

Spicy sausage - KIELBASA

Spicy Stew - OLIO

Spider, to biologist - ARANEID

Spider's nest - NIDUS

Spigot - SPILE

Spinachlike plant - ORACH

Spine - RACHIS

Spinel variety - BALAS

Spiny anteater - ECHIDNA

Spiny lizard - IGUANA

Spiny lobster - LANGOUSTE

Spiny plant - ALOE

Spiny sea creature - URCHIN

Spiny leafed flower - AGAVE

Spiny-shelled
gastropod - MUREX

Spiny shrub - FURZE
or GORSE

Spiny trees - ACACIAS

Spiral-horned antelope ELAND,
KUDU or NYALA

Spiral-horned buck - ADDAX

Spiral-horned sheep - ARGALI

Spiral-shelled mollusk -
NAUTILUS, TRITON or
WHELK

Spire ornament - EPI

Spirit of the time - ZEITGEIST

Spiritual leader - RABBI
or REBBE

Spitchcock - EEL

Split - RIVE

Splitting tool - FROE

Spoil - VITIATE

Sponge - CADGE

Sponsorship - EGIS

Spoor - PISTE

Spore sac - ASCUS

Spotted cat - PARD

Spotted reddish deer - SIKA

Spotted wildcat - MARGAY
or SERVAL

Spread hay to dry - TED

Spreads news of - BRUITS

Spring flower - SCILLA

Sprinkles - SPARGES

Sprite - FAY or PERI

Spumous - SUDSY

Spur part - ROWEL

Spurious wing - ALULA

Square - ISOGON

Square column - ANTA

Square stone - ASHLAR

Sri Lanka
export - TOURMALINE

Sri Lanka native - TAMIL

St. Kitts sister island - VEVIS

St. Petersburg's river - NEVA

St. Theresa's home - AUILA

Stable worker - HOSTLER
or OSTLER

Staccatos opposite - LEGATO

Staffordshire's river - TRENT

Stage leap - JETE

Staircase post or
    support - NEWEL

Stairway in Italy - SCALA

Stairway to a river - GHAT

Stand of trees - COPSE

Stannum - TIN

Stanzas of sonnets - SESSTETS

Star in Aquila - ALTAIR

Star in Argo - CANOPUS

Star in Auriga - CAPELLA

Star in Cannes - ETOILE

Star in Cetus - MIRA

Star in Cygnus - DENEB

Star in Draco - ADIB

Star in Eridanus - ACHERNAR

Star in Gemini - CASTOR

Star in Lyra - VEGA

Star in Nice - ETOILE

Star in Orion - RIGEL

Star in Persius - ALGOL

Star in Scorpio - ANTARES

Star in Taurus - ALDEBARAN

Star in Virgo - SPICA

Star of France - ETOILE

Star: Pref. - ASTR

Starch - AMYLOSE

Starch tree - SAGO

Starchy foodstuffs - SAGOS

State: Fr. - ETAT

State in Indian - ASSAM

State of drowsiness - KEF

State of being
    old - SENESCENT

Stately dance - PAVAN

Statue support - SOCLE

Steel gray element - NIOBIUM

Steel making
    furnace - BESSEMER

Steel mill by-product - DROSS

Steep slope - SCARP

Steller altar - ARA

Stem angle - AXIL

Stench - FETOR or MALODER

Stenuation - SNEEZE

Steppenwolf author - HESSE

Steps for crossing a fence - STILE

Steps to a river bank - GHAT

Steroids - LIPIDS

Steveadore's group - ILA

Stew - SLUMGULLION

Stew pot - OLLA

Stiff hair - SETA

Stimulating nut - KOLA

Stir up sediment - ROIL

Stirrup bone - STAPES

Stomachs of
    ruminants - OMASA

Stone Age
    implement - NEOLITH

Stone coffin - CIST or KIST

Stone fruit - DRUPE

Stone marker - STELA

Stone landmark or mound - CAIRN

Stone splinter - SPALL

Stonecrop plant - SEDUM

Stoppage - STASIS

Stores fodder - ENSILES

Storksbill - GERANIUM

Stout club - CUDGEL

Strait of Messina monster - SCYLLA

Stranger: pref. XENO

Strap on a saddle - LATIGO

Stratagem - RUSE

Stravinski ballet - AGON

Straw for hats - SENNIT

Straw mats - TATANIS

Strawberry geranium - SAXIFRAGE

Stray calf - WAIF

Stray dog - PYE

Stream overflows - FRESHETS

Street kid - GAMIN

Street show - RAREE

Street urchin - WAIF

Stretch material LYCRA

Strict herbivore - VEGAN

String in Bologna - SPAGO

Stringed instruments - VIOLS

Stringed keyboard instrument - CLAVIER

Strip blubber - FLENSE

Strip of gears - UNRIG

Strip tease - ECDYSIAT

Striped antelope - NYALA or KUDU

Strong fiber - BAST or RAMIE

Strong-scented herb or plant - RUE

Strong suit - METIER

Student's cubicle - CARREL

Student's language aid - PONY

Stuffed grape leaves - DOLMA

Stuffs oneself - STODGES

Sturdy chiffon - NINON

Subartic forest - TAIGA

Subatomic particle - BARYON, HADRON, MESON, MUON, NUTRINO, PION, or POSITRON

Subordinate diety - DAEMON

Sub-Saharan region - SAHEL

Successor of Moses - JOSHUA

Successor of Ramses - SETI

Sudden flood - SPATE

Sudden uprising - PUTSCH

Suez port - SAID

Sugar in tea: e.g. - SOLUE

Sugarcane byproduct - BAGASSE

Sulawesi - CELEBES

Sultanate on Borneo - BRUNEI

Summary - PRECIS

Summer capital of India - SIMLA

Summer ermine - STOAT

Summerlike - ESTIVAL

Summet - VERTEX

Summons to prayer - AZAN

Sun dial essential
    part - GNOMON

Sun flower - HELIANTHUS

Sun god - ATEN

Sun hat - TOPI

Sun helmet - TERAI

Sun: pref. - HELIO

Sunken fence - HAHA

Sunni leader - IMAM

Sunscreenasdditive or
    Ingredient - PABA

Supernatural power - MANA
    Supreme Surf sound - ROTE

Surgical
    antiseptic - THIMEROSAL

Surgical insert - STENT

Surgical instrument -
    PROBANG or TROCAR

Surgical knife - LANCET

Surgical probe - STYLET

Surround - EMBAY

Surveying
    instument - ALIDADE

Survivor - RELICT

Sushi bar condiment - WASABI

Sushi wrapping - NORI

Suspenders - GALLUSES

Swamp gas or thing - MIASMA

Swan Genus - OLOR

Swan Lake maiden - ODILE

Sward - SOD

Swedish coin - ORE

Swedish seaport - MALMO

Sweet flag - CALAMUS

Sweet bun or roll - BRIOCHE

Sweet Spanish wine - MALAGA

Sweetheart - INSMORATA

Sweetly melodic - ARIOSO

Swift falcon - PEREGRINE

Swift horses - HOUYHNHNMS

Swiftness - CELERITY

Swimming - NATANT

Swindle - MULCT

Swindler - GANEF

Swiss canton - BASEL,
    LUCERNE
or URI

Swiss cheese - GUYERE

Swiss city - BERNE

Swiss dish - RACLETTE

Swiss river - AARE or AAR

Swiss snowfield - FIRN

Swollen - TURGID

Sword handle - HAFT

Symbol of life - ANKH

Synagogue - SCHUL or SHUL

Synagogue platform - BEMA
    or BEMATA

Synecdoche - TROPE

Synthesizer - MOOG

Synthetic alumina-based gem - BOULE

Synthetic fabric - ARNEL

Synthetic garnet - YAG

Synthetic rubber - BUTYL

Synthetic rubber ingredient - STYRENE

Syphonic movement - RONDO or SCHERZO

Syrinx - PANPIPE

Table constellation - MENSA

Table linen - NAPERY

Table scrap - ORT

Tahitian seaport - PAPEETE

Tahitian wrapped skirt - PAREU

Tail bone - COCCYX

Tailless cat - MANX

Tailless mammal - LORIS

Tailless rabbit relative - PIKA

Taillike - CAUDAL

Tailor: Lat. - SARTOR

Taiwan Strait island - AMOY or MATSU

Taj Mahal site - AGRA

Taking effect legally - NISI

Tale - CONTE

Talk raucously - YAWP

Talkative - PRATE

Tall cactus - SAGUARO

Tall coarse herb - COW PARSNIP

Tall seasoning plant - LOVAGE

Tallow acid - OLEIC

Tamarisk - ATLE

Tammany bigwig - SACHEM

Tangy fish sauce - ALEC

Tapestry - ARRAS

Tapestry thread - WEFT

Tapioca sourse - CASSAVA

Taradiddle - FIB or LIE

Taro root - EDDO

Taro's tuber - CORM

Tarsal bones - CUBOIDS

Tastiest turtle part - CALIPASH

Tasty - SAPID

Tasty crust - GRATIN

Tasty dish - VIAND

Ta-ta in Turin - CIAO

Tautog or whitefish -CHUB

Tautomeric compound - ENOL

Tawny - ECRU

Tawny thrush - VEERY

Tea - BOHEA

Tea plant - CAMOMILE

Tear away - AVULSE

Tearful - LACHRYMOSE

Tearful woman - NIOBE

Technology hater - LUDDITE

Tedium - ENNUI

Teeth: pref. - DENTI or DENTO

Temple - FANE or NAOS

Ten Commandments - DECALOGUE

Ten decibels - BEL

Ten to the 100th power - GOOGOL

Ten year period - DECENNIUM

Tenant farm in Scotland - CROFT

Tenant farmer in India - RYOT

Tendon-bone connector - BURSA

Tennessee flower - IRIS

Tennis situation - ADIN

Terminal portion of the small Intestine - ILEUM

Termagant VERAGO

Testify - DEPONE

Teton Sioux tribe - OGLALA

Tetra variation - NEON

Teutonic god - WOTAN

Teutonic god of thunder - DONAR

Teutonic sky god - TIU

Teutonic war god - WOTAN

Texas armadillo - PEBA

Texas border city - DEL RIO

Texas border river - SABINE

Texctile dyeing substance- EOSIN

Tex-Mex treat - FAJITA

Thailand money - BAHTS

That: Fr. - CETTE

That: Sp. - ESA

That is: Lat. - IDEST

Thatched-roofed hut - JACAL

Thatching palm - NIPA

The act of measuring - MENSURATION

The fifty first psalm - MISERERE

The forearm - CUBITUS

The Furies - ERINYES or EUMENIDES

The great unwashed - PLEBS

The gums - ULA

The Last Super room - PENACLE

The Museof astonomy - URANIA

The Norse gods - AESIR

The soul - ANIMA

Theatre area - RIALTO

Theatre curtain or drop - SCRIM

Theban god - AMENRA

Then: Fr. - DONC

Thermal energy unit - JOULE

These: Fr. - CES

Theseus's wife - PHAEDRA

Thessaly Mountain -OSSA

Thick piled rug - RYA

Thick waterproof fabric - LODEN

Thickening agent - AGAR or SAGO

Thicket - COPPICE or COPSE

Thighbone - FEMUR

Thin fibrous bark - TAPPA

Thin line - STRIA

Thin material - ORGANZA

Thin membrane - PELLICLE

Third canonical hour - TERCE

Third generation Japanese-American - SANSEI

Third in rank - TERTIARY

This: Sp. - ESTA

Thistlelike plant - TEASEL

Thoroughgoing - ARRANT

Those: Fr. - CES

Thousandth of an inch - MIL

Thrall, of old - ESNE

Thrash - LARRUP

Trattoria dessert - SPUMONI

Thread: pref. - NAMATO

Three masted sailing ship - XEBEC

Threefold - TRINE

Three-headed dog - CERSERUS

Three-legged ornamental table - TEAPO

Thoroughwort - BONESET

Three lines of poetry - TERCET

Three-panel picture - TRIPTYCH

Threesome - TRIAD

Three sided harp - TRIGON

Three stringed instruments - REBEC or SAMISET

Three toes bird - RHEA

Three toed sloths - AIS

Three trios - ENNEA

Three wheeled rickshaw - CYCLO

Thrifty - PROVIDENT

Throat dangler - UVULA

Throughout, musically - SEMPRE

Throwback - ATAVISM

Thumb of the nose - SNOOK

Thrushlike warbler - OVENBIRD

Thus - SIC

Tiara - DIADEM

Tiberius' tailor - SARTOR

Tibetan animals - YAKS

Tibetan Buddhism - LAMAISM

Tibetan antelope or gazelle - GOA

Tibetan goat - SEROW

Tick - ACARID

Tidal bore - EAGRE

Tidal wave - TSUNAMI

Tiger genus - FELID

Tight curls - FRIZZ

Tile shaping stand - CRISS

Timbuktu's country - MALI

Time being - NONCE
Time keeper - HOROLOGER
Tinge with gold - AUREATE
Tinny - STANNIC
Tiny blood vessel - VENULA
Tiny dumplings - GNOCCI
Tiny Japanese
    mushroom - ENOKI
Tiny marine animal - ROTIFER
Tirade - SCREED
Titanium ore - RUTILE
Titled Italian family - ESTE
To be - ESSE
To be: Fr. - ETRA
To endure - ABY
To the end, in music - ALFINE
To the point - ADREM
Toast for the
    holidays - WASSAIL
Tobacco kiln - OAST
Tocsin - ALARM
Today: Sp. - HOY
Together musicaly - ADUE
Toil - TRAVAIL
Tokyo airport - NARITA
Tokyo, long ago - EDO
Tokyo rice roll - SUSHI
Tolkien beastie - ORC
Tolkien creature - HOBBIT
Tolkien forest creature - ENT
Tolkien ring bearer - FRODO

Tomalley source - LOBSTER
Tomboy - HOYDEN
Tonguelike organ - LINGUA
Too much, musically -
    TANTO or TROPPO
Tool for bending or shaping
    metal - SWAGE
Tooth material - APATITE
Tooth shaped - DENTOID
Toothless - EDENTATE
Torch cup - CRESSET
Tortilla cooker - COMAL
Tough, durable wood - LARCH
Tough fiber - BAST
Tough fibrous plant - HEMP
Tough grass - ESPARTO
Touring car - PHAETON
Toward the mouth - ORAD
    or ORADE
Tower guard - WARDER
Town in Belgium - YPRES
Town in Italy - EBOLI
Town in Montana - MISSOULA
Town in Oklahoma - ADA
Town near Padua - ESTE
Town near Salerno - EBOLI
Town on Lake
    Maggiore - LOCARNO
Town on Lake
    Victoria - ENTEBBE
Town on the
    Penobscot - ORONO

Town on the Uzbeck - OSH
Town on the Vire - St. Lo
Track alternative - OTB
Trail mix - GORP
Trained personnel - CADRE
Trajectory shape - PARABOLA
Tranquil - IRENIC
Transition - SEGUE
Transparent fabric - TOILE
Transparent gemstone - BERYL
Transparent olivine - PERIDOT
Transparent sea creature - SALPA
Transparent
    substance - HYALINE
Transplant - ECESIS
Trap SPRINGE
Trattoria dessert - TORTONI
Trash - DRECK
Tree frog - HYLA
Tree: pref. - DENDRO
Tree-like cactus - CHOLLA
Tree protruberamce - KNUR
Tree resembling the
    elm - ZELKOVA
Tree sap spigot - SPILE
Tree shaded
    promenade - ALAMEDA
Tree snake - LORA
Tree stump - BOLE
Tree tissue - XYLEM
Tree toad - HYLA
Tree trunk - BOLE

Tree trunk canoe - PIOGUE
Tree used for
    plywood - OBECKE
Tree with a large
    trunk - BAOBAB
Tree with nutlike seeds - PINON
Tree with whitish
    wood - HORNBEAM
Tree worshiper - ANIMIST
Treelike cactus - SAGUARO
Trellis for shrubs - ESPELIER
Trelliswork arbors - PERGOLAS
Tremblor - SEISM
Tremor condition - PALSY
Trendy tea - CHAI
Triangle with 3 unmeven
    sides - SCALENE
Triangular - DELTAIC
Triangular hat - TRICORN
Triangular kerchief or
    shawl - FICHU
Triangular sail - LATEEN
Tribal chief - SACHEM
Tribal healer - SHAMAN
Tribal historian - GRIOT
Tribe of Israel - ASHER,
    DAN, GAD, JUDA,
    LEVI or SIMION
Tribe unit - SEPT
Tribunal of prelates - ROTA
Trident shaped letter - PSI
Trifles - DOITS

Trig. Angle - ARCSINE

Trig. Function - COSEC

Trigon - HARP

Trigonometric function - SINE

Trilled call - CHIRR

Trimming cord - GIMP

Trinity - TRIUNE

Trinket - BIBELOT,
    GAUD, GEWGAW
    or TCHOTCHKE

Tristan's love - ISEULT
    or ISOLDE

Troche - PASTILLE

Trojan king - PRIAM

Trojan War hero - AENEAS

Trojan War name - NESTOR

Troop's camp - ETAPE

Tropical Asian tree - TOON

Tropical bird - TOUCAN

Tropical blackbird - ANI

Tropical bloomer - CANNA

Tropical butterfly - ZEBRA

Tropical desert - BIOME

Tropical disease - YAWS

Tropical fibers - ISTLES

Tropical fish - SCAD

Tropical flower - PROTEA

Tropical fruit - ACKEE

Tropical lizard - ANOLE
    or IGUANA

Tropical palm - ARECA

Tropical parrot - MACAW

Tropical rainforest - BIOME

Tropical resin - ELEMI

Tropical rodent - AGOUTI

Tropical shrub - ACACIA,
    CASSIA, FICUS,
    LANTANA or SENNA

Tropical tern - NOADY

Tropical tree - AKEE, BALSA,
    CACAO, COLA,
    MANGROVE, PALM
    or TAMERIND

Tropical tuber - TARO

Tropical wildcat - EYRA

Tropical wood - EBOMY

Troubador love song - ALBA

Troup's rest area - ETAPE

Troy, to the Greeks - ILIUN

True finch - SISKIN

Trump in card games - BASTA

Trumpet pennant - TABARD

Truncated pyramid - FRUSTUM

Truthful - VERIDICAL

Tuba - HELICON

Tubular pasta - PENNE

Tudor queen - MARY

Tuesday's god - TYR

Tumultuous uprising - EMEUTE

Tuna, at a Sushi bar - AHI

Tundra - BIOME

Tunes: Sp. - AIRES

Tunic of chain
    mail - HAUBERK

Tunisean seaport - SFAX

Turbot - BRILL

Turf - GREENSWARD

Turkic people - TATARS

Turkic tongue - ALTAIC

Turkish bigwig - BEY or PASHA

Turkish cap - CALPAC

Turkish cavalryman - SPAHI

Turkish chamber - ODA

Turkish coin - PARA

Turkish decree - IRADE

Turkish garment - CAFTAN

Turkish general or title -
AGHA, AMEER or BEY

Turkish hospis or
hostel - IMARET

Turkish inn - IMARET
or SERAI

Turkish leader - AGA

Turkish liqueur - RAKI

Turkish officer - EMEER

Turkish official or title -
AGHA or PASHA

Turkish palace - SERAI

Turkish regiment - ALAI

Turkish saber - YATAGHAN

Turkish soldier - SPAHI

Turkish title - DEY or EFFENDI

Turkish unit of weight - OKA

Turmoil - WELTER

Turn on a pivot SLUE

Turn outward - SPLAY

Turns inside out - EVERTS

Turtle shell - SCUTE

Tuscan river - ARNO

Twenty third OT book - ISAIAH

Twice baked bread - RUSK

Twice, musically - BIS

Twig broom - BESOM

Twill weaves fabric - TOILE

Twilled fabric - SERGE

Twinned crystal - MACLE

Twisted pasta - ROTINI

Two dimenional - PLANAR

Two faced god - JANUS

Two handed card
game - ECARTE

Two handed jar - AMPHOR

Two handed soup
bowl - ECUELLE

Two player card
game - BEZIQUE

Two: Sp. - DOS

Two toed sloth - UNAU

Two wheel cart - TUMBREL

Two wheeled carriage - CALESA

Two year old sheep - TEG

Twosome - DYAD

Type measure - PICA

Type of algae - DIATON

Type of antelope - SAIGA

Type of apple - WINESAP

Type of bean - HARICOT

Type of beetle - CHAFER or SCARAB

Typre of camera - SLR

Type of daisy - OXEYE or SHASTA

Type of feather - PINNA

Type of flask or vessel - DEWAR

Type of flower cluster - CYME

Type of Larva - REPIA

Type of lily - SEGO

Type of mushroom - CEP or ENOKI

Type of pair - DYAD

Type of shark - TOPE

Type of sugar - HEXOSE

Type of tie - BOLA

Type of triangle - SCALENE

Type of whale - SCRAG

Type of wheat - SPELT

Type stroke or typeface detail - SERIF

Typee sequel - OMOO

Types of deer - ROES

Tyro - NAIF

Tyrolian garb - DIRNDLE

Ukrainian seaport - ODESSA

Ultimate battle - RAGNAROK

Ulysses's home - ITHICA

Umbrella - AEGIS

Unaccented part - ARSIS

Uncle of Levi - ESAU

Uncle of Saul - NER

Unctuous flattery - SMARM

Underground chamber - KIVA

Understanding - KEN

Understood - IMPLICIT

Underworld region - EREBUS

Underworld River - STYX

Undressed hide - KIP

Uneven – EROSE

Unfilled part of a wine cask - ULLAGE

Unflappable - STOLID

Unfledged bird - EYAS

Unglazed chine - BISCUITWARE

Unhealthy atmosphere - MIASMA

Unicorn constellation - MONOCEROS

Uninteresting - VAPID

Unique - SUI GENERIS

Unit of compacitance - FARAD

Unit of conductance - MHO

Unit of electric charge - COULOMB

Unit of energy - BEV, BTU, ERG, JOULE, RAD or WATT

Unit of flux - TESLA

Unit of force - DYNE

Unit of heat - THERM

Unit of illumination - LUX or PHOT

Unit of induction - TESLA

Unit of land
measure - MORGEN

Unit of light - LUMEN

Unit of loudness - PHON
or SONE

Unit of magnetic flux -
TESLA or WESER

Unit of potential - VOLT

Unit of pressure - TORR

Unit of radiation - REM

Unit of radiation
exposure - ROENTGEN

Unit of radioactivity - CURIE

Unit of refraction - DIOPTER

Unit of volumn - STERE

Unit of wisdom - PEARL

Unit of work - ERG

Units of illumination - LUCES

Units of vers - MORAS

Universal soul - ATMAN

Unless, in law - NISI

Unnatural sleep - SOPOR

Unquestioning
follower - MYRMIDON

Unshod - DISCALCED

Unspoken - TACIT

Unstable meson - KAON

Unsubstantial
image - EIDOLON

Untamed - FERAL

Untanned hide - KIP

Unwelcomed one - PARIAH

Upas tree poison - ANTIAR

Upholstery fabric - FRISE

Upon: Fr. - SUR

Upper jaw - MAXILLA

Upside down "e" - SCHWA

Uraeus - ASP

U.S.A.F. org. - SAC

U.S.N. officers: abbr. - CDRS

U.S. playwright - INGE

U.S.S.R. co-op - ARTEL

Utah lake city - OREM

Utah lily - SEGO

Utah mountain range - UINTA

Vaccines - SERA

Vacuum tube gas - ARGON

Vagabond - PICARD

Vague rumor - ONDIT

Vain - OTIOSE

Valley in Britain - COOMB

Vampire - LAMIA

Vanished - EVANESCED

Variable star - ALGOL

Variety of chalcedony - SARD

Variety of grass - FESCUE

Variety of
hornblende - URALITE

Variety of lettuce - COS

Variety of lily - SEGO

Variety of peach - FREESTONE

Variety of sheep - MERINO

Variety of whale - SEI

Various areas - LOCA

Varnish ingredient - ANINE,
     COPAL, ELEMI, LAC,
     RESIN or TUNG OIL

Varnish material - ELEMI

Vase handle - ANSA

Vase on a pedestal - TAZZA

Vat - TUN

Vatican palace - LATERAN

Vedigris - PATINA

Vegas constellation - LYRA

Veil worn by Muslim
     women - YASHMAK

Velvet finish - PANNE

Venetian district - RIALTO

Venetian gold coin - DECUT

Venomous snake -
     FERDELANCE, KRAIT
     or TAIPAN

Ventilated felt hat - TERAI

Venus as the evening
     star - HESPERUS

Verbena plant - LANTANA

Verdi opera - ERNANI

Vermin poisin - RATSBANE

Vernacular - ARGOT

Verse with 17 syllables - HAIKU

Very: German - SEHR

Very hairy - PILOSE

Very, in music - ASSAI
     or MOLTO

Very, in Vichy - TRES

Very loud,
     musically - FORTISSIMO

Very necessary
     things - DESITERATA

Very pale dry sherry - FINO

Very pale green - CELADON

Very successful - BUFFO

Vesicle - CYST

Vessel - DEWAR

Vessel or duct - VAS

Vessels - PROA or XEBEC

Vestment - ORALE

Vetch - TARE

Vet's dose - BOLUS

Vicious woman - ARRIDAN

Victim of Artemus - ORION

Vienna, to Germans - WIEN

Vietnam city - HANOI or HUE

Vietnamese attire or
     dress - AODAI

Vigor - BRIO

Vigorously - AMAIN
     or CON BRIO

Viking poet - SKALD

Vile rumor CANARD

Village - DORP or THORP

Vinegary: pref. - ACETO

Vineyard - CRU

Viol part - CHOLE

Violin bow part - FROG

Violin of the middle
ages - REBEC

Virgil creation - IDYLL

Virgil epic - AENEID

Virgil's hero - AENEAS

Virginia rabbit
stew - BRUNSWICK

Virginia willow - COSIER
or ITEA

Virgo's brightest star - SPICA

Vishnu incarnation -
AVATAR or RAMA

Visigoth sacker of
Rome - ALARIC

Visored helmet - ARMET

Vitamin A - RETINOL

Vivacity - BRIO

Voiceless - SURD

Volcanic crater - CAULDERA

Volcanic earth - TRASS

Volcanic glass - OBSIDIAN

Volcanic material - MAGMA

Volcanic rock - BASALT
or TRASS

Volcanic valley - ATRIO

Volcano goddess - PELE

Volcano in Peru - EL MISTI

Volcano near Manilla - TAAL

Volcano on Antartica - EREBUS

Volga feeder - OKA

Volitile solvent - ACETAL

Voltage: Abbr. - EMF

Volumn - TOME

Voluptuaries - SYBARITES

Voodoo - MOJO

Voodoo amulets or
spells - MOJOS

Voodoo fetish - OBEAH

Vouchsafe - DEIGN

Vortex - GYRE

Votive stone - STELE

Vulcan's chimney - AETNA

WWII rifle - GARAND

Wading bird - IBIS, RAIL,
SORA or STILT

Wagnarian goddess - ERDA

Wagnerian melod - LEITMOTIF

Wagon shaft - THILL

Wail - ULULATE

Waist coat - GILET

Wales Lake or pool - LLYN

Walk-on-water lizard - BASILISK

Walkway between rows
of trees - ALLEE

Wall handing - ARRAS

Wall treatment - WAINSCOT

Walls of ripened
fruit - PERICARD

Wampum - PEAG

Wander about - DIVACATE

Wanton - PAPHIAN

Ward off - FORFEND

Warlock - NECROMANCER

Warm brown tone - SEPIA

Warm sweetened wine - NEGUS

Warning, old style - ALARUM

Warning bell - TOCSIN

Washington City or
river - YAKIMA

Wasp - VESPID

Waste allowance - TRET

Water: Sp. - AGUA

Water buffalo - ARNA

Water-carved gulch - ARROYO

Water colored with
gum - GOUACHE

Water goddess - EGERIA

Water nymph - NAIAD
or NEREID

Water pipe - HOOKA

Water wheel - NORIA

Watered silk - MOIRE

Waterfall - LINN or SAULT

Waterloo Marshall - NEY

Waterproof wool cloth - LODEN

Wattle - DEWLAP

Watusi garmet - DASHIKI

Wavy, in heraldry - UNDE

Waxy: pref. - CER

Weak - EFFETE

Wealthy one - NABOB

Weapon handle - HAFT

Weasel cousin - ERMINE
or MARTEN

Weasel relative - MINK
or TAYRA

Weather baloon - SONDE

Weaver's bobbin - PIRN

Weaver's reed - SLEY

Web footed bird - SOLAN

Weblike membrane - TELA

Web-site workers - SYSOPS

Weed of the mint
family - HENBIT

Weeper of myth - NIOBE

Weevil - CURCULIO

Weight allowance -
TARE or TRET

Weighty volumn - TOME

Welfare - WEAL

Well-groomed - SOIGNE

Well in France - BIEN

Welsh county - GWENT

Welsh wales - OYMRU

West African desert - NAMIB

West African language - HAUSA

West African monkey - MONA

West coast oak - ENCINA

West Indian palm - GRUGRU

West Indian plant - ANIL

West Indian shrub - INGA

West Indies fish - ABOMA

West Indies island - SABA

West Indies magic - OBEAH

Western Pacific
republic - PALAU

Western Samoan capital - APIA

Western Samoan
currency - TALA

Wet compress - STUPE

Wetland - BIOME

Whale constellation - CETUS

Whale herd - GAM or POD

Whalebone - BALEEN

Whales and
dolphins - CETACEANS

Whales' blowhole - SPIRACLE

Whatnot - ETAGERE

Wheat used for livestock
feed - SPELT

Wheel assembly - BOGIE

Whimper - PULE

Whimpering cry - MEWL

Whimsical humor- DROLLERY

Whine and
complain - KVETCH

Whip handle - CROP

Whip used for
flogging – KNOUT

White fish - CISCO

White lie - TARADIDDLE

White meat
mold - GALANTINE

White metallic
element - INDIUM

White oak - ROBLE

White of the eye - SCLERA

White poplar - ABELE
or ALDER

White sage - RAMONA

White sauce - BECHAMEL

White Sea arm - ONEGA BAY

White sheep - MERINO

White spotted rodent - PACA

White wine - MACON

Whiten - ETIOLATE

Whole - UNITARY

Wicker basket - SKEP

Wickerwork encased
bottle - DEMIJOHN

Wickerwork willow - OSSIER

Wide mouth - MAW

Wife of Abraham - SARAH

Wife of Amphion - NIOBE

Wife of Balder - NANNA

Wife of Brutus - PORTIA

Wife of Cadmus - HARMONIA

Wife of Caesar - UXOR

Wife of Ceausescu - ELENA

Wife of Cronus - RHEA

Wife of David Bowie - IMAM

Wife of Dionysus - ARIADNE

Wife of Dyland
Thomas - CAITLIN

Wife of Esau - ADAH

Wife of Ethan - UMA

Wife of Geraint - ENID

Wife of
Hephaestus - APHRODITE

Wife of Hercules - HEBE

Wife of Homer - MARGE

Wife of Hyperion - THEA
Wife of Iago - EMILIA
Wife of Jacob - LEAH
   or RACHEL
Wife of Jason - MEDEA
Wife of Jupiter - HERA
   or JUNO
Wife of Julius - CALPURNIA
Wife of Lamech - ADAH
Wife of Lohengrin - ELSA
Wife of Menelaus - HELEN
Wife of Nero - OCTAVIA
Wife of Oberon - TITANIA
Wife of Odysseus - PENELOPE
Wife of Orpheous - EURYDICE
Wife of Osiris - ISIS
Wife of Ovid - UXOR
Wife of Paris - OENONE
Wife of Petruchio - KATE
Wife of Priam - HECUBA
Wife of Prince Valiant - ALETA
Wife of Saturn - OPS
Wife of Sir Geraint - ENID
Wife of Siva - KALI
Wife of Theseus - PHAEDRA
Wife of Thor - SIF
Wife of Tyndareus - LEDA
Wife of Uranus - GAIA
Wife of Vulcan - VENUS
Wife of Wagner - COSIMA
Wife of Woody - SOONYI

Wife to Caesar - UXOR
Wifely - UXORIAL
Wig - PERUKE
Wild - FERAL
Wild ass - KIANG or ONAGER
Wild buffalo - ARNEE
Wild cat with tufted
   ears - CARACAL
Wild dog of India - DHOLE
Wild edible mushroom - CEP
Wild goat - IBEX or TAHR
Wild goose - BRANT
Wild herb - YARROW
Wild ox - ANOR, ANOA,
   GAUR or YAK
Wild sheep - AOUDAD,
   ARGALI, SHA or URIAL
Wild silkworm - ERIA
Wildebeest - GNU
Willingly - FAIN
Willow - OSIER
Willow genus - ITEA
Wimper - PULE
Wind blown soil - LOESS
Wind instrument - OCARINA
Windflower - ANEMONE
Window divider - MULLION
Wine blender - OENO
Wine bottle or flask - OLPE
Wine cabinet - CELLARET
Wine cask - TUN
Wine from Spain - MALAGA

Wine grape - COLOMBARD
    or PINOT

Wine pouch - BOTA

Wine: pref. - OEN or OENO

Wine press residue - MARC

Wine sediment - LEES

Wine Stewart - SOMMELIER

Wine vessels - AMAS

Winemaking
    byproduct - ARGOL

Wing - ALA

Wing part - ALULA

Wing: Fr. - AILE

Winged - ALATE or ALAR

Winged ant - ALATE

Winged elm - WAHOO

Winged god - EROS

Winged goddess - NIKE

Winged horse - ARION
    or PEGASUS

Winged wader - STILT

Winglike - ALAR,
    ALATE or OLAR

Winglike structure - ALA

Wings - ALAE

Wink - NICTITATE

Winter apples - RUSSETS
    or WINESAPS

Winter coat material - LODEN

Winter melon - CASABA

Wipe out - EFFACE

Wire measuure - MIL

Wiry African
    grasses - ESPARTOS

Wise lawyer - SOLON

Wise Man - MAGUS

Wishbone - FOURCHETTE

Wispy clouds - CIRRI

Witch: Sp. - BRUJA

Witch bird - ANI

Witchcraft - OBEAH

Witchs day - SABBAT

Witch's diety - HECATE

Witchs' home - ENDOR

With: Fr. - AVEC

With: prefix - SYL

With child - GRAVID

With the bow, musically - ARCO

With full force - AMAIN

Within: Pre. - INTRA

With notched edges - EROSE

Withered - SERE

Within: Pre. - INTRA

Witty - JOCOSE

Witty remark - MOT

Wizard - MAGE

Wolfhound - BORZOI

Wolfsbane - ACONITE

Women's fur cape - PELERINE

Women's shoe - CHOPINE

Woman's shoulder scarf - FICHU

Wonder worker - MAGUS
    or THAMATURGE

Wonk - NERD

Wood knot - KNAR

Wood nymph - DRYAD

Wood sorrel - OCA,
  OKA or OXALIS

Wooded grove - RABBET

Wooden bench - SETTLE

Wooden goblet - MAZER

Wooden pegina masonary
  wall - NOG

Woodland diety - FAUN,
  PAN or SATYR

Woodpile measure - STERE

Woods nyph - DRYAD

Woodwind inventor - SAX

Woody - ALLER

Woody fibre - BAST

Woody plant tissue - XYLEM

Woody's son - ARLO

Woof - WEFT

Wool coat - LODEN

Wool: Lat. or Sp. - LANA

Wooly - HIRSUTE or LANOSE

Word form for "all" - OMNI

Word form for
  "ancient" - PALEO

Word form for beyond - META

Word form for
  "billionth" - NANO

Word form for "bird" -
  AVI or ORNITH

Word form for "blood" - HEMO

Word form for
  "blossom" - FLOR

Word form for "blue" - CYANO

Word form for "bone" - OSTEO

Word form for "bristle" - SETI

Word form for "bull" - TAURO

Word form for "Chinese" - SINO

Word form for "coil" - SPIRO

Word form for "crop" - AGRO

Word form for
  "culture" - ETHNO

Word form for "ear" - OTO

Word form for "earth" - GEO

Word form for "egg" - OVI

Word form for
  "environment" - ECO

Word form for "equal" - PARI

Word form for "false" - PSEUD

Word form for "farming" - AGRI

Word form for "five" - PENTA

Word form for "flight" - AERO

Word for for "foot" - PEDO

Word form for
  "healing" - IATRO

Word form for
  "heavens" - URANO

Word form for "high" - ALTI

Word form for "inner" - ENTO

Word form for
  "image" - ICONO

Word form for "large" - MARCO

Word form for male - ANDO

Word form for "Mars" - AREO

Word form for "milk" - LACT

Word form for "mouth" - ORI

Word form for "nationality" - ETHNO

Word form for "nerve" - NEURO

Word form for "nose" - NASO

Word form for "one billionth" - NANO

Word form for "outer" or "outside" – ECTO

Word form for "peculiar" - IDIO

Word for for "people" - ETHNO

Word form for "personal" - IDIO

Word form for "recent" - NEO

Word form for "right" - ORTH

Word form for "sacred" - HIERO

Word form for "skin" - DERM

Word for for "sleep" - HYPNO

Word form for "small" - MICRO

Word form for "straight" - ORTHO

Word form for "soil" - AGRO

Word form for "sun" - HELIO

Word form for "ten" - DECA

Word form for "thought" IDEO

Word form for "twenty" - ICOSA

Word form for "vinegar" - ACETO

Word form for "wine" - OENO

Word form for "within" - ENTO

Word of mouth - PAROL

Word origin - ETYMON

Word's last syllable - ULTIMA

Work hard - MOIL

Working class member or stiff - POLE

Workshop - ATELIER

World's deepest lake - BAIKAL

World's smallest nation - NAURU

Worn out - EFFETE

Worshiper of Vishnu - BHAKTA

Worsted fabric - ETAMINE

Woven fabric - WEFT

Wrangle - BRABBLE

Wrapped in waxy cloth - CERED

Wreath for the head - ANADEM

Wrinkled - RUGOSE

Wrinkles - RUCKS

Wrist bone - TRAPEZOID

Wrist bones - CARPI

Writer's works - OEUVE

Writing desk - ESCRITOIRE

Written exposition - TREATISTE

Wrong doer - MISCREANT

Wrong: Pref. - MIS

Xiamen - AMOY

X-ray discoverer - ROENTGEN

X-ray measurements - REMS

Xylophone's relative - CELESTAS

Yacht pole - FID

Yale students - ELIS

Yaren's atoll - NAURU

Yashmak - VEIL

Yearling sheep - TEG

Yeast enzyme - LACTASE

Yeast-raised coffee
  cake - KUCHEN

Yellow billed rail - SORA

Yellow clay - ADOBE

Yellow fever mosquito - AEDES

Yellow fruit - PAWPA

Yellow plumlike fruit - LOQUAT

Yellow primrose - OXLIP

Yellowish green - BISCAY
  or RESEDA

Yellowish pigmant - OCHRE

Yellowish pink - RUFOUS

Yellowish red dye - ANATTO

Yemen seaport - ADEN

Yiddish synagogue - SHUL

Yiddish thief - GANEF

Yoga posture - ASANA

Yogert fruit drink - LASSI

Yorkshire River - AIRE or URE

Young actress - ONGENUE

Young barracuda - SPET

Young cod - SCROD

Young eel - ELVER

Young falcon - EYAS

Young female swine - GILT

Young fowl - POULT

Young fox - KIT

Young: Fr. - JEUNE

Young goat - KID

Young Guinea fowl - KEET

Young haddock - SCROD

Young hare - LEVERET

Young hawk - EYAS

Young herring - BRIT

Young hog - SHOAT

Young oyster - SPAT

Young pig - ELT or SHOAT

Young salmon - GRILSE, PARR,
  SAMLET or SMOLT

Young sheep - TEGS or YEAN

Young sow - GILT

Young swan – CYGNET

Young turkey - POULT

Young wolf - WHELP

Youthful - CALLOW

Yucca cousin - AGAVE

Yucca-like plant - SOTOL

Yugoslavian money -PARA

Yuletime quaff - WASSAIL

Zebu's genus - BOS

Zen enlightenment - SATORI

Zen paradox - KOAN

Zeno's home - ELEA

Zeus' blood - ICHOR

Zeus' mother - RHEA

Zhivago love - LARA

Zinger - REPOSTE

Zoroastrian sacred
    texts - AVESTA

Zoroastrians - PARSIS

Zulu warriors - IMPI

PEOPLE IN PUZZLES

Abolitionist Harriet - TUBMAN

Accordionist Floren - MYRON

Actor Ackland - KOSS

Actor Acord - ART

Actor Adam - ARKIN

Actor Adams - EVAN

Actor Adrian - ZMED

Actor Afleck - BEN or CASEY

Actor Alain - DELON

Actor Alastair - SIM

Actor Albright - NEGRON

Actor Alejandro - REY

Actor Alex - CORD

Actor Ames - LEON

Actor Andrew - SHUE

Actor Andrews - DANA

Actor Antonio - SABAT

Actor Armand - ASSANTE

Actor Arnold - STANG or TOM

Actor Asimov - ISAAC

Actor Asther - NILS

Actor Astin - SEAN

Actor Auberjonois - RENE

Actor Avery - VAL

Actor Ayres - LEW

Actor Axton - Hoyt

Actor Azaria - HANK

Actor Bana - ERIC

Actor Baker – JOE DON

Actor Ballard - ALIMI

Actor Banderas - ANTONIO

Actor Bannen - IAN

Actor Barker - LEX

Actor Barry - Gene

Actor Bates - ALAN

Actor Bean - SEAN

Actor Beery - NOAH
  or WALLACE

Actor Benedict - DIRK

Actor Bellows - GIL

Actor Benicio Del - TORO

Actor Bentley - WES

Actor Billy - ZANE

Actor Black - CLINT

Actor Blore - ERIC

Actor Bogosian - ERIC

Actor Booth - EDWIN

Actor Borgnine - ERNEST

Actor Bostwick - BARRY

Actor Bragher - ANDRE

Actor Branagh - KENNETH

Actor Brasselle - KEEFE

Actor Braugher - ANDRE

Actor Brazzi - ROSSANO

Actor Brendon - FRASER
  or SMALL

Actor Brian - KEITH

Actor Bridges - BEAU,
  JEFF or LLOYD

Actor Brody - ADAM

Actor Brolin - JOSH

Actor Brooks - ALBERT

Actor Bruce - DERN,
  NIGEL or WILLIS

Actor Buckholz - HORST

Actor Buddy - EBSEN

Actor Burgess - MEREDITH

Actor Burton - LEVAR
  or RICHARD

Actor C. Thomas - HOWELL

Actor Cain - DEAN

Actor Cameron - KIRK

Actor Carell - STEVE

Actor Cariou - LEN

Actor Carl - WEATHERS

Actor Carridine - DAVID
  or KEITH

Actor Carroll - LEO G.

Actor Carver - BRENT

Actor Carvey - DANA

Actor Cary - ELWES

Actor Casper Van - DIEN

Actor Chad - EVERETT

Actor Channing - TATUM

Actor Charleson - IAN

Actor Cheatle - RON

Actor Cheech - MARIN

Actor Christian - SLATER

Actor Christopher - LLOYD
  or REEVE

Actor Clint - WALKER

Actor Clive - OWEN

Actor Cronyn - HUME

Actor Claude - AKINS
  or RAINS

Actor Clu - GULAGER

Actor Cobb - LEE J

Actor Conrad - Nagel,
  ROBERT or VEIDT

Actor Conreid - HANS

Actor Coppel - BERNIE

Actor Cord - ALEX

Actor Corddry - ROB

Actor Corin - NEMEC

Actor Cory - HAIM

Actor Cosner - KEVIN

Actor Crane - BOB

Actor Cronyn - HUME

Actor Crothers - SCATMAN

Actor Culken - KIERAN

Actor Cuny - ALAIN

Actor Curry - TIM

Actor Curtis - TONY

Actor D. B. SWEENEY

Actor Daly - TIM

Actor Damon - MATT

Actor Dan - DURYEA

Actor Danson - TED

Actor David Ogden - STIERS

Actor Davis - BRAD or OSSIE

Actor Davenport - NIGEL

Actor Day - Lewis - DANIEL

Actor Dean - CAIN

Actor Del Tor - BENICIO

Actor Delois - DOM

Actor Delon - ALAIN

Actor Denis - OHARE

Actor Denver - PYLE

Actor Depardieu - GERARD

Actor Derek - JACOBI

Actor Deving - ADAM

Actor Diamond - DUSTIN

Actor Diggs - TAYE

Actor Dillon - MATT
    or MELINDA

Actor Donahue - TROY

Actor Donald - CRISP

Actor D'Onofrio - VINCENT

Actor Douglas - KIRK

Actor Dourif - BRAD

Actor Dow - TONY

Actor Dullea - KEIR

Actor Duryea - DAN

Actor Ed - CROSS

Actor Edmund - KEAN

Actor Elba - IDRLS

Actor Eldred - GREGORY
    PECK

Actor Elizondo - HECTOR

Actor Edwards - VINCE

Actor Elwes - CARY

Actor Ely - RON

Actor Epps - OMAR or MIKE

Actor Eric - BANA or BLORE

Actor Erik - ESTRADA

Actor Erwin - STU

Actor Esai - MORALES

Actor Estevez - EMELIO

Actor Ethan - HAWKE

Actor Everett - SLOANE

Actor Farrell - COLIN

Actor Fernando - REY
    or LAMAS

Actor Ferrer - MEL

Actor Fiennes - RALPH

Actor Firth - COLIN

Actor Fishburn - LAWRENCE

Actor Franco - NERO

Actor Frederic - MARCH

Actor Frobe - GERT

Actor Gabby - HAYES

Actor Gabriel -BYRNE

Actor Gallagher - Peter

Actor Garcia - ANDY

Actor Garfield - ANDREW

Actor Gary - COLE or
    OLDMAN

Actor George - ARLISS,
    EADES, HEARN,
    SANDERS or TAKEI

Actor Gerard - GIL

Actor Gibson - MEL

Actor Gilliam - STU

Actor Glenn - SCOTT
    or STRANGE

Actor Goldblum - JEFF

Actor Gosling - RYAN

Actor Gossett - LOU

Actor Graves - PETER

Actor Green - LORNE or SETH

Actor Gregory - PECK

Actor Gross - ARYE

Actor Guinness - ALEC

Actor Gulager - CLU

Actor Guttenberg - STEVE

Actor Gyllenhaal - JAKE

Actor Haas - LUKAS

Actor Hadley - REED

Actor Haim - COREY

Actor Handler - EVAN

Actor Hanff - HELENE

Actor Hardison - KADEEM

Actor Harmon - MARK

Actor Harris - MEL

Actor Harrison - REX

Actor Hartnett - JOSH

Actor Hauer - RUTGER

Actor Hawk - ETHAN
   or NATHAN

Actor Hawthorn - NIGEL

Actor Haysbert - DENNIS

Actor Heflin - VAN

Actor Henreid - PAUL

Actor Herbert - LOM

Actor Herschel - BERNARDI

Actor Heydaya - PAN

Actor Hill - DULE

Actor Hirsch - EMILE

Actor Hoffman - DUSTIN

Actor Holm - IAN

Actor Homolka - OSCAR

Actor Horsley - LEE

Actor Howard - DUFF,
   KEN or TREVOR

Actor Hugh - LAURIE

Actor Hunter - IAN

Actor Irwin - STU

Actor Ivor - NOVELLO

Actor Jack or Tim - HOLT

Actor Jacobi - DEREK or LOU

Actor Jacques - TATI

Actor Jaffe - SAM

Actor Jake - WEBBER

Actor James - CAAN,
   SPADER or WOODS

Actor Jannings - EMIL

Actor Jarod - LETO

Actor Jason - BATEMAN

Actor Jeremy - IRONS

Actory Jerome - COWAN

Actor Jerry - ORBACH

Actor Jimmy - SMITS

Actor Joe - PESCI

Joe_____Baker - DON

Actor Joel - GREY

Actor John - SHEA

Actor
   John_____Davies - RHYS

Actor Johnny - DEPP

Actor Johnson - DON

Actor Jonathan - PRYCE

Actor Jones - DEAN

Actor Jose - FERRER

Actor Josh - GAD

Actor Jude - LAW

Actor Julia - RAUL

Actor Karas - ALEX

Actor Katz - OMRI

Actor Kaufman - ANDY

Actor Keach - STACY

Actor Keaton - BUSTER

Actor Keir - DULLEA

Actor Kelly - GENE

Actor Kenneth - BRANAGH

Actor Kilmer - VAL

Actor Kingsley - BEN

Actor Kinnear - GREG

Actor Kinski - KLAUS

Actor Kirby - BRUNO

Actor Klemperer - WERNER

Actor Kline - KEVIN

Actor Kopell - BERNIE

Actor Koteas - ELIAS

Actor Kotto - YAPHET

Actor Kristofferson - KRIS

Actor Kruger - OTTO

Actor LaBeouf - SHIA

Actor Ladd - ALAN

Actor Lasalle - ERIQ

Actor Laurie - HUGH

Actor Law - JUDE

Actor Leary - DENIS

Actor LeBlanc - MATT

Actor Lee Browne - ROSCOE

Actor Liam - NEESON

Actor Linden - HAL

Actor Liota - RAY

Actor Lloyd - NOLAN

Actor Logue - DONAL

Actor Lowe - CHAD
    or ROBERT

Actor Lucas - HAAS

Actor Ludwig - EMIL

Actor Luke - KEYE

Actor Lyon - Ben

Actor
    M_____Walsh - EMMET

Actor MacDonald - CAREY

Actor MacLachlan - KYLE

Actor MacMurray - FRED

Actor Maguire - TOBEY

Actor Mantegna - JOE

Actor March - HAL

Actor Mark - ADDY

Actor Mark_____Baker - LINN

Actor Markham - MONTE

Actor Martin - LANDAU,
    RITTor ROSS

Actor Marvin - LEE

Actor Masi OKA

Actor Matt - DAMON
    or DILLON

Actor Matthau - WALTER

Actor Max Von - SYDOW

Actor Maxwell - GAIL

Actor Maynard - KEN

Actor McBride - CHI

Actor McCowen - ALEC

Actor McGregor - EWAN

Actor McKellen - IAN

Actor McKern - LEO

Actor McRaney - GERALD

Actor McShane - IAN

Actor Mel - FERRER

Actor Merlin - OLSEN

Actor Michael - ANSARA, CAINE, J.

FOX, PARE or R

Actor Milo - O'SHEA

Actor Minaco - AINO

Actor Mineo - SAL

Actor Mintz - ELI

Actor Misha - AUER

Actor Mitchell - SASHA

Actor Mix - TOM

Actor Molinaro - AL

Actor Montalban - RICARDO

Actor Montand - YVES

Actor Moore - DUDLEY or SHEMAR

Actor Morales - ESAI

Actor Moranis - RICK

Actor Morgan - FREEMAN or HARRY

Actor Morita - PAT

Actor Moses - GUNN

Actor Mr. T. - TERO

Actor Mullavey - GREG

Actor Muni - PAUL

Actor Murphy - AUDIE or EDDIE

Actor Murray - DON

Actor Navarro of old - RAMON

Actor Nazimova - ALLA

Actor Neeson - LIAM

Actor Nelson - JUDD

Actor Neville - BRAND

Actor Nicky - KAT

Actor Nicolas - LEA

Actor Nolan - LLOYD

Actor Nolte - NICK

Actor Norton - Edward

Actor Novarro - RAMON

Actor Novello - IVOR

Actor O'Brien - EDMOND or HUGH

Actor O'Donnell - CHRIS

Actor Ogilvy - IAN

Actor Omar - EPPS

Actor O'Shea - MILO

Actor Pacino - AL

Actor Palminteri - CHAZZ

Actor Parker - FESS

Actor Patrick - BERGIN

Actor Paul - MUNI

Actor Pendleton - NAT

Actor Perlman - RON

Actor Perry - LUKE

Actor Peter - BOYLE,
GRAVES or O'TOOLE

Actor Philip - AHN

Actor Phillippe - RYAN

Actor Pop - IGGY

Actor Portier - SIDNEY

Actor Portman - ERIC

Actor Power - TYRONE

Actor Powers - BOOTHE

Actor Price - LONNY
or VINCENT

Actor/Producer
Peter - USTINOV

Actor Quinn - AIDAN
or ANTHON

Actor Rachins - ALAN

Actor Rainer - LUISE

Actor Raines - CLAUDE

Actor Ramis - HAROLD

Actor Ramon - BIERI

Actor Ray - ALDO or LIOTTA

Actor Reeves - KEANU

Actor Reginald - OWEN

Actor Regis - PHILBIN
or TOOMEY

Actor Reynolds - BERT
or RYAN

Actor Rhames - VING

Actor Rhodes - HARI
or HARRY

Actor Richard - BELZER,
EGAN, GERE or KIEL

Actor Richmond - DEON

Actor Rickman - ALAN

Actor Rifkin - RON

Actor Rip - TORN

Actor Ritchard - CYRIL

Actor Ritter - JOHN or TEX

Actor Robbe-Grillet - ALAIN

Actor Robert - ERIC,
DONAT or RYAN

Actor Roberts - ERIC

Actor Robins - TIM

Actor Rogan - SETH

Actor Roger - REES

Actor Romero - CESAR

Actor Roscoe - ATES

Actor Roth - ELI

Actor Rupert - EVERETT

Actor Russ - TAMBLYN

Actor Russell - KURT

Actor Ryan - ONEAL

Actor Santoni - RENI

Actor Scheider - ROY

Actor Savage - FRED

Actor Schreiber - LIEV

Actor Scott - BAIO or BAKULA

Actor Sean - ASTIN or PENN

Actor Seth - ROGEN

Actor Sewell - RUFUS

Actor Sharif - OMAR

Actor Shepard - SAM

Actor Shimerman - ARMIN

Actor Silver - RON

Actor Silvers - PHIL

Actor Singer - LORI or MARC

Actor Sizemore - TOM

Actor Skinner - OTIS

Actor Slaughter - TOD

Actor Sloane - EVERETT

Actor Smith - WIL

Actor Sotto - VIC

Actor Spiner - BRENT

Actor Stamp - TERENCE

Actor Stephen - BOYD or REA

Actor Steve - MCQUEEN

Actor Steven - SEAGAL
or WEBBER

Actor Stevenson - MCLEAN

Actor Stoltz - ERIC

Actor Stu - IRWIN

Actor Studi - WES

Actor Summerville - SLIM

Actor Sutherland - DONALD
or KEIFFER

Actor Tamblyn - RUSS

Actor Tamiroff - AKIM

Actor Tayback - VIC

Actor Terry - KISER

Actor Thicke - ALAN

Actor Thinnes - ROY

Actor Tim - HOLT

Actor Tognazzi - UGO

Actor Tom - ARNOLD,
EWELL, HULCE
or WOPAT

Actor Turhan - BEY

Actor Urban - CARL

Actor Ustinov - PETER

Actor Vallone - RAF

Actor Van Cleef - LEE

Actor Van Peebles - MARIO

Actor Verne - TROYER

Actor Victor - BUONO
or MATURE

Actor Vigoda - ABE

Actor Villechaise - HERVE

Actor Ving - RHAMES

Actor Visnjic - GORAN

Actor Vito - SCOTTI

Actor Voight - JON

Actor Waggoner - LYLE

Actor Wahl - KEN

Actor Walker - CLINT

Actor Wallace - BEERY or REID

Actor Wallach - ELI

Actor Wally - COX

Actor Walsh - M. EMMET

Actor Walston - RAY

Actor Warner - OLAND

Actor Warren - OATES

Actor Washington - DENZEL

Actor Weaving - HUGO

Actor Welles - ORSON

Actor Wendell - COREY

Actor Werner - OSKAR

Actor Wesley - ADDY

Actor Wheaton - WIL

Actor White - JALEEL

Actor Willem - DAFOE

Actor William - CLARK GABLE

Actor William - HAINES,
    INGE,   KATT,
    or SCOTT

Actor Williams - TREAT

Actor Williamson - NICOL

Actor Wilson - OWEN

Actor Woods - JAMES

Actor Wooly - SHEB

Actor Worthington - SAM

Actor Wyle - NOAH

Actor Yaphet - KOTTO

Actor Young - GIG

Actor Ziering - IAN

Actress Ada - REHAN

Actress Adams - AMY or EDIE

Actress Adoree - RENEE

Actress Aimee - ANOUK

Actress Adrienne - BARBEAU
    or CORRI

Actress Albright - LOLA

Actress Alexander - ERIKA

Actress Alicia – ANA or WATT

Actress Allen - KAREN

Actress Alley - KIRSTIE

Actress Allgood - SARA

Actress Ally - SHEEDY

Actress Alonzo - CONCHITA

Actress Altieri - ELENA

Actress Alvarado - TRINI

Actress Alyssa - MILANO
    or PEET

Actress Amanda -
    BEARSE, PEET
or PLUMMER

Actress Amis - BOZ

Actress Amy - MADIGAN

Actress Anders - LUANA

Actress Anderson - LONI
    or PAMELA

Actress Andersson - BIBI

Actress Andress - URSELA

Actress Angela - BASSETT
    or LANSBURY

Actress Angelina - JOLIE

Actress Anjelica - HUSTON

Actress Ann - ARCHER
    or DOREN

Actress Anna - HELD or STEN

Actress Anna May - WONG

Actress Anne - HECHE

Actress Annette - O'TOOLE

Actress Annie - POTTS

Actress Anouk - AIMEE

Actress Archer - ANNE

Actress Argento - ASIA

Actress Ari - MEYERS

Actress Arlene - DAHL

Actress Armstrong - BESS

Actress Arquette - ROSANNA

Actress Arthur - BEA

Actress Ashley - OLSEN

Actress Astor - MARY

Actress Audra - LINDLEY

Actress Aulin - EWA

Actress Bainter - FAY

Actress Baird - CORA

Actress Balin - INA

Actress Bancroft - ANNE

Actress Bara - THEDA

Actress Barbara - BARRY
    or BOSSAN

Actress Barkin - ELLEN

Actress Barrie - MONA

Actress Barrymore - ETHEL

Actress Bartok - EVA

Actress Basinger - KIM

Actress Bassett - ANGELA

Actresss Becinsale - Kate

Actress Bedard - IRENE

Actress Belknap - ANNA

Actress Benning - ANNETTE

Actress Berle - REID

Actress Bergen - CANDICE

Actress Berger - SENTA

Actress Bernadette - PETERS

Actress Berry - HALLE

Actress Beryl - REID

Actress Best - EDNA

Actress Beulah - BONDI

Actress Black - KAREN

Actress Blair - LINDA

Actress Blakley - RONEE

Actress Blanchett - CATE

Actress Bloom - CLAIRE

Actress Blythe - ANN
    or DANNER

Actress Blunt - EMILY

Actress Bondi - Beulah

Actress Bonet - LISA

Actress Bow - CLARA

Actress Braun - TAMARA

Actress Brega - SONIA

Actress Brennan - EILEEN

Actress Brewster - PAGET

Actress Brianne - LEARY

Actress Brittany - SNOW

Actress Burke - BILLIE
    or DELTA

Actress Burstyn - ELLEN

Actress Burton - KATE

Actress Busch - MAE

Actress Byre - ROSE

Actress Caldwell - ZOE

Actress Cameron - DIAZ

Actress Campbell - MAIA,
    NEVE or TISHA

Actress Candy - AZZARA

Actress Cannon - DYAN

Actress Capshaw - KATE

Actress Cardinale - CLAUDIA

Actress Carey - AMIE

Actress Carman - ELECTRA

Actress Carol - KANE

Actress Caroline - RHEA

Actress Carrie - NYE

Actress Carrere - TIA

Actress Carter - DIXIE,
    LINDA or NELL

Actress Cate - BLANCHETT

Actress Cates - PHOEBE

Actress Catherine - BELL

Actress Catherine_____-
    Jones - BELL
or ZETA

Actress Chalke - SARAH

Actress Chandler - ESTEE

Actress Charlotte - RAE

Actress Chase - ILKA

Actress China - CHOW

Actress Chong – RAE DAWN

Actress Christina - RICCI

Actress Christine - ELISE
    or LAHTI

Actress Clair - DANES

Actress Claire - INA

Actress Clarke - MAE

Actress Claudia - McNeil

Actress Close - GLENN

Actress Collette - TONI

Actress Conn - DIDI

Actress Copley - TERI

Actress Cortland - OPAL SUE

Actress Croft - LARA

Actress Crouse - LINDSAY

Actress Curtain - JANE

Actress Cusack - JOAN

Actress Daly - TYNE

Actress Dame Edith - EVANS

Actress Damita - LILI

Actress Dana - IVEY or PLATO

Actress Danes - CLAIRE

Actress Daniels - BEBE

Actress Danner - BLYTHE

Actress Danning - SYBIL

Actress Darby - KIM

Actress Dash - STACY

Actress Davis - ESSIE,
    GEENA or VIOLA

Actress Dawber - PAM

Actress_____Dawn
    Chong - RAE

Actress Debi - MAZAR

Actress Debra - PAGET

Actress Delaney - KIM

Actress Delaria - LEA

Actress Delta - BURKE

Actress Demornay - REBECCA

Actress Dench - JUDI

Actress Dennings - KAT

Actress Diamond - SELMA

Actress Diane - LADD or LANE

Actress Dianne - WIEST

Actress Dickenson - ANGIE

Actress Dillon - MELINDA

Actress Divorak - ANN

Actress Dolenz - AMI

Actress Dolorea - DEL RIO

Actress Donahoe - AMANDA

Actress Donahue - ELINOR

Actress Doris - DAY

Actress Dorothy - MALONE
or PROVINE

Actress D'Orsay - FIFI

Actress Downey - ROMA

Actress Dressler - MARIE

Actress Duce - ELEONORA

Actress Dunaway - FAYE

Actress Duncan - SANDY

Actress Dunne - IRENE

Actress Durbin - DEANNA

Actress Eartha - KITT

Actress Edna - BEST

Actress Eggar - SAMANTHA

Actresss Ekberg - ANITA

Actress Ekland - BRITT

Actress Elaine - STRITCH

Actress Eleniak - ERIKA

Actress Eleonora - DUSE

Actress Elg - TAINA

Actresss Elizabeth - ASHLEY,
PENA, REASER or SHUE

Actress Ella - RAINES

Actress Ellen - DEGENERES

Actress Emma - SAMMS

Actress Erin - MORAN

Actress Esther - MOIRE
or ROLLE

Actress Eva - LONGORIA

Actress Evans - LINDA

Actresss Eve - ARDEN

Actress Everhart - ANGIE

Actress Fairchild - MORGAN

Actress Faris - ANNA

Actess Faye - ALICE

Actress Feldon - VERNA

Actress Feldshuh - TOVAH

Actress Felicia - FARR

Actress Ferrel - TYRA

Actress Fionnula - FLANAGAN

Actress Fiore - ELENA

Actress Fiorentino - LINDA

Actress Fischer - JENNA

Actress Fleming - RHONDA

Actress Fletcher - LOUISE

Actresss Flynn Boyle - LARA

Actress Foch - NINA

Actress Follows - MEGAN

Actress Fontanne - LYNNE

Actress Fonteyn of
old - MARGOT

Actress Foster - JODIE

Actress Freeman - MONA

Actress Fricker - BRENDA

Actress Frost - SADIE

Actress Garbo - GRET

Actress Gay Harden - MARCIA

Actress Gaye - NONA

Actress Genevieve - BUJOLD

Actress Georgia - ENGEL

Actresss Geraldine - PAGE

Actress Gershon - GINA

Actress Gertrude - BERG

Actress Getty - ESTELLE

Actress Gia - SCALA

Actress Gibbs - MARLA

Actress Gilbert - MELISSA
    or SARA

Actress Gill - THEA

Actress Gilpin - PERI

Actress Gimpel - ERICA

Actress Glen - CLOSE

Acress Goddard - PAULETTE

Actress Gold - MISSY

Actress Goldberg - WHOOPI

Actress Gomez - SELENA

Actress Goodman - DODY

Actresss Graff - ILENE

Actress Grant - LEE

Actress Gray - ERIN or NAN

Actress Grayner - ARI

Actress Green - EVA

Actress Gretchen - MOL

Actress Gretta - GARBO

Actress Grier - PAM

Actress Grimes -TAMMY

Actress Gwyn - NELL

Actress Gyllenhaal - MAGGIE

Actress Hagan - UTA

Actress Hall - DEIDRE

Actress Harmon - ANGIE

Actress Harper - TESS

Actress Harris - ZELDA

Actress Hartley - MARIETTE

Actress Hartman - LISA

Actress Hasso - SIGNE

Actress Hatcher - TERI

Actress Hawn - GOLDIE

Actress Hayek - SALMA

Actress Hayley - MILLS

Actress Hayworth - RITA

Actress Headly - GLENNE

Actress Heche - ANNE

Actress Heckart - EILEEN

Actress Helen
    _____Carter - BONHAM

Actress Helen - HAYES,
    MIRREN, SLATERS
    or TWELVETREES

Actress Helgenberger - MARG

Actress Hendren - TIPPI

Actress Henner - MARILU

Actress Hilary - SWANK

Actress Hildegarde - NEFF

Actress Holden - AMANDA

Actress Holm - CELESTE

Actress Holmes - KATIE

Actress Hooks - JAN

Actress Hunt - HELEN or LINDA

Actress Hunter - HOLLY, KIM or TYLO

Actress Hussey - OLIVIA

Actress Huxtable - ADA

Actress Hymes - LEILA

Actress Ina - BALIN

Actress Iona - SKYE

Actress Irene - PAPAS

Actress Jackson - GLENDA or KATE

Actress Jane - CARR

Actress Janet - MCTEER

Actress Janis - ELSIE or PAIGE

Actress Jeanne - EAGLES

Actress Jeanette - NOLAN

Actress Jeffreys - ANNE

Actress Jennifer - ALBA, BEALS, LOPEZ or SALT

Actress Jessica - ALBA, LANGE or TANDY

Actresss_____Jessica Parker - SARAH

Actress Jill - HENNESSEY or WHELAN

Actress Jillian - ANN

Actress Joan - CHEN

Actress Jo Ann - PFLUG

Actress Joanne - DRU or KERNS

Actress Jodie - FOSTER

Actress Johnson - CELIA

Actress Jolie - ANGELINA

Actress Jones - CAROLINE

Actress Jovovich - MILLA

Actress Joyce - DEWITT

Actress Judd - ASHLEY

Actress Judi - DENCH

Actress Judith - IVEY

Actress Julia - ORMOND, ROBERTS or STILES

Actress Jurado - KATY

Actress Kaminska - IDA

Actress Kate - HEPBURN or REDDING

Actress Katherine - ERBE

Actress Kathy - BATES

Actress Katie - SAGAL

Actress Kazan - LAINIE

Actress Kedrova - LILA

Actress Keanon - STACI

Actress Keeton - DIAME

Actress Kelly - HU or MOIRA

Actress Kennedy - MIMI

Actress Kidman - NICOLE

Actress King - MABEL

Actress Kirshner - MIA

Actress Kirsten - DUNST

Actress Knightly - KEIRA

Actress Kristen - ILENE

Actress Kruger - ALMA

Actress Kunis - MILA

Actress Kurtz - SWOOZIE

Actress Ladd - DIANE
or CHERYL

Actress Lake - VERONICA

Actress LaMarr - HEDY

Actress Lancaster - ELSA

Actress Landi - ELISSA

Actress Landry - LILLIE

Actress Langdon - SUE ANE

Actress Lansbury - ANGELA

Acrtress Larter - ALI

Actress Lasser - LOUISE

Actress Laughlin - LORI

Actress Laura - DERN

Actress Laurie - PIPER

Actress Lawless - LUCY

Actress Lawrence - CAROL

Actress Lea - DELARIA

Actresss Leah - REMINI

Actress Leachman - CLORIS

Actress Lee - LILA or RUTA

Actress_____Lee
Nolin - GENA

Actress Legienne - EVA

Actress Leigh - JANET
or VIVIEN

Actress Lena - OLIN

Actress Lenore - ULRIC

Actress Lenska - RULA

Actress Leoni - TEA

Actress Leslie - CARON

Actress Lillie - BEA

Actress Linda - DANO, EDER,
LAVIN or PURL

Actress Lindley - AUDRA
or CAROL

Actress Lindsay - CROUSE,
LOHAN

or WAGNER

Actress Linney - LAURA

Actress Lisa - RINNA

Actress Lisi - VIRNA

Actress Locke - SONDRA

Actress Lockhart - JUNE

Actress Locklear - HEATHER

Actress Logan - ELLA

Actress Lollobrigida - GINA

Actress Lonette - MCKEE

Actress Long - NIA or Shelley

Actress Longoria - EVA

Actress Lords - TRACY

Actress Lotte - LENYA

Actress Loughlin - LORI

Actress Louise - FLETCHER,
LASSER or STUBBS

Actress Luana - ANDERS

Actress Lucy - ARNEZ or LIU

Actress Luise - RAINER

Actress Lupino - IDA

Actress Lupone - PATTI

Actress Lyon - SUE

Actress MacDowel - ANDIE

Actress Madeleine - STOWE

Actress Madigan - AMY

Actress Madlyn - RHUE

Actress Magnani - ANNA

Actress Malone - JENA

Actress Manoff - DINAH

Actress Maples - MARLA

Actress Marceau - SOPHIE

Actress Marisa - TOMEI

Actress Markey - ENID

Actress Marlee - MATLIN

Actress Marsh - JEAN

Actress Marsha - HUNT

Actress Martha - HYER

Actress Martin - ANDREA,
   NAN or PAMELA SUE

Actress Martinelli - ELSA

Actress Mary - ASTOR or URE

Actress Maryam - DABO

Actress Mary Kay - PLACE

Actress Mason - MARSHA

Actress Massey - ILONA

Actress Matlin - MARLEE

Actress Maude - ADAMS

Actress May - ELAINE

Actress Mazar - DEBI

Actress McCambridge -
   MERCEDES

Actress McClanahan - RUE

Actress McClurg - EDIE

Actress McKenna - SIOBHAN

Actress McKeon - NANCY

Actress Meadows -
   AUDREY or JANE

Actress Meg - RYAN or TILLY

Actress Mendez - EVA

Actress Menken - ADAH

Actress Mercedes - RUEHL

Actress Merkel - UNA

Actress Merkerson - EPETHA

Actress Merrill - DINA

Actress Messing - DEBRA

Actress Metcalf - LAURIE

Actress Meyer - Dina

Actress Meyers - ARI

Actress Mia - SARA

Actress Michael - LEARNED

Actress Milano - ALYSSA

Actress Miles - SARAH
   or VERA

Actress Mimi - ROGERS

Actress Mimieu - YVETTE

Actress Minnelli - LIZA

Actress Mitzi - GAYNOR
   or MCCALL

Actress Molly - PICON

Actress Monk - DEBRA

Actress Montez - LOLA

Actresss Moore - MELBA
   or TERRY

Actress Moran - ERIN

Actress Moreau - JEANNE

Actress Moreno - RITA

Actress Morris - ANITA

Actress Munson - ONA

Actress Myer - DINA

Actress Myers - ARI

Actress Naldi - NITA

Actress Nancy - KWAN
   or OLSON

Actress Nazimova - ALLA

Actress Neagle - ANNA

Actress Negri - POLA

Actress Nell - GWYN

Actress Nelligan - KATE

Actress Nettleton - LOIS

Actress Neuwirth - BEBE

Actress NG - IRENE

Actress Nia - PEEBLES

Actress
   Nicole_____Parker - ARI

Actress Nicki - MINAJ

Actress Nicollette - SHERIDAN

Actress Nielsen - ASTA
   or BRIGITTE

Actress Normand - MABEL

Actress North - SHEREE

Actress O'Connor - UNA

Actress Ogrady - GAIL

Actress Olin - LENA

Actress Oliver - EDNA MAY

Actress Olivia d'_____ - ABO

Actress Olivia - HUSSEY

Actress O'Neal - TATUM

Actress Ortiz - ANA

Actress O'Shea - TESSIE

Actress Ostereald - BIBI

Actress Owen - RENA

Actress Pacula - JOANNA

Actress Page - ERICKA
   or GERALDINE

Actress Palmer - BETSY or LILLI

Actress Pam - Grier

Actress Pamela -
   ANDERSON, DES
BARRES or REED

Actress Panabaker - KAY

Actress Papas - IRENE

Actress Paquin - ANNA

Actress Park-Lincoln - LAR

Actress Parker - POSEY or SUSY

Actress Parsons - ESTELLE

Actress Pataky - ELSA

Actress Patsy - KENSIT

Actress Patti - LUPONE

Actress Paula - PRENTISS

Actress Pedrova - OLGA

Actress Peeples - NIA

Actress Peggy - CASS

Actress Penelope - CRUZ

Actress Perez - ROSIE

Actress Perrson - ESSY

Actress Petty - LORI

Actress Pfeiffer- DEDEE

Actress Phillips - SIAN

Actress Phoebe - CATES

Actress Pier - ANGELI

Actress_____ Pinket
   Smith - JADA

Actress Piper - LAURIE

Actress Pitts - ZASU

Actress Plato - DANA

Actress Plumb - EVE

Actress Plummer - AMANDA

Actress Poehler - AMY

Actress Polo - TERI

Actress Portia de - ROSSI

Actress Portman - NATALIE

Actress Potts - ANNIE

Actress Pounder - CCH

Actress Powers - MALA

Actress Prentiss - PAULA

Actress Purviance - EDNA

Actress Rachael Leigh - COOK

Actress Rainer - LUISE

Actress Raines - ELLA

Actress Ramirez - MARISA

Actress Redgrave - LYNN
   or VANESSA

Actress Reed Hall - ALAINA

Actress Rehan - ADA

Actress Reid - BERYL or TARA

Actress Reinking - ANN

Actress Reischl - GERI

Actress Remini - LEAH

Actress Rena - SOFER

Actress Renee - ADOREE

Actress Reva - ROSE

Actress Richards - DENISE

Actress Richardson - MIRANDA
   or NATASHA

Actress Rinna - LISA

Actress Rita - GAM or
   MORENO

Actress Ritter - THELMA

Actress Roberts - TANYA

Actress Robin - GIVENS

Actress Rogers - MIMI

Actress Roker - ROXIE

Actress Roony - MARA

Actress Rosalind - CHAO

Actress Rosie - O'DONNELL
   or PEREZ

Actress Rossum - EMMY

Actress Rowlands - GENA

Actress Rossellini - ISABELLA

Actress Ruby - KEELER

Actress Rule - JANICE

Actress Russel - KERI

Actress Russo - RENE

Actress Ruth - ROMAN

Actress Ryan - JERI or MEG

Actress Ryder - WINONA

Actress Sagal - KATIE

Actress Saldana - ZOE

Actress Sally - FIELD

Actress Sally Ann - HOWES

Actress Salma - HAYEK

Actress Salome - JENS

Actress Salonga - LEA

Actress Sammantha - EGGAR

Actress Samms - EMMA

Actress Sara - MIA

Actress Sara Jessica - PARKER

Actress Sarandan - SUSAN

Actress Scacchi - GRETA

Actress Scala - GIA

Actress Schell - MARIA

Actress Schneider - ROMY

Actress Sedgwick - EDIE
or KYRA

Actress Sevigne - CHLOE

Actress Shane - LIN

Actress Sharon - GANS, GLESS,
STONE or TATE

Actress Shawkat - ALIA

Actress Shearer - MOIRA

Actress Sheedy - ALLY

Actress Sheppard - DELIA

Actress Sherilyn - FENN

Actress Shields - BROOKE

Actress Shire - TALIA

Actress Shirley - AURORA

Actress Shue - ELISABETH

Actress Siddons - SARAH

Actress Signe - HASSO

Actress Signoret - SIMONE

Actress Silverstone - ALICIA

Actress Silvia - SIDNEY
or SYMS

Actress Singer - LORI

Actress Skye - IONE

Actress Slezak - ERIKA

Actress Smart - JEAN

Actress Smith - JACLYN,
MAGGIE

or TASHA

Actress Sobieski - LEELEE

Actress Sofer - RENA

Actress Sommer - ELKE

Actress Sondra - LOCKE

Actress Sonya - BRAGA

Actress Sorvino - MIRA

Actress Spacek - SISSY

Actress Spelling - TORI

Actress Stanley - KIM

Actresss Stapleton - JEAN

Actress Stella - ADLER

Actress Stephanie - BEECHAM

Actress Stevens - INGER
or STELLA

Actress Stewart - ALANA

Actress Stimson - SARA

Actress Stone - SHARON

Actress Strassman - MARCIA

Actress Streep - MERYL

Actress Stritch - ELAINE

Actress Struthers - SALLY

Actress Sue_____Langdon - AN

Actress _____Sue
Martin - PAMELA

Actress Susan - ANTON,
DEY or LUCCI

Actress Susie - AMIS

Actress Suvari - MENA

Actress Suzanne - SOMERS

Actress Swenson - INGA

Actress Swinton - TILDA

Actress Sykes - WANDA

Actress Ta - LEONI

Actress Taina - ELG

Actress Talbot - NITA

Actress Talia - SHIRE

Actress Talmadge - NORMA

Actress Tamblyn - AMBER

Actress Tatania - ALI

Actress Taylor - ELIZABETH, LILI, MAUI, RENEE or REGINA

Actress Tea - LEONI

Actress Tessie - O'SHEA

Actress Texada - TIA

Actress Thomas - MARLO

Actress Thompson - EMMA, LEA or SADA

Actress Thorndyke - SYBIL

Actress Thurman - UMA

Actress Tierney - Gene or MAURA

Actress Tilly - MEG

Actress Tippi - HEDREN

Actress Tomei - MARISA

Actress Tracy - ULLMAN

Actress Trevor - CLAIRE

Actress Trudie - STYLER

Actress Tuesday - WELD

Actress Turner - LANA

Actress Tushingham - RITA

Actress Turturro - AIDA

Actress Tyler - LIV

Actress Tyson - CICELY

Actress Ullman - LIV

Actresss Una - MERKEL

Actress Uta - HAGAN

Actress Valentine - KAREN

Actress Valli - ALIDA

Actress Van Devere - TRISH

Actress Van Doren - MAMIE

Actress Vardalus - NIA

Actresss Velez - LUPE

Actress Verdon - GWEN

Actress Verdugo - ELENA

Actress Veronica - HAMIL or LAKE

Actress Vidal - THEA

Actress Virginia - MADSEN or MAYO

Actress Virna - LISI

Actress Vivian - LEIGH or VANCE

Actress Volz - NEDRA

Actress Wallace - DEE

Actress Wannamaker - ZOE

Actress Ward - SELA

Actress Wasikowska - MIA

Actress Watson - EMILY or EMMA

Actress Watts - NAOMI

Actress Weist - DIANNE

Actress Wendy - BARRIE

Actress Wettig - PATRICIA

Actress Whitman - MAE

Actress Wilde - OLIVIA

Actress Williams - CARA, EDY, ESTHER, JOBETH or KELLY

Actress Wilson - RITA

Actress Winger - DEBRA

Actress Winningham - MARE

Actress Winona - RYDER

Actress Winslet - KATE

Actress Winwood - ESTELLE

Actress Wisikowski - MIA

Actress Witherspoon - CORA or REESE

Actress Witt - ALICIA

Actress Wood - LANA

Actress Woodard - ALFRE

Actress Woods - NAN or REN

Actress Worth - IRENE

Actress Wray - FAY

Actress Wright - TERESA

Actress York - SUSANNAH

Actress Yothers - TINA

Actress Zellweger - RENEE

Actress Zeta-Jones - CATHARINE

Actress Zetterling - MAI

Actress Ziemba - KAREN

Admiral Zumait - ELMO

Albert & Tipper - GORE

Alda - ROBERT or ALAN

Alex & Felix - ADLER

Ali - BABA

Allen - TIM

Allen or Tim - CONWAY

Aluminum discoverer - OERSTED

American naturalist - MUIR

Amin - IDI

Amy or James - LOWELL

Anarchist Goldman - EMMA

Andrea_____Sarto - DEL

Andretti - MARIO

Angus - DEI

Animator Avery - TEX

Animator Bluth - DON

Animator Groening - MATT

Announcer Costas - BOB

Annoucer Dawson - LEN

Announcer Don - PARDO

Anthologist Alberto - MANGUEL

Anthropologist Fossey - DIAN

Anthropologist Margaret - MEAD

Anthropologist Montagu - ASHLEY

Anthropologist Morris - DESMOND

Anthropologist Strauss - LEVI

Aoki of Golf - ISAO

Archibald of basketball - NATE

Architect Alva - AALTO

Architect Benjamin - LAROBE
Architect
    Brammante - DONATO
Architect
  · Buckminster - FULLER
Architect Christopher - WREN
Architect Frank - GEHRY
Architect I. M. _____ - PEI
Architect Jacobsen - ARNE
Architect James - HOBAN
Architect Jones - INIGO
Architech
    Leoh_____Pei - MING
Architect Maya - LIN
Architect Mies van de - ROHE
Architect Oscar - NIEMEYER
Architect Pei - IEOH
Architect Pelli - CESAR
Architect Richard - MEIER
Architect Saarinen -
    EERO or ELIEL
Architect Samuel - SLOAN
Architect Soleri - PAOLO
Architect Van der Rohe - MIES
Architect Wagner - OTTO
Architect William Van - ALEN
Arlene or Roald - DAHL
Art collector Broad - ELI
Art deco designer - ERTE
Artist Adams - OLETA
Artist Alex - KATZ
Artist Alexander - CALDER

Artist Andrew - WYETH
Artist Annigoni - PIETRO
Artist Arp - HANS
Artist Beardsley - AUBREY
Artist Ben - SHAHN
Artist Bonheur - ROSA
Artist Cezanne - PAUL
Artist Chagal - MARC
Artist Del Sarto - ANDREA
Artist Duffy - RAOUL
Artist Edgar - DEGAS
Artist Edouard - MANET
Artist Edvard - MUNCH
Artist Elbers - JOSEF
Artist Emily - CARR
  · Artist Eric - SLOANE
Artist Fernand - LEGER
Artist Frans - HALS
Artist Fransisco - GOYA
Artist Franz - MARC
Artist Frida - KAHLO
Artist Gaugan - PAUL
Artist Grant - WOOD
Artist Guido - RENI
Artist Gustave - DORE
Artist Hals - FRANZ
Artist Harring - KEITH
Artist Homer - WINSLOW
Artist Hopper - EDWARD
Artist Hudson - NAN
Artist James - ENSOR

Artist Jan - STEEN or
 VERMEER
Artist Jasper - JOHNS
Artist Jean - ARP
Artist Joan - MIRO
Artist John - SARGENT
Artist Jose de - RIBERA
Artist Kahlo - FRIDA
Artist LaLique - RENE
Artist Lewitt - SOL
Artist Lichtenstein - ROY
Artist Magritte - RENE
Artist Mark - ROTHKO
Artist Matisse - HENRI
Artist Max - ERNST
Artist Modigliani - AMEDEO
Artist Mondrian - PIET
Artist Monet - CLAUDE
Artist Nadelman - ELIE
Artist Neiman - LEROY
Artist Nolde - EMIL
Artist Paul - KLEE
Artist Picasso - PABLO
Artist Poussin - NICOLAS
Artist Renoir - AUGUSTE
Artist Rivera - DIEGO
Artist Rockwell - KENT
 or NORMAN
Artist Rouseau - HENRI
Artist Sedgewick - EDIE
Artist Smit - ARIE

Artist Theo - JENSEN
Artist Van - GOGH
Artist Vermeer - JAN
Artist Verones - PAOLO
Artist Warhol - ANDY
Artist Watteau - ANTOINE
Artist Wyeth - JAMIE
Asner or Wynn - ED
Astrologer Dixon - JEAN
Astrologer Goodman - LINDA
Astrologer John - DEE
Astrologer Sidney - OMARR
Astronaut Armstrong - NEAL
Astronaut Buzz - ALDRIN
Astronaut Carpenter - SCOTT
Astronaut Collins - EILEEN
Astronaut Dr. Mae - JEMISON
Astronaut Fisher - ANNA LEE
Astronaut Gagarin - YURI
Astronaut Garriott - OWEN
Astronaut Grissom - GIL or GUS
Astronaugh James - VOSS
Astronaut Jamison - MAE
Astronaut Jernigan - TAMARA
Astronaut Judith - RESNICK
Astronaut Roosa - STU
Astronaut Sally - RIDE
Astronaut Shannon - LUCID
Astonaut Slaton - DEKE
Astronaut Sullivan - KATHRYN
Astronaut Walter - SCHIRRA

Astronomer Brahe - TYCHO
Astronomer Hubble - EDWIN
Astronomer Johannes - KEPLER
Astronomer Lowell - PERCIVAL
Astronomer Martin - REES
Astronomer Penzias - ARNO
Astronomer Sir Martin - RYLE
Astronomer Tycho - BRAHE
Atheist Madalyn
    Murray - OHAIR
Attorney Dershowitz - ALAN
Attorney Gloria - ALLRED
Attorney Melvin - BELLI
Attorney Roy - COHN
Auberjonois - RENE
Author Abba - EBAN
Author Achebe - CHINUA
Author Adler - FREDA
    or RENATA
Author Alan - PATON
Author Alcott - LOUISA
Author Alexandra - SHANA
Author Algren - NELSON
Author Alice - ADAMS
Author Alighieri - DANTE
Author Alison LURIE
Author Allende - ISABEL
Author Alther - LISA
Author Alvin - TOFFLER
Author Ambler - ERIC
Author Amis - MARTIN

Author Amistead - MAUPIN
Author Amy - TAN
Author Anais - NIN
Author Anchee - MIN
Author Andersen - HANS
Author Andre - GIDE
    or MAUROIS
Author Andric - IVO
Author Angelou - MAYA
Author Anita - LOOS
Author Ann - RULE
Author Anna - SEWELL
Author Anya - SETON
Author Arendt - HANNAH
Author Arthur - CLARKE
Author Asch - SHOLEM
Author Asimov - ISAAC
Author Asquith - ROS
Author Auel - JEAN
Author Austen - JANE
Author Ayn - RAND
Author Babel - ISAAC
Author Bacon - DELIA
Author Bagnold - ENID
Author Balzac - HONORE
Author Barker - CLIVE
Author Bates - ARLO
Author Beattie - ANN
Author Beckett - SAMUEL
Author Belloc - HILAIRE
Author Bellows - SAUL

Author Belva - PLAIN

Author Berenstain - STAN

Author Bernard - MALAMUD

Author Betti - UGO

Author Bierce - AMBROSE

Author Binchly - MAEVE

Author Blixen - KAREN

Author Bloom - ALLAN

Author Blume - JUDY

Author Blyton - ENID

Author Booth - TARKINGTON

Author Boyle - KAY or TISH

Author Bracken - PEG

Author Braveman - KATE

Author Bret - ELLIS or HARTE

Author Brookner - ANITA

Author Brown - DAN or DEE

Author Buchanan - EDNA

Author Buck - PEARL

Author Buscaglia - LEO

Author
    Butler - ROBERT- OLEN

Author Cainan - ETHAN

Author Caldwell - ERSKINE

Author Caleb - CARR

Author Calvino - ITALO

Author Canette - ELIAS

Author Capek - KAREL

Author Capet - KARE

Author Capote - TRUMAN

Author Carl - SAGAN

Author Carnegie - DALE

Author Carolyn - KEENE

Author Carr - CALEB

Author Carson - RACHEL

Author Castaneda - CARLOS

Author Castillo - ANA

Author Cather - WILLAS

Author Chaim - POTOK

Author Chalmers - IRENA

Author _____Chandler
    Harris - JOEL

Author Charles - READE
    or OLSON

Author Chomsky - NOAM

Author Chopin - KATE

Author Clark - BLAISE

Author Clancy - TOM

Author Cleveland - AMORY

Author Clifford - ODETS

Author Colin - CAPP

Author Collins - WILKIE

Author Comfort - ALEX

Author Connell - EVAN

Author Conrad - JOSEPH

Author Cornelius - RYAN

Author Coulter - ANN

Author Cross - AMANDA

Author Currie - EDWINA

Author Cussler - CLIVE

Author Dahl - ROALD

Author Daniel - KEYES

Author Davis - ADELLE

Author De Beauvoir - SIMONE

Author De Foe - DANIEL

Author De Hartog - JAN

Author De La Roche - MAZO

Author Deighton - LEN

Author Delillo - DON

Author Desmond - MORRIS

Author Devereau - JUDE

Author Dexter - PETE

Author Dian - FOSSEY

Author Dideon - JOAN

Author Dillard - ANNIE

Author Dinesen - ISAK

Author Don - DeLILLO

Author _____Donald
    Walsch - NEALE

Author Du Maurier - DAPHNE

Author
    Earl _____Biggers - DERR

Author Eberhart - MIGNON

Author Eda - LESHAN

Author Edward D. - HOCH

Author Edwin - OCONNOR

Author Eleanor - ESTES

Author Eliau - ARIE

Author Elinor - GLYN
    or WYLIE

Author Elkin - STANLEY

Author Elizabeth - BOWEN

Author Ellen - RASKIN

Author Ellison - HARLAN
    or RALPH

Author Ellsberg - DANIEL

Author Emily - CARR

Author Ephron - DELIA
    or NORA

Author Eric - BERNE

Author Erica - JONG

Author Erich - SEGAL

Author Ernest - POOLE

Author Ernie - PYLE

Author Esquivel - LAURA

Author Eudora - WELTY

Author Fannie - FLAGG

Author Fallaci - ORIANA

Author Farley - MOWAT

Author Faust - GOETHE

Author Fielding - HENRY

Author Fitzgerald - ZELDA

Author Fleming - IAN

Author Follett - KEN

Author Fforde - JASPER

Author Fosse - DIAN

Author France - ANATOLE

Author Francoise - SAGAN

Author Frank - ASCH
    or NORRIS

Author Franz - KAFKA

Author Frederik - POHL

Author Fromm - ERIC

Author Fugard - ATHOL

Author Gail - PARENT

Author Gardner - EARL

Author Garson - KANIN

Author Gay - TALESE

Author George - ELIOT,
 ORWELL, SAND
 or SOROS

Author Germaine - GREER

Author Germaine de - STAEL

Author Gertrude - STEIN

Author Gibbons - KAYE

Author Gilchrist - ELLEN

Author Gish - JEN

Author Glasgow - ELLEN

Author Glyn - ELINOR

Author Godden - RUMER

Aauthor Godwin - GAIL

Author Goncharov - IVAN

Author Gore - VIDAL

Author Grafton - SUE

Author Graham - GREENE

Author Grass - GUNTER

Author Gray - ZANE

Author Greene – GAEL
 or GRAHAM

Author Greg - EGAN

Author Guest - JUDITH

Author H. H. Munroe - SAKI

Author Hagan - UTA

Author Haley - ALEX

Author Hammond - INNES

Author Hamsun - KNUT

Author Hanff - HELENE

Author Harland – ELLISON

Author Harper - LEE

Author Havelock - ELLIS

Author
 Hawthorn - NATHANIEL

Author Heine - HEINRICH

Author Henrik - IBSEN

Author Henry - ROTH

Author Herman - HESSE

Author Heyerdahl - THOR

Author Hillerman - TONY

Author Hite - SHERE

Author Hoag - TAMI

Author Hoff – BENJAMIN
 or SYD

Author Hoffer - ERIC

Author Hoffman - ABBIE

Author Hood - ANN

Author Horatio - ALGER

Author Hubbard – L. RON

Author Hulme - KERI

Author Hunter - EVAN

Author
 Hurston _____NEALE -
 ZORA

Author Huxley - ALDOUS

Author Ian - FLEMING
 or MCEWAN

Author Ingall Wilder - LAURA

Author Ira - LEVIN

Author Isaac - ASIMOV

Author Jack - LONDON

Author _____ Jackson
Braun - LILIAN

Author Jacob - RIIS

Author Jaffe - RONA

Author James - AGEE, ATLAS,
MANN or PATTERSON

Author Janowitz - TAMA

Author Jane - SMILEY

Author Jaquelin - SUSANN

Author Jay - ANSON

Author Jean - AUEL or RHYS

Author Jean Paul -SARTRE

Author Jeffrey - ARCHER

Author Jessamyn - WEST

Author Johann - WYSS

Author Johanna - SPYRI

Author John Dickson - CARR

Author John Dos - PASSOS

Author John - LECARRE,
LYLY or UPDIKE

Author John Kennedy - TOOLE

Author Jones - LEROI

Author Jong - ERICA

Author Jorge - AMADO

Author
Jorge_____Borges - LUIS

Author Josephine - TEY

Author Joyce - JAMES

Author Joyce Carol - OATES

Author Kafka - FRANZ

Author Kanter - SETH

Author Kauffman - BEL

Author Ken - KESEY

Author Kesey - KEN

Author Khoury - ELIAS

Author Kingsley - AMIS

Author Knight - ERIC

Author Kogawa - JOY

Author Koontz - DEAN

Author Kundera - MILAN

Author Lamott - JUNE

Author Langdon - JANE

Author Lathen - EMMA

Auther Lee - HARPER

Author _____ Lee
Hope - LAURA

Author Leguin - URSALA

Author Lesage - ALAIN

Author Leon - ROOKE or URIS

Author Leonard - ELMIR
or ELMORE

Author Leshan - EDA

Author Lesssing - DORIS MAY

Author Levin - IRA

Author Lin - YUTANG

Author Lindbergh - ANNE

Author Lipman - ELINOR

Author Lofting - HUGH

Author Lofts - NORAH

Author Loos - ANITA

Author Louisa May - ALCOTT

Author Ludlum - ROBERT

Author Ludwig - EMIL

Author Lurie - ALISON

Author Lustbader - ERIC

Author Maalouf - AMIN

Author MacDonald - ROSS

Author Malraux - ANDRE

Author Margaret - ATWOOD

Author Marian - ENGEL

Author Mario - PUZO

Author Marsh - NGAIO

Author Martin - AMIS

Author Mary Lee - SETTLE

Author Maurice - EVANS

Author May - ROLLO

Author McBain - ED

Author McCaffrey - ANNE

Author McCann - COOLUM

Author McClintock - NORAH

Author McCourtney - LORENA

Author McCullers - CARSON

Author McCullough - COLLEEN

Author McDermott - ALICE

Author Melville - HERMAN

Author Melvin - BELLI

Author Michael - ENDE
or INNES

Author Michaels - FERN

Author Mihel - KORDA

Author Miller - SUE or HENRY

Author Mills - ENOS

Author Milne - ALAN

Author Milosz - CZESLAW

Author Montez - LOLA

Author Morrison - TONI

Author Munro - ALICE

Author Murdoch - IRIS

Author Nathaniel - WEST

Author Nelson - ALGREN

Author Neville - SHUTE

Author Ngaio - MARSH

Author Nicolas - GAGE

Author Nin - ANAIS

Author Nino - RICCI

Author Noel - BEHN
or COWARD

Author Norman - MAILER

Author Norman
Vincent - PEALE

Author O'Brien - EDNA

Author Octavio - PAZ

Author Odets - CLIFFORD

Author O'Faolain - SEAN

Author O'Flaherty - LIAM

Author Olesha - YURY

Author Oz - AMOS

Author Packard - VANCE

Author Pamela_____Barres - DES

Author Parent - GAIL

Author Paretsky - SARA

Author Pasternak - BORIS

Author Paton - ALAN

Author Pauline - KAMEL

Author Peter - MAAS

Author Peters - ELLIS

Author Philip - ROTH

Author Piandello - LUIGI

Author Pierre - LOTI

Author Plain - BELVA

Author Potock - CHAIM

Author Prosper - MERIMEE

Author Proust - MARCEL

Author Prudhomme - ENOLA

Author Puzo - MARIO

Author Pyle - ERNIE

Author Quick - AMANDA

Author Quidland - ANNA

Author Radcliffe - ANN

Author Randy - SHILTS

Author Rawlings - MARJORIE

Author Rebecca - WEST

Author Rice - ANNE or ELMER

Author Richard - ADAMS
    or SCARRY

Author Richard Henry - DANA

Author Roald - DAHL

Author Robbe-Grillet - ALAIN

Author Robert - RUARK
    or STONE

Author Robert_____Butler -
    OLEN

Author Roberts - NORA

Author Robertson - DAVIES

Author Robinson - EDEN

Author Roger St. Johns - ADELA

Author Rombauer - IRMA

Author Rosten - LEO

Author Roth - PHILIP

Author Rule - ANN

Author S. S. Van - DINE

Author Sanchez - SONIA

Author Sandel - CORA

Author Santha Rama - RAU

Author
    Sarah_____Jewett - ORNE

Author Schreiner - OLIVE

Author Scott - O'DELL
    or TUROW

Author Sebold - ALICE

Author Segal - ERICH

Author Sendak - MAURICE

Author Seton - ANYA

Author Sewell - ANNA

Author Shaw - IRWIN

Author Sheehy - GAIL

Author Sheldon - SIDNEY

Author Shelley - MARY

Author Shere - HITE

Author
    Sherwood - ANDERSON

Author Shilts - RANDY

Author Sholem - ASCH

Author Shreve - ANITA

Author Siddhartha - HESSE

Author Sidney - SHELDON

Author Siegel - BERNIE

Author Sillitoe - ALAN

Author Silvia - PLATH

Author Simenon - Georges

Author Simpson - MONA

Author Sinclair - ROSS
   or UPTON

Author Sir Thomas - ELYOT

Author Skvorecky - JOSEF

Author Snicket - LEMONY

Author Sophie - KERR

Author Spryri - JOHANNA

Author Stanislaw - LEM

Author Stein - GERTRUDE

Author Steinhauer - OLIN

Author Stephen - CRANE

Author Stephenson - NEAL

Author Stewart - ALSOP

Author Stoker - BRAM

Author Stout - REX

Author Sturluson - SNORRI

Author Susan - ISAACS
   or SONTAG

Author Suzanne - SOMERS

Author Talese - GAY

Author Tamblyn - RUSS

Author Tan - AMY

Author Tarbell - IDA

Author Tasha - TUDOR

Author Tertz - ABRAM

Author Thomas - MARLO
   or PAINE

Author Tillie - OLSON

Author Tofler - ALVIN

Author Tolstoy - LEO

Author Toni - MORRISON

Author Trilling - LIONEL

Author Truman - CAPOTE

Author Turgenov - IVAN

Author Turkel - STUDS

Author Tyler - ANNE

Author Umberto - ECO

Author Updike - JOHN

Author Uris - LEON

Author Ursula - LEGUIN

Author Urquhart - THOMAS

Author Victoria - HOLT

Author Vonnegut - KURT

Author Walker - ALICE
   or PERCY

Author Wallace - LEW

Author Wally - AMOS

Author Walter - FARLEY
   or PATER

Author Walton - IZAAK

Author Waugh - ALEC
   or EVELYN

Author Weldon - FEY

Author Welty - EUDORA

Author West - NATHANAEL

Author Wharton - EDITH

Author White - T. H.

Author Wilde - OSCAR

Author Wilder - THORNTON

Author Wiesel - ELIE

Author William - GIBSON

Author William H. - WHYTE
Author Winegarten - RENEE
Author Wister - OWEN
Author Wolf - NAOMI
Author Wolfert - IRA
Author Wolff - TOBIAS
Author Wouk - HERMAN
Author Yurik - SOL
Author Yutang - LIN
Author Zola - EMILE
Author Zona - GALE
Author Zora _____Hurton -
    NEALE
Auto pioneer Carl - BENZ
Auto pioneer Ransom - OLDS
Auto racer Gordon - JEFF
Auto racer Kyle - Busch
Auto racer Petty - KYLE
    or RICHARD
Auto racer Prost - ALAIN
Automaker Ferrari - ENZO
Automaker
    Maserati - ERNESTO
Aviator Balbo - ITALO
Aviator Chennault - CLAIRE
Aviator Earhart - AMELIA
Aviator Garros - ROLAND
Aviator Post - WILEY
B. C. Cartoonist - HAUNT
Baba - ALI
Bacteriologist Dubos - RENE
Bacteriologist Jonas - SALK

Bakkaruba Alicia - ALONZO
Ballpoint pen inventor
    Lazlo - BIRO
Ballarina Alonzo - ALICIA
Ballarina Fonteyn - MARGOT
Ballarina Galina - ULANOVA
Ballarina Karsavina - TAMARA
Ballarina Markova - ALICIA
Ballarina Markarova - NATALIA
Ballarina Melissa - HAYDEN
Ballarina painter - DEGAS
Ballarina Pavlova - ANNA
Ballarina Plisetskaya - MAYA
Ballarina Rambeat - MARIE
Ballarina Shearer - MOIRA
Ballarina Spessivtzeve - OLGA
Ballet dancer
    Youskevitch - IGOR
Ballet dancer Bruhn - ERIC
Ball player Dykstra - LEN
Bandleader Baxter - LES
Bandleader Cugot - Xavier
Bandleader Edmundo - ROS
Bandleader Fields - SHEP
Bandleader Kay - KYSER
Bandleader King - PEEWEE
Bandleader Lawrence - WELK
Bandleader Les - ELGART
Bandleader Lester - LANIN
Bandleader Lewis - TED
Bandleader Miller - GLENN

Bandleader Puente - TITO
Bandleader Ray - EBERLE
Bandleader Tito - PUENTE
Bandleader Waring - FRED
Bandleader Winding - KAI
Banjoist Fleck - BELA
Bannister or Moore - Roger
Barak of Israel - EHUD
Barbera's partner - HANNA
Baritone Paquale - AMATO
Baritone Robert - MERRILL
Baseball great Buck - O'NEIL
Baseball great
    Honus - WAGNER
Baseball great Irvin - MONTE
Baseball great Moore - EARL
Baseball great Ralph - KINER
Baseball great Rod - CAREW
Baseball great Tony -
    GWYNN or OLIVA
Baseball great Vaughan - ARKY
Basseball Legend
    Honus - WAGNER
Baseball manager Piniella - LOU
Baseball pitcher Hideki - IRABU
Baseball pitcher Tiant - LUIS
Baseball player
    Clemente - ROBERTO
Baseball shortstop
    Vizquel - OMAR
Baseball star
    Garciaparra - NOMAR

Baseball star Suzuki - ICHIRO
Baseballer Frankie - FRISCH
Baseballer Fred - LYNN
Baseballer Hodges - GIL
Baseballer Johnny - SAIN
Baseballer Magglio or
    Rey - ORDONEZ
Baseball's Alcindor - LEW
Baseball's Alejandro - PENA
Baseball's Alex - OCHOA
Baseball's Amos - OTIS
Baseball's Bando or Maglie - SAL
Baseball's Banks - ERNIE
Baseball's Bauer - HANK
Baseball's Boggs - WADE
Baseball's Boone - BRET
Baseball's Boyer - CLETE
    or KEN
Baseball's Bud - SELIG
Baseball's Buddy - ROSAR
Baseball's Carew - ROD
Baseball's Carlton - FISK
Baseball's Cey - RON
Baseball's Combs - EARLE
Baseball's Darling - RON
Baseball's Del - ENNIS
Baseball's Dent - Bucky
Baseball's Doubleday - ABNER
Baseball's Durocher - LEO
Baseball's Dykstra - LEN
Baseball's Felipe - ALOU

Baseball's Garciapara - NOMAR

Baseball's Gibson - BOB

Baseball's Grove - LEFTY

Baseball's Guerrero - PEDRO

Baseball's Hank - BAUER

Baseball's Hershiser - OREL

Baseball's Hideo - NOMO

Baseball's Howard - ELSTON

Baseball's Hosmer - ERIC

Baseball's Jeter - DEREK

Baseball's Jones - CLEON

Baseball's Jorge - POSADA

Baseball's Jose - CANSECO

Baseball's Lopes - DAVEY

Baseball's Maglie - SAL

Baseball's Mannie - RAMIREZ

Baseball's Martinez -
    PEDRO or TINO

Baseball's Matsui –
    HIDEKI or KAZ

Basebell's Moses - EDWIN

Baseball's Musial - STAN

Baseball's Olivares - OMAR

Baseball's Ordonez - REY

Baseball's Ott - MEL

Baseball's Palmiero - RAFAEL

Baseball's Petrocelli - RICO

Baseball's Piniella - LOU

Baseball's Preacher - ROE

Baseball's Rafael - PALMIERO

Baseball's Ramirez - MANNIE

Basesball's Raul - IBANEZ

Baseball's Ricky - LEDEE

Baseball's Ripken - CAL

Baseball's Rizzuto - PHIL

Baseball's
    Roberto - CLEMENTE

Baseball's Robin - YOUNT

Baseball's Rodriguez -
    ALEX AROD
or IVAN

Baseball's Ron - GANT

Baseball's Roush - EDD

Baseball's Rusty - STAUB

Baseball's Sal - BANDO

Baseball's Sandberg - RYNE

Baseball's Sandy - ALOMAR

Baseball's Slaughter - ENOS

Baseball's Speaker - TRIS

Baseball's Tommie - AGEE

Baseball's Tony - PENA

Baseball's Travis - LEE

Baseball's Vizquel - OMAR

Baseball's Warren - SPAHN

Baseball's Wilhelm - HOYTE

Baseball star
    Galarraga - ANDRES

Baseball star Rebecca - LOBO

Baseball star Yastremski - CARL

Basketball coach Pat - RILEY

Basketball great Thomas - ISIAH

Basketball star Baylor - ELGIN

Basketball star Larry - BIRD

Basketball star Ming - YAO
Basketball star Malone - KARL
Basketball's Birdsong - OTIS
Basketball's Gilmore - ARTIS
Basketball's Jason - KIDD
Basketbell's Kemp - SHAWN
Basketball's Olajuwan - AKEEM
Basketball's Patrick - EWING
Basketball's Robertson - OSCAR
Basketball's Thurmond - NATE
Basketball's Unseld - WES
Basketball's Walter - KARA
Basketball's Yastremski - CARL
Bass player Chandler - CHAS
Basso Cesare - SIEPI
Basso Chaliapin - FEADOR
Basso Pinza - EZIO
Bathyspherist William - BEEBE
Beattie or Blyth - ANN
Beatty of films - NED
Best or Ferber - EDNA
Betsy or Arnold - PALMER
Betsy or Diana - ROSS
Beverly or George - SANDERS
Bhutto of Pakastan - BENAZAR
Bike racer Lemond - GREG
Biochemist Tiselius - ARNE
Biographer Hawes - ESME
Biographer Leon - EDEL
Biographer Ludwig - EMIL
Biographer Strachey - LYTTON

Biographer Walton - IZAAK
Biologist Metchnikoff - ELIE
Biologist Rachel - CARSON
Biologist Stephan Jay - GOULD
Blake of TV - AMANDA
Body builder Ferrigno - LOU
Bohr - AAGE NIELS
Bonheur or Ponselle - ROSA
Botinist Gray - ASA
Botinist Mendal - GREGOR
Boulanger of music - NADIA
Bowler Dick - WEBER
Boxer Ali - LAILA
Boxer Archie MOORE
Boxer Barkley - IRAN
Boxer Benvenuti - NINO
Boxer Firpo - LUIS
Boxer Griffith - EMILE
Boxer Holyfield - EVANDER
Boxer Johansson - ENGEMAR
Boxer Laila - ALI
Boxer Marvin - HAGLER
Boxer Max - BAER
Boxer Mayweather - FLOYD
Boxer Primo - CARNERA
Boxer Riddick - BOWE
Boxer Roberto - DURAN
Boxer Rodriguez - IVAN
Boxer Schmelling - MAX
Boxer Spinks - LEON
Boxer Stevenson - TEO

Boxer Tyson - MIKE

Boxer Willard - JESS

Boxing champ Billy - CONN

Boxinng champ Hawes - ESME

Boxing champ Riddick - BOWE

Boxing great
    Carlos - PALOMINO

_____Breckonridge - MYRA

Bridge expert Charles - GOREN

Bridge expert Oswald - JACOBY

Bridge Guru Culbertson - ELY

British actor Peter - CUSHING

British composer - ELGAR
    or ARNE

British playwrite
    Barstow - STAN

British PM Tony - BLAIR

Broadcaster Linda - ELLERBEE

Bronte's governess - EYRE

Brooks or Brundage - AVERY

Bruce & Laura - DERN

Bryant or Baker - ANITA

Bulba - TARAS

Buster or Diane - KEATON

Cabinet maker
    Phyfe - DUNCAN

Cager Frazier - WALT

Cager Gilmore - ARTIS

Cager Montore - EARL

Cager Thomas - ISIAH

Caldwell of Broadway - ZOE

Cambodia's Lon - NOL

Camera maven Land - EDWIN

Camus - ALBERT

Canadian actor Cariou - LEN

Canadian songstress -
    K.D. LANG

Cantor or Murphy - EDDIE

Car maker
    Maserati - ERNESTO

Card game expert
    John – SCARNE

Caricaturist Damier - HONORE

Cartoonist Addams - CHAS

Cartoonist Berke - BREATHED

Cartoonist Browne - DIK

Cartoonist Bushmiller - ERNIE

Cartoonist Caniff - MILT

Cartoonist Chast - ROZ

Cartoonist Drake - STAN

Cartoonist Drucker - MORT

Cartoonist Ed - DODD

Cartoonist Feifer - JULES

Cartoonist Foster - HAL

Cartoonist Gardner - REA

Cartoonist Gary - LARSON

Cartoonist Goldberg - RUBE

Cartoonist Gould - CHESTER

Cartoonist Groening - MATT

Cartoonist Guisewite - CATHY

Cartoonist Hoff - SYD

Cartoonist Hollander - NICOLE

Cartoonist Johnny - HART

Cartoonist Keane - BIL

Cartoonist Kelly - WALT
Cartoonist Key - TED
Cartoonist Lazarus - MELL
Cartoonist Malden - BILL
Cartoonist Peter - ARNO
Cartoonist R. - CRUMB
Cartoonist Russell - MYERS
Cartoonist Silverstein - SHEL
Cartoonist Soglow - OTTO
Cartoonist Tex - AVERY
Cartoonist Thomas - NAST
Cartoonist Trudeau - GARRY
Cartoonist Walker - MORT
Cartoonist Will - EISNER
Cartoonist Wilson - GAHAN
Cartoonist Winsor - MCCAY
Carvey or Delaney - DANA
Cecil B. or Agnes De - MILLE
Cellist Casals - PABLO
Cellist Ma - YOYO
Cellist Nathanial - ROSEN
Cellist Rostropovich - SLAVA
Cellist Starker - JANOS
Central idea, in music - TEMA
Chairperson Greenspan - ALAN
Chan portrayer Sidney -TOLER
Chan portrayer
    Warren - OLAND
Chang's twin - ENG
Channel swimmer
    Gertrude - EDERLE

Channing - CAROL
Chanteuse Edith - PIAF
Chaplin - Charles or OONA
Chef Deen - PAULA
Chef Ducasse - ALAIN
Chef Emeril - LAGASSE
Chef Jacques - PEPIN
Chemist Mendeleev - DMITRI
Chemist Otto - HAHN
Chemist Pauling - LINUS
Chemist Remsen - IRA
Chess Champ
    Capablanca - JOSE
Chess champ Mikhail - TAL
Chess champion
    Nimzowitsch - ARON
Chess great Spassky - BORIS
Chessmaster Anatoly - KARPOV
Chessmaster Kasparov -
    GARY or TAL
Chess player
    Lasker - EMANUEL
Choreographer Ailey - ALVIN
Choreographer Alvin - AILEY
Choreographer
    Antonio - GEDES
Choreographer Bausch - PINA
Choreographer Bob - FOSSE
Choreographer
    Champion - GOWER
Choreographer
    Cunningham - MERCE

Choreographer de
Mille - AGNES
Choreographer Fosse - BOB
Choreographer
Frederick - ASHTON
Choreographer
Graham - MARTHA
Choreographer Jose - LIMON
Choreographer Lubovitch - LAR
Choreographer Michael - KIDD
Choreographer Pan - HERMES
Choreographer Paula - ABDUL
Choreographer Reinking - ANN
Choreographer Ruth -
ST. DENIS
Choreographer Shawn - TED
Choreographer Sir
Frederick - ASHTON
Choreographer Ted - SHAWN
Choreographer Tetley - GLEN
Choreographer Tharp - TWYLA
Choreographer White - ONNA
Chou En - LAI
Chris of tennis - EVERT
Cinematographer
Charles - LANG
Cinematographer
Nykvist - SVEN
Cinematographer Tony - IMI
Clapton of song - ERIC
Clare Boothe - LUCE
Clarinetist Artie - SHAW

Clark of country - ROY
Clockmaker Terry - ELI
Clockmaker Thomas - SETH
Clothier Straus - LEVI
Coach Amos Alonzo - STAGG
Coach Chuck - NOLL
Coach Ditka - MIKE
Coach Ebank - WEEB
Coach Jackson - PHIL
Coach Karolyi - BELA
Coach Parseghian - ARA
Coach Pat - RILEY
Coach Paterno - LOE
Coach Rockner - KNUTE
Coburg - SAXE
Colonial patriot Silas - DEANE
Colomnist Bobeck - ERMA
Columnist Buckwald - ART
Columnist Cassini - IGOR
Columnist Charen - MONA
Columnist Estrich - SUSAN
Columnist Frank
Pierce - ADAMS
Columnist George - WILL
Columnist Goodman - ELLEN
Columnist Greenfield - MEG
Columnist Herb - CAEN
Columnist
Huffington - ARIANNA
Columnist Joseph - ALSOP
Columnist Klein - EZRA

Columnist Leshan - EDA
Columnist Maureen - DOWD
Columnist Maxwell - ELSA
Colomnist Mike - ROYKO
Colomnist Miller - JUDITH
Columnist Molly - IVINS
Colomnist Nooonan - PEGGY
Columnist Pyle - ERNIE
Colomnist Reese - HELOISE
Columnist Robert - KOVAK
Columnist Wilson - EARL
Comedian
    Amsterdam - MOREY
Comedian Bernie - MAC
Comedian Bill - DANA
Comedian Bishop - JOEY
Comedian Bob - HOPE
Comedian Carrey - JIM
Comedian Cohen - MYRON
Commedian Cook - DANE
Commedian Daniel - TOSH
Comedian David - BRENNER
Comedian Deleria - LEA
Comedian Denis - LEARY
Comedian Dwyer - BIL
Comedian George -
    CARLIN or GOBEL
Comedian Green - TOM
Comedian Izzard - EDDIE
Commedian L'ange - ARTIE
Comedian MacDonald - NORM

Comedian Margaret - CHO
Comedian Myron - COHEN
Comedian Philips - EMO
Comedian Richard - BELZER
Comedian Rock - CHRIS
Comedian Shandling - GARY
Comedian Shore - PAULY
Comedian Silverman - SARAH
Comedic actor James - COCO
Comedienne ANNE - MEARA
Comedienne Butler - BRETT
Comedienne Charlotte - RAE
Comedienne Degeneres - ELLEN
Comedienne Dunn - NORA
Comedienne Fields - TOTIE
Comediene Gasteyer - ANA
Comediene Georgia - ENGEL
Comedienne Judy - CANOVA
Comediene Margaret - CHO
Comedienne Martha - RAYE
Comedienne May - ELAINE
Comedienne McClurg - EDIE
Comedienne O'Donnell - ROSIE
Comedienne O'Shea - TESSIE
Comedienne Peggie - CASS
Comedienne Radner - GILDA
Comedienne
    Rosie - ODONNEL
Comedienne Sykes - WANDA
Comedienne Taylor - RENEE

Comedienne Wanda - SYKES

Comedienne
    Witherspoon - CORA
Commentator Rowland - EVANS
Comic actor Oakie - JACK
Comis actor John - CLEESE
Comic actor Sandler - ADAM
Comic Allen - STEVE
Comic Amsterdam - MOREY
Comic Anderson - LOUIS
Comic Ann - MEARA
Comic Auerbach - ARTIE
Comic Bill - DANA
Comic Boosler - ELAINE
Comic Brad - HALL
Comic Bruce - LENNY
Comic Buddy - HACKETT
Comic Butler - BRETT
Comic Caplan - GABE
Comic Carey - DREW
Comic Carolla - ADAM
Comic Carvey - DANA
Comic Cahppelle - DAVE
Comic Chris - ROCK
Comic Crosby - NORM
Comic Dangerfield - RODNEY
Comic David - SPADE
Comic Fannie - FLAGG
Comic Foxsworthy - JEFF
Comic Freberg - STAN

Comic Gobel - GEORGE
Comic Hartmen - PHIL
Comic Hill - BENNY
Comic Idle - ERIC
Comic Janeane - GAROFALO
Comic Jaques - TATI
Comic Johnson - ARTE
Comic Johny - YUNE
Comic Joslyn - ALLYN
Comic Judy - TUNUDA
Comic Kamen - MILT
Comic Kaplan - GABE
Comic Kibibble - ISH
Comic Kilborn - CRAIG
Comic Kineson - SAM
Comic Kovacs - ERNIE
Comic Lily - TOMLIN
Comic Lovitz - JON
Comic Mandel - HOWIE
Comic Margaret - CHO
Comic Maron - MARC
Comic Meara - ANNE
Comic Miller - DENNIS
Comic Nora - DUNN
Comic O'Donnell - ROSIE
Comic Perlman - RHEA
Comic Philips - EMO
Comic Radner - GILDA
Comic Rich - HAL
Comic Richard - JENI
Comic Rickles - DON

Comic Rudner - RITA

Comic Russell - NIPSEY

Comic Sandler - ADAM

Comic Sherman - ALLAN

Comic Stewart - JON

Camic Wanda - SYKES

Comic Wilson - FLIP

Comic Youngman - HENNY

Comical Schreiber - AVERY

Commentator Colmes - ALAN

Commentator
    Limbaugh - RUSH

Commentator Phil - SIMMS

Commentator Rooney - ANDY

Compose Aaron - COPLAND

Composer Ahbez - EDEN

Composer Alban - BERG

Composer Albeniz - ISAAC

Composer
    Albinonini -TOMASO

Composer
    Alessandro - SCARLATTI

Composer Anderson - LEROY

Composer Andre - MATHIEU

Composer Arensky - ANTON

Composer Arlen - HAROLD

Composer Bacharach - BURT

Composer Bartok - BELA

Composer Bedrich - SMETANA

Composer
    Benjamin - BRITTEN

Composer Berg - ALBAN

Composer Berlioz - HECTOR

Composer Bernstein - ELMER

Composer Blake - EUBIE

Composer Boulez - PIERRE

Composer Brian - ENO

Composer Bruch - MAX

Composer Bruckner - ANTON

Composer Burlioz - HECTOR

Composer Cage - JOHN

Composer Camille
    Saint - SAENS

Composer Carl - NIELSEN
    or ORFF

Composer _____ Carlo
    Menotti - GIAN

Composer Cesar - CUI

Composer Charles - IVES

Composer Claude - DEBUSSY

Composer Copland - AARON

Composer
    Corelli - ARCANGELO

Composer Corngold - ERICH

Composer Coward - NOEL

Composer Daniel - AUBER

Composer DeBussy - CLAUDE

Composer Delibes - LEO

Composer Di
    Capua - EDUARDO

Composer Dimitri - TIOMKIN

Composer Dohnanyi - ERNO

Composer
    Domenico - SCARLATTI

Composer Dvorak - ANTON

Composer Edouardo - LALO

Composer Edward - ELGAR

Composer Edvard - GRIEG

Composer Elfman - DANNY

Composer Elton - JOHN

Composer Eric - COATES

Composer Erik - SATIE

Composer Ethelbert - NEVIN

Composer Eugene - YSAYE

Composer Faith - PERCY

Composer Fauer - GABRIEL

Composer Ferde - GROFE

Composer Francis - LAI

Composer Franck - CESAR

Composer Franz - LEHAR

Composer Frederick - LOWE

Composer Friml - RUDOLF

Composer Garner - ERROLL

Composer Georges - BIZET
    or ENESCO

Composer Giacomo - PUCCINI

Composer
    Giancarlo - MENOTTI

Composer Giuseppi - VERDI

Composer Glass - PHILIP

Composer Gordon - CREE

Composer Grieg - EDVARD

Composer Grofe - FERDA

Composer Gustav - HOLST
    or MAHLER

Composer Haba - ALOIS

Composer Harold - ARLEN

Composer Hayes - ISAAC

Composer Hector - BERIOZ

Composer Heft - NEAL

Composer
    Heitor - VILLALOBOS

Composer Hovhaness - ALAN

Composer Howard - HANSON

Composer Jacques -
    BREL or IBERT

Composer Janacek - LEOS

Composer Jean-
    Marie - LECLAIR

Composer Jean-
    Phillippe - RAMEAU

Composer Jeff - NEVIN

Composer Jones - ISHAM

Composer Joseph - HAYDN
    or MEYER

Composer Josquin_____
    Pres - DES

Composer Jule - STEIN
    or STYNE

Composer Jules - MASSENET

Composer Karl - ORFF

Composer Kern - JEROME

Composer
    Khachaturian - ARAM

Composer Kit - ORY

Composer Kodaly - ZOLTAN

Composer Korngold - ERICH

Composer Kurt - WEILL

Composer Lalo - EDOUARD

Composer Lateef - YOUSEF

Composer Laura - NYRO

Composer Legrand - MICHEL

Composer Lehman - ENGEL

Composer Leonard - COHEN

Composer Leos - JANACEK

Composer Lieberman - ROLF

Composer Lucas - FOSS

Composer Luigi - NONO

Composer Mahler - GUSTAV

Composer Markovitch - IHOR

Composer Mascagni - PIETRO

Composer Maurice -
JARRE or RAVEL

Composer Max - REGER
or STEINER

Composer Mendelssohn - FELIX

Composer Menken - ALAN

Composer Milhaud - DARIUS

Composer Milton - AGER

Composser Morricone - ENNIO

Composer
Mussorgsky - MODESTE

Composer Mustgrave - THEA

Composer Muzio - CLEMENTI

Composer Ned - ROREM

Composer Newborn - IRA

Composer Newman - RANDY

Composer Nino - ROTA

Composer Novello - IVOR

Composer Nuno - JAIME

Composer Orff - CARL

Composer Peter - NERO

Composer Philip - GLASS

Composer
Ponchielli - AMILCARE

Composer Porter - COLE

Composer Prokofiev - SERGEI

Composer Puccini - GIACOMO

Composer Puente - TITO

Composer Quincy - JONES

Composer
Rachmanninoff - SERGEY

Composer Randy - NEWMAN

Composer Ravel - MAURICE

Composer
Respighi - OTTORINO

Composer Richard - DRIGO
or WAGNER

Composer Rimsky -
Korsakov - NIKOLAI

Composer Rorem - NED

Composer Rota - NINO

Composer Rubenstein - ANTON

Composer Rudolph - FRIML

Composer Saint-
Saens - CAMILLE

Composer Sammy - FAIN

Composer Satie - ERIK

Composer
Scarlatti - ALESSANDRO

Composer Schifrin - LALO

Composer Schoenberg - ARNOLD

Composer Schumann - ROBERT

Composer Shostakovich - DMITRI

Composer Sibelius - JEAN

Composer Siegmeister - ELIE

Composer Sir Edward - ELGAR

Composer Speaks - OLEY

Composer Strauss - JOHANN or OSKAR

Composer Stravinski - IGOR

Composer Styne - JULE

Composer Taylor - DEEMS

Composer Thomas - ARNE

Composer Thomson - VIRGIL

Composer Tiompkin - DMITRI

Composer Tchaikovsky - PETER ILICH

Composer Ulysses - KAY

Composer Victor - HERBERT

Composer Villa-Lobos - HEITOR

Composer Von Dohnanyi - ERNST

Clomposer Weben - ATON

Composer Weill - KURT

Composer William - BOYCE

Composer Zimbalist - EFREM

Computer pioneer Lovelace - ADA

Concertist Campbell - TEVIN

Conductor Alberto - EREDE

Conductor Anderson - LEROY

Conductor Andre - PREVIN

Conductor Ansermet - ERNEST

Conductor Antal - DORATI

Conductor Barenboim - DANIEL

Conductor Boulanger - NADIA

Conductor Boult - ADRIAN

Conductor Caldwell - SARAH

Conductor Claudio - ABBADO

Conductor Czell - GEORGE

Conductor Davis - COLIN

Conductor de Waart - EDO

Conductor Dorati - ANTAL

Conductor Erno - PAPEE

Conductor Fritz - REINER

Conductor Georg - SOLTI

Conductor Hefti - NEAL

Conductor Herbert - KARAJAN

Conductor James - LEVINE

Conductor Jarvi - NEEME

Conductor Klemperer - OTTO

Conductor Kostelanetz - ANDRE

Conductor Koussevetzky - SERGE

Conductor Kubelik - RAFAEL

Conductor Kurt - ADLER, MASUR or WIELL

Conductor Lehman - ENGEL

Conductor Leibowitz - RENE

Conductor Leinsdorf - ERICH

Conductor Lukas - FOSS

Conductor Markovitch - IGOR

Conductor Marriner - NEVILLE

Conductor Mehta - ZUBIN

Conductor
    Mitropoulos - DIMITRI

Conductor Ormandy - EUGENE

Conductor _____ Pekka
    Salonen - ESA

Conductor Pierre - Boulez

Conductor Previn - ANDRE

Conductor Riccardo - MUTI

Conductor Seiji - OZAWA

Conductor Sir
    Thomas - BEECHAM

Conductor Solti - GEORG

Conductor
    Toscanini - ARTURO

Conductor Walter - BRUNO

Conductor Zubin - MEHTA

Congressman Gingrich - NEWT

Conservationist John - MUIR

Contralto
    Marian - ANDERSON

Convey - BERT

Cook Rombauer - IRMA

Coolidge of song - RITA

Cornelia_____Skinner - OTIS

Cornetist Beiderbecke - BIX

Corporal O'Reilly - RADAR

Cosmetician Curtis - HELENE

Cosmonaut Gagarin - YURI

Cosmonaut Leonov - ALEXI

Cosmonaut Markarov - OLEG

Coty M. - RENE

Count in music - BASIE

Country's Brooks - GARTH

Country's Jennings - WAYLON

Country star McCann - LILA

Country star West - DOTTIE

Couric of NBC - KATIE

Cousteau's middle name - YVES

Couturiere Schiaparelli - ELSA

Cover girl Carol - ALT

Coward or Harrison - NOEL

Cowboy Rogers - ROY

_____"Crazy Legs"
    Hirsch - ELROY

Critic Barnes - CLIVE

Critic Ebert - ROGER

Critic Greene - GAEL

Critic Harold - ROSENBERG

Critic Hentoff - NAT

Critic John - SIMON

Critic Kael - PAULINE

Critic Kenneth - TYNAN

Critic Maslin - JANET

Critic Pauline - KAEL

Critic Reed - REX

Critic Sheraton - MIMI

Critic Susan - SONTAG

Critic Taylor - DEEMS

Critic Trilling - LIONEL
Critic Walter - KERR
Crooner King Cole - NAT
Crooner Michael - BOLTON
Crooner Perry - COMO
Cruise - TOM
Cuban patriot Jose - MARTI
Cubist Fernand - LEGER
Cubist Rubic - ERNO
Cuthbertson of bridge - ELY
Cyclist Armstrong - LANCE
Cyclist Ballanger - FELICIA
Cyclist Floyd - LANDIS
Cyclist Lemond - GREG
DDE's arena - ETO
Da Gama - VASCO
Dadaist Hans - ARP
Dadaist Jean - ARP
Dadaist Max - ERNST
Dallas - STELLA
Daly of TV - TYNE
Dame Everage - EDNA
Dame Myra - HESS
Dame Sitwell - EDITH
Dancer Abdul - PAULA
Dancer Alvin - AILEY
Dancer Bausch - PINA
Dancer Ben - VEREEN
Dancer Castle - IRENE
Dancer Coles - HONI
Dancer Cunningham - MERCE

Dancer DeMille - AGNES
Dancer Duncan - ISADORA
Dancer Gilda - GRAY
Dancer Honi - COLES
Dancer Jean Marie - RENEE
Dancer Jose - LIMON
Dancer Kaye - NORA
Dancer Leanide - MASSINE
Dancer Lola - MONTEZ
Dancer McKechne - DONNA
Dancer Miller - ANN
Dancer Montez - LOLA
Dancer Ninjinski - VASLAV
Dancer Pavlova - ANNA
Dancer Petit - ROLAND
Dancer Prowse - JULIET
Dancer Reinking - ANN
Dancer Rita - MORENO
Dancer Robbins - JEROME
Dancer Shawn - TED
Dancer Sheara - MOIRA
Dancer Taina - ELG
Dancer Tamblyn - RUSS
Dancer Ted - SHAWN
Dancer Vaslav - NIJINSKY
Dancer Vereen - BEN
Dancer Verdon - GWEN
Daniel of the LPGA - BETH
Danson or Koppel - TED
David Bowie's wife - IMAM
Dawson or Deighton - LEN

De Balzac - HONORE

Decathlete Johnson - RAFER

Decorator De Wolf - ELSIE

Deejay Casey - KASEM

Degeneres - ELLEN

De Leon - PONCE

De Valera - EAMON

Dennis - DAY

Dentist Dr. Ida - GRAY

Derek or Diddley - BO

Descartes - RENE

Designer Alvar - AALTO

Designer Antonio - CASTILLO

Designer Arpel - ADRIEN

Designer Ashley - LAURA

Designer Bartley - LUELLA

Designer Beaton - CECIL

Designer Bill - BLASS

Designer Calvin - KLEIN

Designer Cassini - OLEG

Designer Cerutti - NINO

Designer Charles - EAMES

Designer Clairborne - LIZ

Designer Clark - OSSIE

Designer Danillo - Donati

Designer de Wolfe - ELSIE

Designer Donna - KARAN

Designer Emilio - PUCCI

Designer Geoffrey - BEENE

Designer Gernreich - RUDI

Designer Giorgio - ARMANI

Designer Gucci - ALDO

Designer Hardy - AIMIES

Designer Head - EDITH

Designer Herman - STAN

Designer Herv - LEGER

Designer Hilfiger - TOMMY

Designer Horn - CAROL

Designer Hugo - BOSS

Designer Johnson - BETSEY

Designer Karan - DONNA

Designer Kawakudo - REI

Designer Kenneth - COLE

Designer Klein - ANNE

Desgner Lagerfield - KARL

Designer Lapidus - TED

Designer Laura - ASHLEY

Designer Magli - BRUNO

Designer Mary - QUANT

Designer Melinda - ENG

Designer Miller - NICOLE

Designer Miuccia - PRADA

Designer Mizrahi - ISAAC

Designer Nina - RICCI

Designer Peretti - ELSA

Designer Perry - ELLIS

Designer Picasso - PALOMA

Designer Picone - EVAN

Designer Pierre - CARDIN

Designer Pucci - EMILIO

Designer Rabanne - PACO

Designer Ricci - NINA

Designer Rowan - RENA

Designer Saab - ELIE

Designer Saint Laurent - YVE

Designer Schiaparelli - ELSA

Designer Sharaff - IRENE

Designer Simpson - ADELE

Designer Sui - ANNA

Designer Tahari - ELIE

Designer Vera - WANG

Designer Versace -
    DONATELLA or GIANNI

Designer Von
    Furstenberg - EGON

Designer Wang - VERA

Detective Lupin
    (fiction) - ARSENE

Detective Pinkerton - ALLAN

DeValera - EAMON

Diarist Anais - NIN

Diarist Frank - ANNE

Diarist Samuel - PEPYS

Dicken's pen name - BOZ

Diplomat Hammarskjold - DAG

Diplomat Harriman - PAMELA

Diplomat Mesta - PERLE

Diplomat Silas - DEANE

Deplomat Wallenberg - RAOUL

Diplomat Whitelaw - REID

Director Adrian - LYNE

Director Allegret - MARC

Director Alan - PAKULA

Director Almodovar - PEDRO

Director Amiel - JON

Director Anatole - LITVAK

Director Anderson - WES

Director Andre - MALLE

Director Apatow - JUDD

Director Arthur - PENN

Director Avakian - ARAM

Director Babiyi - REZA

Director Barker - CLIVE

Director Bergman - INGMAR

Director Besson - LUC

Director Blake – EDWARDS

Director Brian de - PALMA

Director Brooks - MEL

Director Browning - TOD

Director Bunuel - LUIS

Director Burrows - ABE

Director Burton - TIM

Director Cameron - CROWE

Director Campion - JANE

Director Chabrol - CLAUDE

Director Clair - RENE

Director Columbus - CHRIS

Director Coppola - SOPHIA

Director Craven - WES

Director Daniel - MANN

Director David - LEANN
    or LYNCH

Director Davis - OSSIE

Director Demme - TED

Director DePalma - BRIAN

Director DeSica - VICTORIO

Director Donen - STANLEY

Director Doug - LIMAN

Director Edel - ULI

Director Edwards - BLAKE

Director - ELI - ROTH

Director Eng - LEE

Director Ephrom - NORA

Director Ferrara - ABEL

Director Forman - MILOS

Director Francesco - ROSI

Director Frank - CAPRA,
     LLOYD or TASHLIN

Director Fritz - LANG

Director Gance - ABEL

Director Garson - KANIN

Director George - A.
     ROMERO or LUCAS

Director Gibbons - CEDRIC

Director Goddard - JEAN LUC

Director Gosnell - RAJAH

Director Grosbard - ULU

Director Gus van - SANT

Director Guthrie - TYRONE

Director Guy - RITCHIE

Director Haines - RANDA

Director Hal - ASHBY

Director Hallstrom - LASSE

Director Harold - RAMIS

Director Heckerling - AMY

Director Herzog - WERNER

Director Hitchcock – ALFRED

Director Hooper - TOBE

Director Howard -
     HAWKS or RON

Director Jaques - TATI

Director
     Jean_____Godard - LUC

Director Joel - COEN

Director Joffe - ROLAND

Director John - CARPENTER,
     HUSTON or SAYLES

Director Jon - AMIEL

Director Jonathan - DEMME

Director Jordan - NEIL

Director Josh - LOGAN

Director Kazan - ELIA

Director Kenton - ERLE

Director King - VIDOR

Director Kubrick - STANLEY

Director Kurosawa - AKIRA

Director Lee - ANG or SPIKE

Director Leone - SERGIO

Director Litvak - ANATOL

Director Louis - MALLE

Director Lubitsch - ERNST

Director Lucas - GEORGE

Director Lumet - SIDNEY

Director Lyne - ADRIAN

Director Malle - LOUIS

Director Mann - DELBERT

Director Marshall - PENNY

Director Martin - RITT

Director May - ELAINE

Director Mazursky - PAUL

Director McAnuff - DES

Director McCarey - LEO

Director Mendez - SAM

Director Mervyn - LEROY

Director Meyer - RUSS

Director Michael - APTED
    or MANN

Director Mike - NICHOLS

Director Mimi - LEDER

Director Minnelli - VINCENTE

Director Mira – NAIR

Director Morris - ERROL

Director Nicholas -
    MEYER or ROEG

Director Norah - EPHRON

Director Noyce - PHILLIP

Director Pakula - ALAN

Director Parker - ALAN

Director Pasolini - PAOLO

Director Peckinpah - SAM

Director Peter - WEIR or YATES

Director Petri - ELIO

Director Pitlik - NOAM

Director Polanski - ROMAN

Director Pollock - SYD

Director Ponti - CARLO

Director Preston - STURGES

Director Quintero - JOSE

Director Raoul - WALSH

Director Reitman - IVAN

Director Renoir - JEAN

Director Resnais - ALAIN

Director Richard - DONNER,
    LESTER or TODD

Director Ridley - SCOTT

Director Riefenstahl - LENI

Director Rietman - IVAN

Director Robert - ALTMAN

Director Robins - JEROME

Director Rohmer - ERIC

Director Roth - ELI

Director Russ - MEYER

Director Russell - KEN

Director Sam - RAIMI

Director Schary - DORE

Director Scott - RIDLEY

Director Sergio - LEONE

Director Shepard - SAM

Director Sidney - LUMET

Director Spielberg - STEVEN

Director Spike - LEE

Director Stanley - DONEN

Director Stone - OLIVER

Director Sturges - PRESTON

Director
    Tarantino - QUENTON

Director Tim – Burton

Director Trevor - NUNN

Director Vadim - ROGER

Director Van Sant - GUS

Director Vittorio - DESICA

Director Von Sternburg - JOSEF

Director Vontrier - LARS

Director Walsh - RAOUL

Director Wenders - WIM

Director Werner - HERZOG

Director Wertmuller - LINA

Director Whitaker - FOREST

Director Woody - ALLEN

Director Zack - SNYDER

Director Zeffirelli - FRANCO

Director Zoltan - KORDA

Discus champion Al - OERTER

Diva Albanes - LICIA

Diva Baker - ANITA

Diva Borodina - OLGA

Diva Callas - MARIA

Diva Gluck - ALMA

Diva Linda - EDER

Diva Maria - CALLAS

Diva Marton - EVA

Diva Merriman - NAN

Diva Mitchell - LEONA

Diva Moffo - ANNA

Diva Ponselle - ROSA

Diva Ranata - SCOTTO

Diva Roberta - PETERS

Diva Sutherland - JOAN

Diva Te Kanawa - KIRI

Diver Louganis - GREG

Divine - ANDY

Doctor Alzheimer - ALOIS

Doctor Westheimer - RUTH

Dolphin Marino - DAN

Don of football - SHULA

Doris - DAY

Doubleday - ABNER

Douglas of film - KIRK

Drama critic Walter - KERR

Dramatist Arthur
    Wing - PINERO

Dramatist Ben - JONSON

Dramatist Blitzstein - MARC

Dramatist Cherkhov - ANTON

Dramatist Clifford - ODETS

Dramatist David - HARE
    or RABE

Dramatist De Vega - LOPE

Dramatist Edward - ALBEE

Dramatist Fugard - ATHOL

Dramatist George - PEELE

Dramatist Guitry - SACHA

Dramatist Hellman - LILLIAN

Dramatist Henly - BETH

Dramatist Henrik - IBSEN

Dramatist Jean Paul - SATRE

Dramatist John
    Millington - SYNGE

Dramatist Jonson - BEN

Dramitist
    Luigi - PIRANDELLO

Dramatist Moss - HART

Dramatist O'Casey - SEAN

Dramatist Thomas - KYD

Drummer Blakey - ART

Drummer Cosy - COLE

Drummer Gene - KRUPA

Drummer Keith - MOON

Drummer Ringo - STARR

Drummer Ulrich - LARS

Drummer Warren - DODDS

Duncan - ISADORE

Durocher - LEO

Dutch painter Karel - APPEL

Earl_____Biggers - DERR

Eban of Israel - ABBA

Economist Eliot - JANEWAY

Economist John_____Mill - STUART

Economist John Maynard - KEYNES

Economist Kenneth - ARROW

Economist Marx - KARL

Economist Short - ADAM

Economist Smith - ADAM

Editor Brown - TINA

Editor Paley - BABE

Editor Whitelaw - REID

Editor Wintour - ANNA

Editor/Writer Peter - DEVRIES

Educator Collins - MARVA

Educator Horace - MANN

Educator Mary McLeod - BETHUNE

Educator Montessori - MARIE

Educator Willard - EMMA

Egypt's Mubarak - HOSNI

Elevator man Otis - ELISHA

Emcee Garroway - DAVE

Emmy winner Falco - EDIE

English composer - ARNE

English philosopher - LOCKE

English poet Matthew - PRIOR

Engraver Albrecht - DURER

En-Lai - CHOU

Entertainer Allen - STEVE

Entertainer Amos - TORI

Entertainer Blossom - DEARIE

Entertainer Brickell - EDIE

Entertainer Brooks - GARTH

Entertainer Eartha - KITT

Entertainer Falana - LOLA

Entertainer Ivor - NOVELLO

Entertainer Josephine - BAKER

Entertainer Kazan - LAINIE

Entertainer Kotto - YAPHET

Entertainer Massey - ILONA

Entertainer Miles - VERA

Entertainer Moffo - ANNA

Entertainer Myra - HESSE

Entertainer O'Shea - TESSIE

Entertainer Rita - MORENO

Environmentalist Dubos - RENE

Ernie of golf - ELS

Essayist Bacon - FRANCIS

Essayist Debotton - ALAIN

Essayist Repplier - AGNES

Essayist Susan - SONTAG

Estaire - FRED and ESTELE

Ethologist Konrad - LORENZ

Evangelist McPherson - AIMEE

Explorer Amundsen - ROALD

Explorer Balboa - VASCO

Explorer Cabral - PEDRO

Explorer De Gama - VASCO

Explorer Eriksson - LEIF

Explorer Hedin - SVEN

Explorer Hernando - DE SOTO

Explorer Heyerdahl - THOR

Explorer James - COOK

Explorer John - RAE

Explorer Johnson - OSA

Explorer Marquette - PROPERS

Explorer Robert - PEARY

Explorer Sabastian - CABOT

Explorer Shackleton - ERNEST

Explorer Sverdrup - OTTO

Explorer Tasman - ABEL

Explorer William - BEEBE

Explorer Zebulon - PIKE

Expressionist Emil - NOLDE

Feminist Carrie - CATT

Feminist Germaine - GREER

Feminist Lucretia - MOTT

Fernando or Lorenzo - LAMAS

Fields - W.C. or GRACIE

Figure-skater Kulik - ILIA

Figure-skater Midori - ITO

Figure-skater Trenary - JILL

Film critic James - AGEE

Film critic Pauline - KAEL

Filmmaker De Laurentis - DINO

Filmmaker Jacque - TATI

Filmmaker Joel or
    Ethan - COEN

Filmmaker Martin - RITT

Filmmaker Van Sant - GUS

Financier Carl - ICAHN

Fire fighter Red - ADAIR

Fitzgerald - ELLA

Fleming or Hunter - IAN

Flemish painter - BOSCH

Flugalhorn player
    Check - MABGIONE

Flutist Herbie - MANN

Flutist Jean Pierre - RAMPAL

Flynn of films - ERROL

Foch or Simone - NINA

Folk singer Burl - IVES

Folk singer Guthrie - ARLO

Folk singer Joan - BAEZ

Folk singer Mitchell - JONI

Folk singer Pete - SEEGER

Folk singer Phil - OCHS
    or SIMMS

Football analyst Hank - STRAM

Football great Bart - STARR

Football great Graham - OTTO

Football great Len - DAWSON

Football great Ronnie - LOTT
Football kicker Jason - ELAM
Footballer Aikman - TROY
Footballer Brian - SIPE
Footballer Don - BEEBE
Footballer Esianson - BOOMER
Footballer Ewbanks - WEEB
Footballer Grier - ROSIE
Footballer Hersh - ELROY
Footballer Jim - NANCE
Footballer Jones - BERT
Footballer Manchetti - GINO
Footballer Pele - EDSON
Footballer Ronnie - LOTT
Footballer Sanders - DEION
Footballer Sayers - GALE
Footballer Staubach - ROGER
Footballer Swann - LYNN
Footballer Terrell - OWENS
Footballer Van
    Brocklin - NORM
Footballer Yepremian - GARO
Ford of fashion - EILEEN
Fountain - PETE
Foxx - REDD
Francis or Dahl - ARLENE
Frankie of music - CARLE
    or LAINE
Franklin or Hogen - BEN
Fraser of tennis - NEALE
French astronomer - PICARD

French composer
    Daniel - AUBER
French composer - LALO
French landscapist - COROT
French novelist, Pierre - LOTI
French novelist Zola - EMILE
French painter - INGRES
French philosopher - SOREL
French revelutionist John
    Paul - MARAT
French sociologist - TARDE
Funnyman Jay - MOHR
Funnyman Martin - SHORT
Gabriel of music - PETER
Gadgeteer Popiel - RON
Game show Monte - HALL
Game show White - VANNA
Gandi - RAJIV
Garfunkel - ART
Garr of filmdom - TERI
General Aarnold - HAP
General Bradley - OMAR
General Clark - WESLEY
General Doubleday - ABNER
General Powell - COLIN
General Rommel - ERWIN
German astronomer - KEPLER
German author - SACHS
German chemist - EIGEN
German composer - WEBER
Gerulaitis, of tennis - VITAS

Gillette - ANITA

Glass maker Antonio - NERI

Gluck of opera - ALMA

Gold medalist Lipinski - TARA

Gold Medalist Latrina - WITT

Gold medalist
    Yagudin - ALEXEI

Gold medalist Mary
    Lou - RETON

Gold medalist
    Miller - SHANNON

Gold medalist Rantanen - HELI

Gold medalist
    Rudolph - WILMA

Golden Glover
    Rodriguez - IVAN

Golf pro Hale - IRWIN

Golfer Alcott - AMY

Golfer Aoki - ISAO

Golfer Ballesteros - SEVE
    or SEVERIANO

Golfer Bernhard - LANGER

Golfer Bob - ESTES or TWAY

Golfer Bobbie - JONES

Golfer Bret - OGLE

Golfer Browne - OLIN

Golfer Bruce - CRAMPTON

Golfer Calvin - PEETE

Golfer Carrie - WEBB

Golfer Christina - KIM

Golfer Craig - SADLER

Golfer Creamer - PAULA

Golfer Crenshaw - BEN

Golfer Curtis - STRANGE

Golfer Dave - MARR

Golfer Davies - LAURA

Golfer Davis - LOVE III

Golfer Didrikson - BABE

Golfer Dutra - OLIN

Golfer Ed - SNEAD

Golfer Ernie - ELS

Golfer Faldo - NICK

Golfer Garcia - SERGIO

Golfer Hale - IRWIN

Golfer Harrington - PADRAIG

Golfer Henke - NOLAN

Golfer Hinckle - LON

Golfer Hogan - BEN

Golfer Irwin - HALE

Golfer Isao - AOKI

Golfer Jay - HAAS

Golfer Jerry - PATE

Golfer John - DALY

Golfer Johnson - ZACK

Golfer Julius - BOROS

Golfer Laura - DAVIES

Golfer Lindley - LETA

Golfer Lopez - NANCY

Golfer Lorena - OCHOA

Golfer Mark - OMEARA

Golfer Mediate - ROCCO

Golfer McIroy - RORY

Golfer Michelle - WIE

Golfer Mickelson - PHIL

Golfer Middlecoff - GARY

Golfer Montgomerie - COLIN

Golfer Morgan - GIL

Golfer Nick - FALDO

Golfer Nicklaus - JACK

Golfer Norman - GREG

Golfer North - ANDY

Golfer Ochoa - LORENA

Golfer Palmer - ARNIE

Golfer Patty - BERG

Golfer Pavin - COREY

Golfer Payne - STEWART

Golfer Peter - THOMSON

Golfer Polter - IAN

Golfer Price - NICK

Golfer Rawls - BETSY

Golfer Rodriquez - CHICHI

Golfer Sabitini - CORY

Golfer Sam - SNEAD

Golfer Sandy - LYLE

Golfer Sarazen - GENE

Golfer Seri - PAK

Golfer Sorenstam - ANNIKA

Golfer Stadler - CRAIG

Golfer Stewart - PAYNE

Golfer Steve - PATE

Golfer Strange - CURTIS

Golfer Sutton - HAL

Golfer Thomas - BJORN

Golfer Thompson - LEXI

Golfer Tom - KITE

Golfer Turner - SHERRI

Golfer Uresti - OMAR

Golfer Vijay - SINGH

Golfer Wadkins - LANNY

Golfer Watson - BUBBA

Golfer Walter - HAGEN

Golfer Weir - MIKE

Golfer Woosnan - IAN

Golf's Baker-Finch - IAN

Gorby's Mrs. - RAISA

Governor Ventura - JESSE

Grammy winner Puente - TITO

Gridiron great Greasy - NEALE

Griffith - ANDY

Guevara - CHE

Guitar master Van
    Halen - EDDIE

Guitarist Allman - DUANE

Guitarist Andre - SEGOVIA

Guitarist Atkins - CHET

Guitarist Barrett - SYD

Guitarist Bob - EGAN

Guitarist Borland - WES

Guitarist Campbell - GLEN

Guitarist Carlo - SANTANA

Guitarist Chet - ATKINS

Guitarist Clapton - ERIC

Guitarist Cooder - RY

Guitarist Delucia - PACO

Guitarist Duane - EDDY

Guitarist Dweezil - KAPPA

Guitarist Farlow - TAL

Guitarist Fender - LEO

Guitarist Flatt - LESTER

Guitarist George - BENSON

Guitarist Harvey - MANDEL

Guitarist Hendrix - JIMI

Guitarist Jeff - BECK

Guitarist Jimmy - PAGE

Guitarist Joe - WALSH

Guitarist John - FAHEY

Guitarist Kaplan - IRA

Guitarist Kottke - LEO

Guitarist
    Lindsey - BUCKINGHAM

Guitarist Lofgren - NILS

Guitarist Mann - AIMEE

Guitarist Montgomery - WES

Guitarist Montoya - CARLOS

Guitarist Nugent - TED

Guitarist Ocasek - RIC

Guitarist Paul - LES

Guitarist Romero - PEPE

Guitarist Santana - CARLOS

Guitarist Segovia - ANDRES

Gutarist Steve - EARLE or VAI

Guitarist Tiny - GRIMES

Guitariest Townsend - PETE

Guitariest Tufnel - NIGEL

Guitarist Walsh - JOE

Guitarist Watson - DOC

Guthrie - ARLO

Gymnast Comaneci - NADIA

Gymnast Dominique - DAWES

Gymnast Kerri - STRUG

Gymnast Korbut - OLGA

Gymnast Miller - SHANNON

Gymnast Rigby - CATHY

Gymnast Shrug - KERRI

Gynt - PEER

Hall-of-Fame pitcher
    Early - WYNN

Hall-of-Famer Al - KALINE

Hall-of-Famer Aparicio - LUIS

Hall-of Famer
    Ashford - EVELYN

Hall-of-Famer Averill - EARL

Hall-of-Famer Banks - ERNIE

Hall-of-Famer Bart - STARR

Hall-of-Famer Baylor - ELGIN

Hall-of- Famer Bobby - DOERR

Hall-of-Famer Bunning - JIM

Hall-of-Famer Cap - ANSON

Hall-of-Famer Carey - MAX

Hall-of-Famer Carl - ELLER

Hall-of-Famer
    Clemente - ROBERTO

Hall-of-Famer Combs - EARLE

Hall-of-Famer Dan - ISSEL

Hall-of-Famer Dawson - LEN

Hall-of-Famer Dick - LEBEAU

Hall-of-Famer Early - WYNN

Hall-of-Famer Earnie - NEVERS

Hall-of-Famer Edd - ROUSH

Hall-of-Famer Ewbank - WEEB

Hall-of-Famer Fingers - ROLLIE

Hall-of-Famer Ford - LEN

Hall-of-Famer Fox - BRETT
or NELLIE

Hall-of-Famer Francis - EMILE

Hall-of-Famer
George - BLANDA,
BRETT, HALAS or SISLER

Hall-of-Famer Gibson - JOSH

Hall-of-Famer Graham - OTTO

Hall-of-Famer Greasy - NEALE

Hall-of-Famer Grimm - RUSS

Hall-of-Famer Groza - LOU

Hall-of-Famer Hayes - ELVIN

Hall-of-Famer Herber - ARNIE

Hall-of-Famer Hirsch - ELROY

Hall-of-Famer Hoyt - WAITE

Hall-of-Famer Jim - THORPE

Hall-of-Famer Johnny - MIZE

Hall-of-Famer Koufax - SANDY

Hall-of-Famer Lefty - GROVE

Hall-of-Famer Long - HOWIE

Hall-of-Famer Lott - RONNIE

Hall-of-Famer Luckman - SID

Hall-of-Famer Lynn - SWANN

Hall-of-Famer
Marchetti - GINO

Hall-of-Famer Mel - OTT

Hall-of-Famer
Mike - SCHMIDT

Hall-of-Famer Monte - IRVIN

Hall-of-Famer Palmer - JIM

Hall-of-famer Pennock - HERB

Hall-of-Famer Ralph - KINER

Hall-of-Famer Rixey - EPPA

Hall-of-Famer Robin - YOUNT

Hall-of-Famer Rod - CAREW

Hall-of-Famer Roush - EDD

Hall-of-Famer Sandberg - RYNE

Hall-of-Famer Thomas - ISIAH

Hall-of-famer Tom - LANDRY

Hall-of-Famer Tony - PEREZ

Hall-of-Famer Traynor - PIE

Hall-of-Famer Unseld - WES

Hall-of-Famer
Wagner - HONUS

Hall-of-Famer Waite - HOYT

Hall-of-Famer Walker - DOAK

Hall-of-Famer Warren -
SAPP or SPAHN

Hall-elm-of-Famer Wilhelm - HOYT

Hall-of-Famer Wilson - PHAT

Hall-of-Famer Yogi - BERRA

Hammett to friends - DASH

Hank of baseball - AARON

Harmonica virtuoso
Larry - ADLER

Harpsichordist Kipnis - IGOR

Harpsichordist
Landowska - WANDA

Hart or Cooper - GARY

Hartman - LISA

Heraldic cross - SALTIRE

Herbie or Horace - MANN

Hershiser of baseball - OREL

Hipnotist Franz - MESMER

Historian Durant - ARIEL

Historian Hannah - ARENDT

Historian
Macaulay - CATHARINE

Historian Max - WEBER

Historian Nevins - ALLAN

Historian Shelby - FOOTE

Historian Toynbee - ARNOLD

Hockey great Potvin - DENIS

Hockey's Bobby - ORR

Hockey's Broten - NEAL

Hockey's Lindros - ERIC

Hockey's Stojanov - ALEK

Hockey star Tikkanen - ESA

Hollywood gossip
Barrett - RONA

Hollywood Moore - DEMI
or DUDLEY

Hoopster Baylor - ELGIN

Hoopster Gilmore - ARTIS

Hoopster Unseld - WES

Hope of Hollywood -
BOB or LANGE

Horatio - ALGER

Horologist Terry - ELLI

Horologist Thomas - SETH

Horoscope columnist
Sydney - OMARR

Horse-drawn coach - FIACRE

Hostess Perle - MESTA

Hotelier Helmesley - LEONA

Humorist Ade - GEORGE

Humorist Barry - DAVE

Humorist Bill - ARPS

Humorist Buckwald - ART

Humorist Cleveland - AMORY

Humorist Dorothy - PARKER

Humorist Geroge - ADE

Humorist Hubbard - KIM

Humorist Joe - HAN

Humorist Keillor - GARRISON

Humorist Lardner - RING

Humorist Lebowitz - FRAN

Humorist Rogers - WILL

Humorist Rosten - LEO

Humorist Sahl - MORT

Humorist Sedaris - AMY

Humorist Sherman - ALLEN

Humorist Sherrin - NED

Humorist Ward - ARTEMUS

Hungarian composer - LEHAR

Hungarian leader -
Kadar - JANOS

Hurler Hideo - NOMO

Hurler Johnson - RANDY

Hurler Moses - EDWIN

Hurler Nehemiah - RENALDO

Hurler Tiant - LUIS

Hurler Warren - SPAHN

Illusionist Burton - LANCE
Illustrator Beardsly - AUBREY
Illustrator Edward - GOREY
Illustrator Maxfield - PARRISH
Illustrator Ronald - SEARLE
Impresario Sol - HUROK
Impressionist David - FRYE
Impressionist Mary - CASSATT
Impressionist Pierre - RENOIR
Industrialist Cyrus - EATON
Industrialist
    Harvey - FIRESTONE
Infamous Amin - IDI
Infamous Helmsley - LEONA
Interviewer Couric - KATIE
Inventor Berliner - EMILE
Inventor Borden - GAIL
Inventor Deforst - LEE
Inventor Elisha - OTIS
Inventor Gray - ELISHA
Inventor Howe - ELIAS
Inventor James - EDES
Inventor Land - EDWIN
Inventor McCormack - CYRUS
Inventor Nikola - TESLA
Inventor Otis - ELISHA
Inventor Popeil - RON
Inventor Sperry - ELMER
Inventor Tesla - NIKOLA
Inventor Tull - JETHRO
Inventor Samuel - MORSE

Inventor Sikorsky - IGOR
Inventor Whitney - ELI
Ireland's De Valera - EAMON
Irene - RYAN
Irish author O'Brien - EDNA
Irwin of the PGA - HALE
Israili Barak - EHUD
Israeli hero Moshe - DAYAN
Italian actress, of old - DUSE
Italian General, Balbo - ITALO
Jackson or Nelligan - KATE
Jacques of song - BREL
James of song - ETTA
Jamie of TV - FARR
Jannings of early films - EMIL
Japanese Nobelist - SATO
Japanese wrestler Sato - AKIO
Jazz artist Crothers - SCATMAN
Jazz fusion guitarist
    Klugh - EARL
Jazz great Art - TATUM
Jazz great Davis - MILES
Jazz great Sandoyal - ARTURO
Jazz great Thelonious - MONK
Jazz guitarist
    Montgomery - WES
Jazz legend Chick - COREA
Jazz musician Adderley - NAT
Jazz musician Austen - LOVIE
Jazz pianist Allison - MOSE
Jazz pianist Jankowski - HORST

Jazz musician Lateef - YUSEF

Jazz pianist Oscar - PETERSON

Jazz singer Anita - O'DAY

Jazz trombonist
    Jack - TEAGARDEN

Jazz trumpeter Baker - CHET

Jazz trumpeter Jones -THAD

Jazzman Aderley - NAT

Jazzman Allison - MOSE

Jassman Baker - CHET

Jassman Beiderbecke - BIX

Jazzman Blake - EUBIE

Jazzman Blakey - ART

Jazzman Chick - COREA

Jazzman Dave - BRUBECK

Jazzman Evans - GIL

Jazzman Frank - WESS

Jazzman Garner - ERROLL

Jazzman Hentoff - NAT

Jazzman Herbie - MANN

Jazzman Hines - EARL

Jazzman _____ Hot Lips
    Page - ORAN

Jazzman Hubert - LAWS

Jazzman Jackson - MILT

Jazzman Kid - ORY

Jazzman Malone - KARL

Jazzman Montgomery - WES

Jazzman Mose - ALLISON

Jazzman Niehaus - LENNIE

Jazzman Rollins - SONNY

Jazzman Russell - PEE WEE

Jazzman Saunders - MERL

Jazzman Shapiro - ARTIE

Jazzman Tatum - ART

Jazzman Thelonious - MONK

Jazzman Tristano - LENNIE

Jazzman Waller - FATS

Jassman Zoot - SIMS

Jeweler LaLique - RENE

Joan of art - MIRO

Jockey Arcaro - EDDIE

Jockey Cordero - ANGE

Jockey Day - PAT

Jockey Julia - KRONE

Jockey Laffit - PINCAY

Jockey Pat - DAY

Jockey Sellers - SHANE

Jockey Smith - ROBYN

Jockey Turcotte - RON

Jockey Valasquez - JORGE

John_____Passos - DOS

John the writer - O'Hara

Johnson - Magic

Josip Broz - TITO

Journalist Abel - ELIE

Journalist Alexander - SHANA

Journalist Alisair - COOKE

Journalist Bierce - AMBROSE

Journalist Blitzer - WOLF

Journalist Bly - NELLY

Journalist Bombeck - ERMA

Journalist Bernstein - CARL
Journalist Brendon - GILL
Journalist Cupcinet - IRV
Journalist Dominick - DUNNE
Journalist Ernie - PYLE
Journalist Fallaci - ORIANA
Journalist Gellhorn - MARTHA
Journalist George - ADE
Journalist Glenny - MISHO
Journalist Hamill - PETE
Journalist Harry - REASONER
Journalist Herb - CAEN
Journalist Hentoff - NAT
Journalist Hill - ERICA
Journalist Horace - GREELEY
Journalist Hume - BRIT
Journalist Jacob August - RIIS
Journalist Lisa - LING
Journalist Joseph - ALSOPS
Journalist Kupcinet - IRV
Journalist Lebowitz - FRAN
Jounalist Marvin - KALB
Journalist Odonnell - NORAH
Journalist Paula - ZAHN
Journalist Pyle - ERNIE
Journalist Riis - JACOB
Journalist Roberts - COKIE
Journalist Roger St. Johns - ADEL A
Journalist Seymor - NERSH
Journalist Shapiro - ARI

Journalist Sheehy - GAIL
Journalist Shriver - MARIA
Journalist Stuart - ALSOPS
Journalist Stewart - ALSOP
Journalist Tarbell - IDA
Journalist Walters - BARBARA
Journalist Whitelaw - REID
Journalist Zahn - PAULA
Judge Lance - ITO
Julius of golf - BOROS
Jurist Fortas - ABE
Jurist Kenneth - STARR
Justice Bader Ginsberg - RUTH
Justice Scalia - ANTONIN
Justice Thomas - CLARENCE
Karenina - ANNA
Keaton - BUSTER
Kennedy or Waters - ETHEL
Kerr - ANITA
King of Hollywood - VIDOR
King of the Faeries - OBERON
Kruger or Preminger - OTTO
LPGA Carner - JOANNE
LPGA Daniel - BETH
LPGA Hall-of-Famer Patty - BERG
LPGA Juli - INKSTER
LPGA Karrie - WEBB
LPGA star Pak - SERI
Lacosta of tennis - RENE
Lady Hamilton - EMMA

Lahr - BERT
Lagosi or Bartok - BELA
Lamarr of old films - HEDY
Lamb - ELIA
Lambchops Lewis - SHARI
Lance of the court - ITO
Lawman Earp - WYATT
Lawyer Dershowitz - ALAN
Legal Lance - ITO
Lendl of tennis - IVAN
Levin or Gershwin - IRA
Lexicographer Partridge - ERIC
Linguist Chomsky - NOAM
Linguist Mario - PEI
Lithographer
    Currie - NATHANIEL
Lithographer James - IVES
Lithographer Redon - ODILON
Lizzy Borden's sister - EMMA
Logician Turning - ALAN
Lollobrigida - GINA
Lon - NOL
Long - HUEY PIERCE
Lorna - DOONE
Lott of politics - TRENT
Luft of song - LORNA
Lyrisist Bergman - ALAN
Lyrisist Carole Bayer - SAGER
Lyrisist David - HAL
Lyisist Gershwin - IRA
Lyrisist Green - ADOLPH

Lyrisist Gus - KAHN
Lyrisist Harbach - OTTO
Lyrisist Harburg - YI
Lyrisist Hart - Lorenz
Lyrisist Kahn - GUS
Lyrisist Lerner - ALAN
Lyrisist Lorenz - HART
Lyrisist Rice - TIM
Lyrisist Taupin - BERNIE
Lyrisist Washington - NED
Madam Bovary - EMMA
Madame de _____ - STAEL
Maestro DeWaart - EDO
Maestro Koussevitzky - SERGE
Maestro Leinsdorf - ERICH
Maestro Lorin - MAAZEL
Maestro Mehta - ZUBIN
Maestro Pekka - SALONEN
Maestro Ricardo - MUTI
Maestro Jeiji - OSWA
Maestro Toscanini - ARTURO
Magician Henning - DOUG
Magician Jillette - PENN
Magnani or Moffo - ANNA
Malcolm_____Warner -
    JAMAL
Malone of baseball - MOSES
Mao_____Tung - TSE
Marathoner Pippig - UTA
Marathoner Rosie - RUIZ
Marathoner Waitz - GRETA

Marathoner, Zatioej - EMIL

Mariah of music - CAREY

Mar_____- Baker - LINN

Markswoman Annie - OAKLEY

Marlon of film - BRANDO

Marquis de - SADE

Marvin - LEE

Masters champion
Mark - OMEARA

Mathematician
Babbage - CHARLES

Mathematician Blaise - PASCAL

Mathematician _____De
Fermat - PIERRE

Mathematician Byron - ADA

Mathematician
Descartes - RENE

Mathematician George - BOOLE

Mathematician Godel - KURT

Mathematician
Gottfried - LIEBNIZ

Mathematician Jon
Von - NEUMANN

Mathematician
Kummer - ERNST

Mathematician Kurt - GODEL

Mathematician
Leonhard - EULER

Mathematician Lovelace - ADA

Mathematician
Marin - MERSENNE

Mathematician Newton - ISAAC

Mathematician Pascal - BLAISE

Mathematician
Robert - HOOKE

Mathematician Stewart – IAN

Mathematician Turing - ALAN

Matty or Felix - ALOU

Maxwell - ELSA

_____ May Alcott - LOUISA

Meg - RYAN

Mentalist Geller - URI

Metcalf of Football - ERIC

Mezzo Frederica von - STADE

Mezzo Obraztsova - ELENA

Mezzo-soprano
Marilyn - HORNE

Mezzo-soprano
Merriman - NAN

Mezzo-soprano Stevens - RISE

McClurg - EDIE

Mies Vander - ROHE

Millay or Ferber - EDNA

Mime Marcel - MARCEAU

Minerologist Frederich - MOHS

Missionary Junipero - SERRA

Missionary
Schweitzer - ALBERT

Mme. Bovary - EMMA

Model Alexis - KIM

Model Banks TYRA

Model Benitez - ELSA

Model Campbell - NAOMI

Model Carangi - GIA

Model Carol - ALT
Model Carre - OTIS
Model Chow - TINA
Model Crawford - CINDY
Model Everhart - ANGIE
Model from Samolea - IMAN
Model Gadot - GAL
Model Garielle - REECE
Model Herzigova - EVA
Model Kate - MOSS
Model Kim - ELEXIS
Model Lanzoni - FABIO
Model McPherson - ELLE
Model Moss - KATE
Model Parker - SUSY
Model Pataky - ELSA
Model Sastre - INES
Model Shayk - IRENA
Model Sims - NAOMI
Model Taylor - MAUI
Model Tyler - LIV
Model Wek - ALEK
Monica of tennis - SELES
Moody in Allen's alley - TITUS
Moore - DEMI, DUDLEY, MARY
TYLER or ROGER
Moran or Gray - ERIN
Moshe of Israel - ARENS
Movie Mogul Adolph - ZUKOR
Movie mogul Laemmle - CARL

Moviie mogul Marcus - LOEW
Movie's Bruce - WILLIS
Mr. Arafat - YASIR
Mr. Sagan - CARL
Mrs. Artie Shaw - LANA
Mrs. Charlie Chaplin - OONA
Mrs. David Bowie - IMAN
Mrs. David Copperfield - DORA
Mrs Gorbachev - RAYSA
Mrs. Marcos - IMELDA
Mrs. Parker-Bowles - CAMILLA
Mrs. Rabin - LEAH
Mrs. Tony Martin - SYD
Ms. LeGallienne - EVA
Ms. Massey - ILONA
Ms. Miles - VERA
Ms. Roger St. Johns - ADELA
Ms. Thorndike - SYBIL
Mubarak of Egypt - HOSNI
Muckraker Tarbell - IDA
Mulrooney of Canada - BRIAN
Munro's pen name - SAKI
Muralist Jose - SERT
Muralist Melchers - GARI
Muralist Rivera - DIEGO
Muscleman Steve - REEVES
Musial - STAN
Music critic Ned - ROREM
Musical Baker - ANITA
Musical Franklin - ARETHA
Musical John - DENVER

Musician Blake - EUBIA
Musician Brian - ENO
Musician Brubeck - DAVE
Musician Chick - COREA
Musician Doherty - PAPAS
Musician Dury - IAN
Musician Lofgren - NILS
Musician Lou - REED
Musician Mischa - Elman
Musician Morissette - ALANIS
Musician Phillips - PAPAS
Musician Redbone - LEON
Musician Renzor - TRENT
Musician Ric - OCASEK
Musician Schifrin - LALO
Musician Shankar - RAVI
Musician Santamaria - MONGO
Musician Willie - COLON
Musico Guisar - TITO
Naldi of silents - NITA
Nat King - COLE
Naturalist Adamson - JOY
Natualist John - MUIR
Navarro of the silents - RAMON
Navigator Vitus - BERING
NBA great Hayes - ELVIN
NBA's Gilmore - ARTIS
NBA's Miller - REGGIE
NBA's Mourning - ALONZO
NBA's Shaquille - ONEAL
Negri of old films - POLA

New age Irish singer - ANYA
News anchor Connie - CHUNG
Newscaster Ellerbee - LINDA
Newsman Bernard - SHAW
Newsman Blitzer - WOLF
Newsman Brit - HUME
Newsman Charles - OSGOODE
Newsman Donaldson - SAM
Newsman Garrick - UTLEY
Newsman Hughes - RUDD
Newsman Huntley - CHET
Newsman Lehrer - JIM
Newsman Marvin - Kalb
Newsman Newman - EDWIN
Newsman Roger - ONEIL
Newsman Sevareid - ERIC
Newsman Ted - KOPPEL
Newsman Vanocur - SANDER
Newsperson
     Alexandria - SHANA
Newswoman Braver - RITA
Newswoman Lindstrom - PIA
Newswoman Logan - LARA
Newswoman Shriver - MARIA
NFL great Kyle - ROTE
NFL kicker Jason - ELAM
Ngo Dinh - DIEM
Nobel bacteriologist - ENDERS
Nobel biochemist
     Servo - OACHOA
Nobel chemist Harold - UREY

Nobel chemist Von
 Baeyer - ADOLF
Nobel physicist Isidor - RABI
Nobel winner Bellow - SAUL
Nobel winner Pavlov - IVAN
Nobelist Alverez - LUIS
Nobelist Andre - GIDE
Nobelist Andric - IVO
Nobelist Bellow - SOL
Nobelist Camilo - CELA
Nobelist Camus - ALBERT
Nobelist Canetti - ELIAS
Nobelist Cassin - RENE
Nobelist Clancy - TOM
Nobelist Cordel - HULL
Nobelist Currie MARIE
Nobelist Dulbecco - RENATO
Nobelist Eisaku - SATO
Nobelist Fermi - ENRICO
Nobelist Finsen - NIELS
Nobelist Fo - DARIO
Nobelist Fredrik - BAJER
Nobelist Glashow - SHELDON
Nobelist Gordimer - NADINE
Nobelist Hahn - OTTO
Nobelist Harold - UREY
Nobelist Henri - BERGSON
Nobelist Hermann - HESSE
Nobelist Isador - RABI
Nobelist Jacobus Van't - HOFF

Nobelist
 John_____Orr - BOYD
Nobelist Joliet-Curie - IRENE
Nobelist Kofi - ANNAN
Nobelist Kurt - ALDER
Nobelist Metchnikoff - ELIE
Nobelist Morrison - TONI
Nobelist Nelly - SACHS
Nobelist Neruda - PABLO
Nobelist Nevil - SHUTE
Nobelist Octavio - PAZ
Nobelist Onsager - LARS
Nobelist Oscar_____Sanchez -
 ARIAS
Nobelist Paul - DIRAC
Nobelist Pavlov - IVAN
Nobelist Penzias - ARNO
Nobelist _____Perez
 Esquivel - ADOLFO
Nobelist Planck - MAX
Nobelist Root - ELIHU
Nobelist Sachs - NELLY
Nobelist Sakharov - ANDREI
Nobelist Sanchez -
 OSCAR ARIAS
Nobelist Servo - OCHOA
Nobelist Shimon - PEREZ
Nobelist Soyinka - WOLE
Nobelist Van Baeyer - ADOLF
Nobelist Wiesel - ELIE
Nobelist Wolfgan - PAULI
Nobelist Yalow - ROSALYN

Nobelist Yasir - ARAFAT
Nolan, of baseball - RYAN
Norwegian Nobelist - LANGE
Novelist Alcott - LOUISA
Novelist Alexandre - DUMAS
Novellist Alphonse - DAUDET
Novelist Amado - JORGE
Novelist Amelia - BARR
Novelist Andre - GIDE
Novelist Andric - IVO
Novelist Anita - BROOKNER
Novelist Anne - TYLER
Novelist Anya - SETON
Novelist Austen - JANE
Novelist Ayn - RAND
Novelist Bainbridge - BERYL
Novelist Barbara - PYM
Novelist Barker - CLIVE
Novelist Barstow - STAN
Novelist Baum - VICKI
Novelist Beattie - ANN
Novelist Bellows - SAUL
Novelist Binchy - MAEVE
Novelist Blasco - IBANEZ
Novelist Brand - MAX
Novelist Bret Easton - ELLIS
Novelist Bronte - EMILY
Novelist Brookner - ANITA
Novelist Buck - PEARL
Novelist Buntline - NED
Novelist Caldwell - ERSKINE

Novelist Caleb - CARR
Novelist Camus - ALBERT
Novelist Canin - NATHAN
Novelist Capec - KAREL
Novelist Carr - CALEB
Novelist Castedo - ELENA
Novelist Cather - WILLA
Novelist Calvino - ITALO
Novelist Charles - READE
Novelist Connell - EVAN
Novelist Conroy - PAT
Novelist Cornelius - RYAN
Novelist Cusler - CLIVE
Novelist Dahl - ROALD
Novelist Danielle - STEE
Novelist DeBalzac - HONORE
Novelist De La Roche - MAZO
Novelist Devries - PETER
Novelist Dorothy - EDEN
Novelist Drury - ALLEN
Novelist Dulbecco - RENATO
Novelist du Maurier - DAPHNE
Novelist
    Easton_____ELLIS - BRET
Novelist Elinor - GLYN
    or WYLIE
Novelist Elizabeth - BOWEN
Novelist Emile - ZOLA
Novelist Ephron - DELIA
    or NORA
Novelist Eric - AMBLER
Novelist Erich - SEGAL

Novelist Ernest K. - GANN

Novelist Eugene - SUE

Novelist Fannie - HURST

Novelist Ferber - EDNA

Novelist Flannery - OCONNOR

Novelist Flaubert GUSTAV

Novelist France - ANATOLE

Novelist Frances
	Parkinson - KEYES

Novelist Frankie - FRISCH

Novelist Franz - KAFKA

Novelist Fuentes - CARLOS

Novelist George - ELIOT
	or SAND

Novelist Georgette - HEYER

Novelist Gerritsen - TESS

Novelist Glasgow - ELLEN

Novelist Glyn - ELINOR

Novelist Gordimer - NADINE

Novelist Gore - VIDAL

Novelist Gould - LOIS

Novelist Grafton - SUE

Novelist Green - GRAHAM

Novelist Gray - ZANE

Novelist Hammond - INNES

Novelist Harper - LEE

Novelist
	Hawthorne - NATHANIEL

Novelist Hay - IAN

Novelist Herman - HESSE

Novelist Highsmith - PATRICIA

Novelist Hoag - TAMI

Novelist Honore - de BALZAC

Novelist Hunter - EVAN

Novelist Hurston - ZORA

Novelist Ishmael - REED

Novelist Jaffe - RONA

Novelist Jamaica - KINCAID

Novelist James - AGEE
	or JONES

Novelist Janowitz - TAMA

Novelist Jean - AUEL

Novelist Jean-Paul - SARTRE

Novelist John - JAKES

Novelist John - Le CARRE
	or O'HARA

Novelist John Dickson - CARR

Novelist
	John_____Passos - DOS

Novelist Jong - ERICA

Novelist Jorge - AMADO

Novelist Josephine - TEY

Novelist Joyce Carol - OATES

Novelist Kafka - FRANZ

Novelist Kathleen - NORRIS

Novelist Kazanantzakis - NIKOS

Novelist Kesey - KEN

Novelist Kiklai - GOGOL

Novelist Kingsley - AMIS

Novelist Kobo - ABE

Novelist Koontz - DEAN

Novelist Kurt - VONNEGUT

Novelist Laurence - STERNE

Novelist Lee - HARPER

Novelist Legerlof - SELMA

Novelist Lequin - URSULA

Novelist Leon - URIS

Novelist Leonard - ELMORE

Novelist Leshan - EDA

Novelist Lessing - DORIS

Novelist Leverson - ADA

Novelist Levin - IRA

Novelist Lindgren - ASTRID

Novelist Lofts - NORAH

Novelist Loren
    D. - ESTLEMAN

Novelist Lurie - ALISON

Novelist Malamud - BERNARD

Novelist Malrau - ANDRE

Novelist Marcel - PROUST

Novelist Margaret - DRABBLE

Novelist
    McCullough - COLLEEN

Novelist McMillan - TERRY

Novelist Mishima - YUKIO

Novelist Morant - ELSA

Novelist Moravia - ALBERTO

Novelist Morrison - TONI

Novelist Murdock - IRIS

Novelist Nelle - ARPERLEE

Novelist Nevada - BARR

Novelist Nevil - SHUTE

Novelist Ngaio - MARSH

Novelist O'Brien - EDNA

Novelist O'Flaherty - LIAM

Novelist Olsen - TILLIE

Novelist Oz - AMOS

Novelist Packer - ANN

Novelist Paretsky - SARA

Novelist Patchett - ANN

Novelist Paton - ALAN

Novelist Peter - BENCHLE,
    MAAS or STRAUB

Novelist Philip - ROTH
    or WYLIE

Novelist Phillpotts - EDEN

Novelist Pierre - LOTI

Novelist Quindlen - ANNA

Novelist Radcliffe - ANN

Novelist Raja - RAO

Novelist Ralph - ELLISON

Novelist Rand - AYN

Novelist Reidbanks - LYNNE

Novelist Remarque - ERICH

Novelist Richler - MORDECAI

Novelist Roald - DAHL

Novelist Roberts - NORA

Novelist Roche - MAZO

Novelist Rohmer - SAX

Novelist Roxana - DEFOE

Novelist Sandel - CORA

Novelist
    Santha_____Rau - RAMA

Novelist Sarah _____
    Jewett - ORNE

Novelist Scott - TUROW

Novelist Sebold - ALICE

Novelist Segal - ERICH
or LORE

Novelist Servero - OCHOA

Novelist Seton - ANYA

Novelist Sewell - ANNA

Novelist Shaw - IRWIN

Novelist Sheldon - SIDNEY

Novelist Shirley Ann - GRAU

Novelist Sholem - ASCH

Novelist Shreve - ANITA

Novelist Shusaku - ENDO

Novelist Sillitoe - ALAN

Novelist Sinclair - UPTON

Novelist Sontag - SUSAN

Novelist Stanley - ELKIN

Novelist Stapleton - OLAF

Novelist Susan - ISAACS
or SONTAG

Novelist Svevo - ITALO

Novelist Tan - AMY

Novelist Tennant - KYLIE

Novelist Tilley - OLSEN

Novelist Turgenev - IVAN

Novelist Turow - SCOTT

Novelist Tyler - ANNE

Novelist Umberto - ECO

Novelist Uris - LEON

Novelist Vicki - BAUM

Novelist Victoria - HOLT

Novelist Vidal - GORE

Novelist Virginia - WOOLF

Novelist Vittorini - ELIO

Novelist Wagner - ELIN

Novelist Walker - ALICE

Novelist Waugh - ALEC
or EVELYN

Novelist Welty - EUDORA

Novelist Wharton - EDITH

Novelist Willa - CATHER

Novelist Wilson ANGUS

Novelist Wister - OWEN

Novelist Wolfert - IRA

Novelist Zola - EMILE

Novelist Zora_____Hurston -
NEALE

Novello of old films - IVOR

O'Casey - SEAN

Olympian Al - OERTER

Olympian Biondi - MATT

Olympian Blair - BONNIE

Olympian Connor - BART

Olympain Devers - GAIL

Olympian Jesse - OWENS

Olympian Jim - THORPE

Olympian Johnson - RAFER

Olympian Lewis - CARL

Olympian Lipinski - TARA

Olympian Nurmi - PAAVO

Olympian Ohno - APOLO

Olympian Street - PICABO

Ollympian Strug - KERRI

Olympian Zatopek - EMIL

Olympic discus champ
Al - OERTER

Olympic great
Comaneci - NADIA

Olympic great Janet - EVANS

Olympic runner
Johnson - RAFER

Olympic runner Jones - LOLO

Olympic skier Alberto - TOMBA

Olympic skier
Maentyranta - EERO

Olympic skier Phil - MAHRE

Olympic skier Sailer - TONI

Olympic swimmer
Bionde - MATT

Olympic swimmer
Ian - THORPE

Olympic swimmer
Janet - EVANS

Olympic track star
Ashford - EVELYN

Onassis, briefly - ARI

Ono - YOKO

Opera bass Tajo - ITALO

Opera singer Bostridge - IAN

Opera singer Gedda - NICOLAI

Opera singer Gluck - ALMA

Opera singer Marilyn - HORNE

Opera singer Quilico - LOUIS

Opera singer Te Kenawa - KIRA

Opera star Tebaldi - RENATA

Operetic Eleanor - STEBER

Orator Chauncey - DEPEW

Orchestrator Jule - STYNE

Organist Braga - ENA

Oscar nominee Edward
James - OLMOS

Oscar winner Dench - JUDY

Oscar winner Gooding - CUBA

Oscar winner Rainer - LUISE

Otis - AMOS or ELISHA

Outfielder Slaughter - ENOS

Page of music - PATTI

Painter Albert
Pinkham - RYDER

Painter Alphonse - MUCHA

Painter Andrea D el - SARTO

Painter Angelico - FRA

Painter Anthony Van - DYCK

Painter Appel - KAREL

Painter Berthe - MORISOT

Painter Bonheur - ROSA

Painter Braque - GEORGES

Painter Brueghel - PIETER

Painter Camille - PISARRO

Painter Carot - JEAN
BAPTISTE

Painter Chagall - MARC

Painter Claude - MONET

Painter Cornelius de - VOS

Painter Daumier - HONORE

Painter Degas - EDGAR

Painter Dufy - RAOUL

Painter Edgar - DEGAS

Painter Eduard - MANET

Painter Emile - NOLDE

Painter Fernand - LEGER

Painter Fiorentino - ROSSO

Painter Francis - BACON

Painter Frank - STELLA

Painter Frans - HALS

Painter Franz - MARC

Painter George - CATLIN
  or INNESS

Painter Georges - SEURAT

Painter Georgia - OKEEFE

Painter
  Gerard_____Borch -TER

Painter Gino - SEVERINI

Painter Guido - RENI

Painter Gustav - KLIMT

Painter
  Guy_____Dubois - PENE

Painter Hals - FRANS

Painter Hans - ARPS

Painter Harring - KEITH

Painter Hieronymus - BOSCH

Painter Hofmann - HANS

Painter Holbein – HANS

Painter Homer - WINSLOW

Painter Hopper- Edward

Painter Jackson - POLLOCK

Painter James - ENSOR

Painter Jan - STEEN

Painter Jan van der - MEER

Painter Jan Van - GOYEN

Painter Jasper - JOHNS

Painter Jean - ARP

Painter Jim - DINE

Painter Joan - MIRO

Painter John – MARIN
  or SLOAN

Painter John Baptiste - COROT

Painter John La_____ - FARGE

Painter John Singer - SARGENT

Painter Jose Maria - SERT

Painter Joseph - STELLA

Painter Katz - ALEX

Painter Klee - PAUL

Painter Klimt - GUSTAV

Painter Krasner - LEE

Painter Larry - RIVERS

Painter Leroy - NEIMAN

Painter Lichtenstein - ROY

Painter Magritte - RENE

Painter Manet - EDOUARD

Painter Mantegna - ANDREA

Painter Mary - CASSATT

Painter Matisse - HENRI

Painter Maurice - UTRILLO

Painter Max - ERNST

Painter Modigliani - AMEDEO

Painter- Mondrian - PIET

Painter Munch - EDVARD

Painter N. C. - WYETH

Painter Neiman - LEROY

Painter Nolde - EMIL

Painter of ballarinas - DEGAS
Painter Paul - KLEE
Painter Picasso - PABLO
Painter Pierre
    Auguste - RENOIR
Painter Rembrandt - PEALE
Painter Remington - FREDERIC
Painter Richard - ESTES
Painter Rivera - DIEGO
Painter Rober - HENRI
Painter Rockwell - NORMAN
Painter Rossetti - DANTE
Painter Rousseau - HENRI
Painter Rossetti - DANTE
Painter Schiele - EGON
Painter Signorelli - LUCA
Painter Sir Joshua - Reynolds
Painter Sir Peter - LELY
Painter Sir William - ORPEN
Painter Soutine - CHAIM
Painter Steen - JAN
Painter Taddeo - GADDI
Painter Tanguy - YVES
Painter Uccello - PAOLO
Painter Van Doesburg - THEO
Painter Van Eyck - JAN
Painter Vereshchagin - VASILI
Painter Vermeer - JAN
Painter Veronese - PAOLO
Painter Wifredo - LAM
Painter Wyeth - ANDREW

Panza - SANCHO
Papas and Ryan - IRENE
Parks or Bonheur - ROSA
Parquet circle - PARTERRE
Pat or Richard - BOONE
Pathologist Sir James - PAGET
Paul of song - ANKA
Peggy of TV - REA
Penn or Connery - SEAN
Percussionist Puente - TITO
Perot - ROSS
Perry of TV - LUKE or COMO
Peter of films - LORRE
Philanthropist
    Andrew - CARNEGIE
Philanthropist Barton - CLARA
Philanthropist
    Brady - DIAMONDJIM
Philanthropist Brooke - ASTOR
Philanthropist Cornell - EZRA
Philanthropist Fisher - AVERY
Philanthropist George - SOROS
Philanthropist
    Hopkins - JOHNS
Philanthropist Rhodes - CECIL
Philanthropist Yale - ELIHU
Philbin - REGIS
Philosopher A J - AYER
Philosopher Auguste - COMTE
Philosopher Bergson - HENRI
Philosopher Blaise - PASCAL
Philosopher David - HUME

Philosopher De Beauvoir - SIMONE

Philosopher Denis - DIDEROT

Philosopher Descartes - RENE

Philosopher Emmanuel - KANT

Philosopher Francis - BACON

Philosopher Georg - HEGEL

Philosopher Georges - SOREL

Philosopher Gottfried - LEIBNIZ

Philosopher Hannah - ARENDT

Philosopher Hume - DAVID

Philosopher Immanuel - KANT

Philosopher Jean Paul - SARTRE

Philosopher John Stuart - LOCKE or MILL

Philosopher Josiah - ROYCE

Philosopher Kierkegaard - SOREN

Philosopher Langer - SUSANNE

Philosopher Lao - TSE

Philosopher Locke - JOHN

Philosopher Mach - ERNST

Philosopher Pascal - BLAISE

Philosopher Smith - ADAM

Philosopher Watts - ALAN

Philosopher Weil - SIMONE

Philosopher Wittgenstein - LUDWIG

Philosopher/writer Hoffer - ERIC

Photographer Adams - ANSEL

Photographer Arbus - DIANE

Photographer Beaton - CECIL

Photographer Cornell - CAPA

Photographer Cunningham - IMOGEN

Photographer Diane - ARBUS

Photographer Dorothea - LANGE

Photographer Gilpin - LAURA

Photographer Goldin - NAN

Photographer Herb - RITTS

Photographer Irving - PENN

Photographer Leibovitz - ANNIE

Photographer Paul - STRAND

Photographer Richard - AVEDON

Photographer Walker - EVANS

Physicist Ampere - ANDRE

Physicist Bohr - NIELS

Physicist Edward - TELLER

Physicist Enrico - FERMI

Physicist Ernst - MACH

Physicist Esaki - LEO

Physicist Fermi - ENRICO

Physicist Geiger - HANS

Physicist Georg - OHM

Physicist Hawking - STEPHEN

Physicist Helsenberg - WERNER

Physicist Isador - RABI

Physicist John - KERR or LOCKE

Physicist Joliot-Curie - IRENE

Physicist Mach - ERNST

Physicist Meitner - LISE

Physicist Max - PLANCK

Physicist Nicola - TESLA

Physicist Niels - BOHR

Physicist Niels - BOHR

Physicist Otto - HAHN

Physicist Rutherford - ERNEST

Physicist Sakharov - ANDRE

Physicis Schrodinger - IRWIN

Physicist Szilard - LEO

Physicist Tann - IGOR

Physicist Wolfgang - PAULI

Pianist Ahmad - NAMEL

Pianist Alicia - KEYS

Pianist Allison - MOSE

Pianist Andre - WATTS

Pianist Argerich - MARTHA

Pianist Art - TATUM

Pianist Arthur - SCHNABEL

Pianist Ax - EMANUEL

Pianist Barenboim - DANIEL

Pianist Bill - EVANS

Pianist Billy - JOEL

Pianist Blake - EUBIE

Pianist Bronstein - EVA

Pianist Brubeck - DAVE

Pianist Bruno - ROSSI

Pianist Eubie - BLAKE

Pianist Chasins - ABRAM

Pianist Chick - COREA

Pianist Claudio - ARRAU

Pianist Cliburn - VAN

Pianist Czerny - KARL

Pianist Diane - KRALL

Pianist Emile - GILELS

Pianist Evans - GIL

Pianist Fats - DOMINO

Pianist Fleisher - LEON

Pianist George - SHEARING

Pianist Gilels - EMIL

Pianist Glenn - GOULD

Pianist Handcock - HERBIE

Pianist Hess - MYRA

Pianist Hines - EARL

Pianist Janis - BYRON

Pianist Jankowski - HORST

Pianist Jorge - BOLET

Pianist Jose - ITURBI

Pianist Katie - WEBSTER

Pianist Kuerti - ANTON

Pianist Laredo - RUTH

Pianist Lewis - RAMSEY

Pianist Lupu - RADU

Pianist Marsalis - ELLIS

Pianist Marx - CHICO

Pianist McCann - LES

Pianist McCoy - TYNER

Pianist Myra - HESS

Pianist Oscar - LEVANT
or PETERSON

Pianist Paderewski - IGNACE

Pianist Peter - NERO

Pianist Previn - ANDRE

Pianist Radu - LUPU

Pianist Rosalyn - TURECK

Pianist Rubinstein - ANTON
or ARTUR

Pianist Rudolph - SERKIN

Pianist Schnabel - ARTUR

Pianist Serkin - PETER
or RUDOLF

Pianist Tatum - ART

Pianist Templeton - ALEC

Pianist Tesh - JOHN

Pianist Thelonious - MONK

Pianist Von Alpenheim - ILSE

Pianist Von Dohnanyi - ERNO

Pianist Watts - ANDRE

Pianist Wilson - TEDDY

Pierre or J. D. - SALINGER

Pike - NEBULON

Pilgrim John - ALDEN

Pinky and Peggy - LEE

Pirate William - KIDD

Pitcher of old Wilhelm - HOYT

Pitcher Al - LEITER

Pitcher Astacio - PEDRO

Pitcher Billy - O'DELL

Pitcher Blackwell - EWELL

Pitcher Blue - VIDA

Pitcher Blyleven - ERT

Pitcher Darling - RON

Pitcher Dave - STIEB

Pitcher David - CONE

Pitcher Drabek - DOUG

Pitcher Fingers - ROLLIE

Pitcher Galarraga - ARMANDO

Pitcher Guidrey - RON

Pitcher Hamel - COLE

Pitcher Hershiser - OREL

Pitcher Hideki - IRABU

Pitcher Hideo - NOMO

Pitcher Jamie - MOYER

Pitcher Jim - PALMER

Pitcher LeMarr - HOYT

Pitcher Mario - SOTO

Pitcher Martinez - PEDRO
or RAMON

Pitcher Milt - PAPPAS

Pitcher Nen - ROBB

Pitcher Orosco JESSIE

Pitcher Ortiz - RUSS

Pitcher Paul - TOTH

Pitcher Quisenberry - DAN

Pitcher Reynolds - ALLIE

Pitcher Robb - NEN

Pitcher Saberhagen - BRET

Pitcher Satchel - PAIGE

Pitcher Seaver - TOM

Pitcher Shawn - ESTES

Pitcher Tiant - LUIS

Place Kicker Benirschke - ROLF

Playwright/Actor
Williams - EMLYN

Playwright Akins - ZOE

Playwright Albee - EDWARD

Playwright Anouilh - JEAN

Playwright Ayckbourn - ALAN

Playwright Barstow - STAN

Playwright Beckett - SAMUEL

Playwright Bernard - SLADE

Playwright Bertolt - BRECHT

Playwright Bogasian - ERIC

Playwright Brendan - BEHAN

Playwright Burrows - ABE

Playwright Calderon - PEDRO

Playwright Capek - KAREL

Playwright Cesaire - AIME

Playwright Chayefsky - PADDY

Playwright Chekhov - ANTON

Playwright Clifford - ODETS

Playwright Connelly - MARC

Playwright Coward - NOEL

Playwright David -
    MAMET or RABE

Playwright Edward - ALBEE

Playwright Eve - ENSLER

Playwright·Eugene -
    IONESCO or ONEILL

Playwright Federico
    Garcia - LORCA

Playwright Fugard - ATHOL

Playwright George - PEELE

Playwright Geraldine - ARON

Playwright Goethe - JOHANN

Playwright Harold - PINTNER

Playwright Hart - MOSS

Playwright Hellman - LILLIAN

Playwright Henley - BETH

Playwrite Henrik - IBSEN

Playwright Horovitz -ISRAEL

Playwright Horton - FOOTE

Playwright Ibsen - HENRIK

Playwright Jean - GENET

Playwright Joe - ORTON

Playwright John - OSBORNE

Playwrite John
    Millington - SYNGE

Playwright Jones - LEROI

Playwright Karel - CAPEK

Playwright Luce - CLARE

Playwright Max – SHULMAN

Playwright Miller - ARTHUR

Playwright Mosel - TAD

Playwright Murray - SCGISGAL

Playwright Norman - MARSHA

Playwright O'Casey - SEAN

Playwright O'Neill - EUGENE

Playwright Paula - VOGEL

Playwright Peter - WEISS

Playwright Pinter - HAROLD

Playwright Pirandello - LUIGI

Plsywright
    Rattigan - TERRANCE

Playwright Rice - ELMER

Playwright Sean - O'CASEY

Playwright Shepard - SAM

Playwright Simon - NEIL

Playwright Spewack - BELLA

Playwright Stoppard - TOM

Playwright Strindberg - AUGUST

Playwright Thomas - KYD

Playwright Victorien - SARDOU

Playwright Wasserman - WENDY

Playwright Wendy - LILL

Playwright William - INGE

Playwright Williams - EMLYN

Playwright Wilson - AUGUST

Playwright Zoe - AKINS

Poet Aiken - CONRAD

Poet Alexander - POPE

Poet Alfred - NOYES

Poet Alfred_____Birney - EARLE

Poet Alice - CARY

Poet Alighieri - DANTE

Poet _____Alington Robinson - EDWIN

Poet Allen - TATE

Poet Amy - LOWELL

Poet Angelou - MAYA

Poet Annibale - CARO

Poet Archibald - MACLEISH

Poet _____Arlington Robinson - ERWIN

Poet Auden - WYSTAN

Poet Aukrust - OLAV

Poet Barak - AMIRI

Poet Birney - EARLE

Poet Bradstreet - ANNE

Poet Breton - ENDRE

Poet/Cartoonist Silverstein - SHEL

Poet Cary - ALICE

Poet Cassady - NEAL

Poet Cavalcanti - GUIDO

Poet Cesaire - AIME

Poet Charles - OLSEN

Poet Clement - MOORE

Poet Conrad - AIKEN

Poet Crane - HART

Poet Cummings - ESTLIN

Poet Dante - ROSSETTI

Poet Dickinson - EMILY

Poet Doolittle - HILDA

Poet Dove - RITA

Poet Dowsen - ERNEST

Poet Earle - BIRNEY

Poet Edgar Lee - MASTERS

Poet Edith - SITWELL

Poet Edwin Arlington - ROBINSON

Poet Edward - LEAR

Poet Elinor - WYLIE

Poet Elizabeth - Bishop

Poet Endre - BRETON

Poet Erin - MOURE

Poet Felicia Dorothea - HEMANS

Poet Frank - OHARA

Poet Fredrico Garcia - LORCA

Poet Frost - ROBERT

Poet Gallagher – TESS

Poet Gary - SNYDER

Poet Gertrude - STEIN

Poet Ginsberg - ALLEN

Poet Giovanni - NIKKI

Poet Glasgow - ELLEN

Poet Guest - EDGAR

Poet Gunn - THOM

Poet Gwen - HARWOOD

Poet Heamie - SEAMUS

Poet Hart - CRANE

Poet Heinrich - HEINE

Poet Hoyt - ELINOR

Poet Hughes - TED

Poet James Whitcomb - RILEY

Poet John - DONNE or KEATS

Poet Jones - LEROI

Poet Jonson - BEN

Poet Joseph - ADDISON

Poet Kahill - GIBRAN

Poet Karlfeldt - ERIK

Poet Khayyam - OMAR

Poet Khosrow - AMIR

Poet Langston - HUGHES

Poet Laura - RIDING

Poet Laureate Dove - RITA

Poet Laureate Nicholas - ROWE

Poet Laureate Mark - STRAND

Poet Laureate Van
    Duyn - MONA

Poet Lazarus - EMMA

Poet _____Lee
    Masters - EDGAR

Poet Levertov - DENISE

Poet Lindsay - VACHEL

Poet_____Lindsay
    Gordon - ADAM

Poet Lizette - REESE

Poet Louise - BOGAN

Poet Lowell - AMY

Poet Ludovico - ARIOSTO

Poet Mandelstan - OSIP

Poet Mare - WALTER DELA

Poet Marianne - MOORE

Poet Mark Van - DOREN

Poet Markham - IRWIN

Poet Matthew - PRIOR

Poet McKuen - ROD

Poet Millarme - STEPHANE

Poet Millay - EDNA

Poet Milton - ACORN

Poet Moore - CLEMENT
    or MARIANNE

Poet Muir - EDWIN

Poet Neruda - JAN or PABLO

Poet Nicholes - ROWE

Poet Piet - HEIN

Poet Noyes - ALFRED

Poet Ogden - NASH

Poet Omar - KHAYYAM

Poet Osbert - SITWELL

Poet Oscar - WILDE

Poet Pablo - NERUDA

Poet Percy - SHELLY

Poet Phyllis - WEBB

Poet Pound - EZRA

Poet Rainer - RILKE

Poet Ralph Waldo - EMERSON

Poet Rich - ADRIENNE

Poet Robert - FROST or WACE

Poet Rossetti - DANTE

Poet Rupert - BROOKE

Poet Sachs - NELLY

Poet Salter - MARYJO

Poet Samuel - COLERIDGE

Poet Sandburg - CARL

Poet Sara - TEASDALE

Poet
     Sarah_____Jewett - ORNE

Poet Seamus - HEANEY

Poet Sexton - ANNE

Poet Sharon - OLDS

Poet Siegfried-·SASSOON

Poet Silverstein - SHEL

Poet Silvia - PLATH

Poet Sitwell - EDITH

Poet Smith - PATTI

Poet St. John_____ - PERSE

Poet St. Vincent Millay - EDNA

Poet Swenson MAY

Poet T. E. - HULME

Poet Tate - ALLAN or NAHUM

Poet Teasdale - SARA

Poet Thomas - DYLAN
     or GRAY

Poet Torquato - TASSO

Poet Ugo - BETTI

Poet Van Duyn - MONA

Poet Voznesenski - ANDREI

Poet W. H. _____ - AUDEN

Poet Walcott - DEREK

Poet Wheeler Wilcox - ELLA

Poet Whitman - WALT

Poet Wilcox - ELLA

Poet Wilfred - OWEN

Poet William Butler - YEATS

Poet Wylie - ELINOR

Poet Wystan Hugh - AUDEN

Poet Yevtushenko - YEVGENY

Poet Young - ELLA

Poetic Percy - SHELLEY

Poetic Siegried - SASSOON

Political analyst
     Meyers - DEEDEE

Political pundit
     John - SUNUNU

Politician Gary - HART

Politician Gingrich - NEWT

Politico Hollings - ERNEST

Polster Roper - ELMO

Ponselle of opera - ROSA

Pop singer Elliot - CASS

Pop singer Gaye - NONA

Pop singer Hendryx - NONA
Pop singer Phoebe - SNOW
Pop singer Tori - AMOS
Pop star Morisette - ALANIS
Popeye's creator Elzie - SEGAR
Portraitist John
    Singer - SARGENT
Portraitiest Rembrandt - PEALE
Pot of Cambodia_____ - POL
Primatologist Fossey - DIAN
Producer Adolph - ZUKOR
Producer Brian - ENO
Producer David - MERRICK
Producer De Laurentis - DINO
Producer Efrom - DELIA
Producer Hayward - LELAND
Producer Hunter - ROSS
Producer Jack - WARNER
Producer Joseph - PAPP
Producter McPharlane - SETH
Producer Phil - SPECTOR
Producer Roach - HAL
Producer Robert - EVANS
Producer Roddenberry - GENE
Producer Schary - DORE
Producer Ziegfeld - FLORENZ
Prohibitionist Carrie - NATION
Prometheus's sister-in-
    law - PANDORA
Prynne - HESTER
Psychiatrist Alfred - ADLER

Psychiatrist Berne - ERIC
Psychiatrist Jung - CARL
Psychic Edgar - CAYCE
Psychic Geller - URI
Psychoanalyst Feud - ANNA
Psychoanalyst Fromm - ERICH
Psychoanalyst Horney - KAREN
Psychoanalyst Wilhelm - REICH
Psychologist Alfred - BINET
Psychologist
    Bettelheim - BRUNO
Psychologist Carl - ROGERS
Psychologist Havelock - ELLIS
Psychologist Jean - PIAGET
Psychologist Jung - CARL
Psychologist Lee - SALK
Psychologist Leshan - EDA
Psychologist May - ROLLO
Psychologist Pavlov - IVAN
Psychologist Piaget - JEAN
Publisher Adolph - OCHS
Publisher Canfield - CASS
Publisher Chandler - KEN
Publisher Conde - NAST
Publisher Katherine - GRAHAM
Publisher William
    Randolph - HEARST
Pugilist Tunny - GENE
Pulitzer Lurie - ALISON
Pulitzer novelist James - AGEE
Pulitzer poet - AIKEN

Pulitzer winner Carl - SEGAN
Pulitzer winner Huxtable - ADA
Pulitzer winner Walker - ALICE
Pundit Coulter - ANN
Puppeteer Fran - ALLISON
Puppeteer Jim - HENSON
Puppeteer Lewis - SHARI
Puppeteer Stu - GILLIAM
Puppeteer Tony - SARG
Puppet master Bil - BAIRD
Quarterback Bradshaw - TERRY
Quarterback Brett - FAVRE
Quarterback
     Daunte - CULPEPPER
Quarterback Dawson - LEN
Quarterback Dilfer - TRENT
Quarterback
     Esiason - BOOMER
Quarterback Favre - BRETT
Quarterback Flutie - DOUG
Quarterback
     Hasselbeck - MATT
Quarterback John - ELWAY
Quarterback Manning -
     ELI or PEYTON
Quarterback Rodney - PEETE
Quarterback Tarkington - FRAN
Quarterback Tony - ROMO
Quincy of music - JONES
Racer Andretti - MARIO
Racer Bobby - UNSER
     or RAHAL

Racer Earnhardt - DALE
Racer Elliott - SADLER
Racer Fabi - TEO
Racer Gordon - JEFF
Racer Jarrett - NED
Racer Lauda - NIKI
Racer Luyendyk - ARIE
Racer Mansell - NIGEL
Racer Mark - MARTIN
Racer Petty - KYLE
Racer Rick - MEARS
Racer Ricky - RUDD
Racer Stirling - MOSS
Racer Teo - FABI
Racer Tom - SNEVA
Racer Yarborough - CALE
Racing great Al - UNSER
Radio hostess Hensen - DIANE
Raines - ELLA
Ralph _____
     Emerson - WALDO
Rap's_____Kim - LIL
Rapper Elliot - MISSY
Rapper Nicki - MINAJ
Rebecca Romijn - STAMOS
Red Cross founder
     CLARA - BARTON
Redding of music - OTIS
Reddy of song - HELEN
Reformer Baker - ELLA
Reformer Bloomer - AMELIA

Reformer Jacob - RIIS

Reporter Hume - BRIT

Reporter Stahl - LESLIE

Reviewer Roger - EBERT

Rhodes - CECIL JOHN

Rigby of song - ELEANOR

Rigg or Ross - DIANA

Ring star Dempsey - JACK

Rock star John - ELTON

Rocker Adams - BRYAN

Rocker Bob - SEGER

Rocker Brian - ENO

Rocker Courtney - LOVE

Rocker DiFranco - ANI

Roocker Green - DAY

Rocker Keith - EMERSON

Rocker Kurt - COBAIN

Rocker Marilyn - MANSON

Rocker Morrison - VAN

Rocker Ocasek - RIC

Rocker Ramone - DEEDEE

Rocker Rose - AXL

Rocker Russel - LEON

Rocker Smith - PATTI

Rocker Steve - EARLE

Rocker Townsend - PETE

Rockney of Notre
    Dame - KNUTE

Roger of baseball - MARIS

Roh_____Wu - TAE

Roman philosopher - SENECA

Rubik - ERNO

Ruby or Sandra - DEE

Runner Alberto SALAZAR

Runner Boldon - ATO

Runner Budd - ZOLA

Runner Coghlan - EMMON

Runner Devers - GAIL

Runner Jim - RYUN

Runner Johnson - RAFER

Runner Keino - KIP

Runner Lewis - CARL

Runner Mary - DECKER

Runner Mota - ROSA

Runner Rudolph - WILMA

Runner Sebastian - COE

Runner Steve - OVETT

Runner Viren - LASSE

Runner Waitz - GETE

Runner Zatopek - EMIL

Running back Johnson - RUDI

Running back
    Ladarian - Tomlinson

Russian poet
    Mandelshtam - OSIP

Sally with a fan - RAND

Sarto, Andrea _____ - DEL

Satirist Belloc - HILAIRE

Satirist Bendan - BEHAN

Satirist Mort - SAHL

Satirist Ward - NED

Satirist Will - DURST

Saxophonist Al - COHN
Saxophonist
    Coleman - ORNETTE
Saxophonist Getz - STAN
Saxophonist Gordon - DEXTER
Saxophonist John - COLTRANE
Saxophonist Mulligan - GERRY
Saxophonist Parker - EVAN
Saxophonist Zoot - SIMS
Scientist Otto - LOWEI
Scientologist Durkheim - EMILE
Scientologist Hubbard - L RON
Scientologist Rimini - LEAH
Screenwriter Ben - HECHT
Screenwriter Clifford - ODETS
Screenwriter Ephron - NORA
Screenwriter Eric - AMBLER
Screenwriter Hecht - BEN
Screenwriter James - AGEE
Screenwriter Lods - ANITA
Screenwriter Roald - DAHL
Sculptor Arp - JEAN
Sculpror Auguste - RODIN
Sculptor Chillida - EDUARDO
Sculptor Epstein - JACOB
Sculptor Henry - MOORE
Sculptor Hesse - EVA
Scultor Jean - ARP
Sculptor Leoni - LEONE
Sculptor Maya - LIN
Sculptor Nadelman - ELIE

Sculptor Nikola - PISANO
Sculptor Noguchi - ISAMU
Sculptor Oldenburg - CLAES
Sculptorr Pisano - NICOLA
Sculptor Sir Jacob - EPSTEIN
Sculptor Taft - LORADO
Sebastian's twin - VIOLA
Seedman Burpee - ATLEE
Senator Hatch - ORRIN
Senator Kefauver - ESTES
Senator Spector - ARLEN
Senator Thurmond - STROM
Sewing machine inventor
    Howe - ELIAS
Sexologist Hite - SHERE
Shaq or Tatum - ONEAL
Sharif or Bradley - OMAR
Shire of Rocky films - TALIA
Shoe designer Maglia - BRUNO
Shore of TV - DINAH
Shortstop Aparicio - LUIS
Shortstop Derek - JETER
Shortstop
    Garciaparra - NOMAR
Shortstop Peewee - REESE
Shortstopp Walt - WEISS
Shroyer of TV - ENOS
Sicilian code of
    silence - OMERTA
Signor Alighieri - DANTE
Silent actor Novello - RAMON
Silent actress Markey - ENID

Silent actress
  Normand - MABEL
Silent film star Theda - BARA
Silent star Leeds - LILA
Silent star Naldi - NITA
Silent star, Negri - POLA
Silents star Novello - IVOR
Singer Abdul - PAULA
Singer Acuff - ROY
Singer Adalina - PATTI
Singer Adam - ANT
Singer Adams - OLETA
Singer Aguilera - CHRISTINA
Singer Aimee - MANN
Singer Akers - Karen
Singer Al - JARREA, JOLSON
  or MARTINO
Singer Alicia - KEYS
Singer Amos - TORI
Singer Anderson - IVIE
Singer Andrews - INEZ
Singer Andy - GIBB
Singer Anita - BAKER,
  LAURIN or O'DAY
Singer Ant - ADAM
Singer Anthony - MARC
Singer Apple - FIONA
Singer Arthur - CONLEY
Singer Axton - HOYTE
Singer Bachman - TAL
Singer Baez - JOAN
Singer Bailey - PEARL

Singer Baker - LAVERN
Singer Bandu - ERYKAH
Singer Bandy - MOE
Singer Barbara - MCNAIR
Singer Barry - LEN or
  MANILOW
Singer Bartoli CELIA
Singer Basil - TONI
Singer Beverly - SILLS
Singer Billy - JOEL,
  OCEAN or VERA
Singer Billy Jo - SPEARS
Singer Black - CILLA or CLINT
Singer Blades - RUBEN
Singer Blakely - RONEE
Singer Bob - DYLAN or SEGER
Singer Bobby - BLAND,
  DARIN or HEBB
Singer Bocelli - ANDREA
Singer Bonnie – RAITT
  or TYLER
Singer Boz - SCAGGS
Singer Braxton - TONI
Singer Brewer - TERESA
Singer Brickell - EDIE
Singer Bridgewater - DEEDEE
Singer Brightman - SARAH
Singer Brooks - GARTH
Singer Brown - JAMES
Singer Bryan - ADAMS
Singer Bryson - PEABO
Singer Burl - IVES

Singer C. C. - PENISTON
Singer Calve - EMMA
Singer Campbell - GLEN
Singer Cantrell - LANA
Singer Cara - IRENE
Singer Carey - MARIAH
Singer Carlisle - BELINDA
Singer Carmen - MCRAE
or ERIC
Singer Carpenter - KAREN
Singer Carr - VICKIE
Singer Carter - DEANA
or NELL
Singer Caruso - ENRICO
Singer Cash - ROSANNE
Singer Cassidy - SHAWN
Singer Cat - STEVENS
Singer Celine - DION
Singer Chaka - KAHN
Singer Chapin HARRY
Singer Cherry - NENEH
Singer Chesney - KENNY
Singer Chet - ATKINS
Singer Chris - ISAAK or REA
Singer Christina - AGUILERA
Singer Chrystal - GAYLE
Singer Clapton - ERIC
Singer Clark - DEE,
ROY or TERRI
Singer Cleo - LAINE
Singer Cocker - JOE
Singer Cohn - MARC

Singer Collins - PHIL
Singer Colombo - RUSS
Singer Cooke - SAM
Singer Coolidge - RITA
Singer Corine Bailey - RAE
Singer Cory - HART
Singer Costello - ELVIS
Singer Crow - SHERYL
Singer Cruz - CELIA
Singer Dalton - LACY
Singer Dame Nellie - MELBA
Singer Damone - VIC
Singer Danny - O'KEEFE
Singer David - BOWIE
Singer Davis - ALANA or MAC
Singer Dee - JOEY, KIKI
or SNIDER
Singer Delange - ELSIE
Singer Del Rey - LANA
Singer Dement - IRIS
Singer Desario - TERI
Singer Diana - ROSS or KRALL
Singer DiFranco - ANI
Singer Doherty - DENNY
Singer Donna - SUMMER
Singer Donner - RAL
Singer Dottie - WEST
Singer Dupree - ROBBIE
Singer Dury - IAN
Singer Eames - EMMA
Singer Easton - SHEENA

Singer Eddie - VEDDER
Singer Edith - PIAF
Singer Eleanor - RIGBY
Singer Emmy Lou - HARRIS
Singer Enzo - STUARTI
Singer Erykah - BADU
Singer Estefan - GLORIA
Singer Etheridge - MELISSA
Singer Etta - JAMES
Singer Evans - SARA
Singer Faith - HILL
Singer Falana - LOLA
Singer Farrell - EILEEN
Singer Feliciano - JOSE
Singer Fernandez - REMO
Singer Fisher - SHUG
Singer Flack - ROBERTA
Singer Ford - ERNIE or LITA
Singer Foxx - INEZ
Singer Francis - CONNIE
Singer Franklin - ARETHA
    or ERMA
Singer Freda - PAYNE
Singer Fricke - JANIE
Singer Furtardo - NELLY
Singer Gabriel – BYRNE
    or PETER
Singer Gale - CHRYSTAL
Singer Gary - NUMAN
Singer Gedda - NICOLAI
Singer Gene - PITNEY

Singer Gentry - BOBBIE
Singer George - STRAIT
Singer Gerhardt - ELENA
Singer Gibb - ANDY
Singer Gibbs - TERRI
Singer Gill - VINCE
Singer Glenn - FREY
Singer Gloria - ESTEFAN
    or GAYNOR
Singer Gluck - ALMA
Singer Gobbi - TITO
Singer Gomez - SELENA
Singer Gore - LESLEY
Singer Gorme - EYDIE
Singer Graham - NASH
Singer Grant – AMY,
    EDDIE or GOGI
Singer Greenbaum - NORMAN
Singer Greenwood - LEE
Singer Griffin - PATTY
Singer Griffith - NANCI
Singer Groban - JOSH
Singer Guthrie - ARLO
    or WOODY
Singer Gwen - STEPHANI
Singer Haggard - MERLE
Singer Hall - TOM T or DARYL
Singer Halliwell - GERI
Singer Harris - EMMY LOU
Singer Harrison - GEORGE
Singer Havens - RICHIE
Singer Hayes - ISAAC

Singer Helen - REDDY
Singer Hendrix - JIMI
Singer Hendryx - NONA
Singer Hill - DRU, FAITH
   or LAURYN
Singer Holiday - BILLIE
Singer Holly - NEAR
Singer Horne - MARILYN
Singer Houston - CISSY
Singer Hunter - ALBERTA
Singer Ian - JANIS
Singer Iglesias - ENRIQUE
Singer India - ARIE
Singer Irene - CARA
Singer Isaac - HAYES
Singer Isadora - PIA
Singer Jackson - ALAN,
   JANET, MICHAEL,
   MAHALIA or WANDA
Singer James - ETTA
   or INGRAM
Singer Janis - IAN
Singer Jaques - BREL
Singer Jarreau - AL
Singer Jason - MTAZ
Singer Jeannie C - RILEY
Singer Jenkins - ELLE
Singer Jennings - WAYLAND
Singer Jenny - LIND
Singer Jerry - VALE
Singer Jerry Lee - LEWIS
Singer Jett - JOAN

Singer Jim - CROCE
Singer Joan - BAEZ or JETT
Singer Joe – ELY or WALSH
Singer Joey - DEE
Singer John - ELTON, MAYER,
   PRINE or WAITE
Singer Jon - SECADA
Singer Jones - ALLAN,
   NORAH or TOM
Singer Joplin - JANIS
Singer Jordan - MONTELL
Singer Josh - WHITE
Singer Judd - NAOMI
   or WYNONNA
Singer Julio - IGLASIAS
Singer K. T. - OSLIN
Singer Kahn - CHAKA
Singer Kaldor - CONNIE
Singer Kamoze - INI
Singer Karen - AKERS
Singer Kathy - MATTEA
Singer Katie - WEBSTER
Singer Kazan - LAINE
Singer Keith - TOBY
Singer Ketchum - HAL
Singer Keys - ALICIA
Singer King - BENE
   or CAROLE
Singer Kingston - SEAN
Singer Kitt - EARTHA
Singer Kitty - WELLS
Singer Knight - GLADYS

Singer Krall - DIANA
Singer Krause - ALISON
Singer Kravitz - LENNY
Singer LaBelle - PATTI
Singer Laine - CLEO
Singer Lambert - ADAM
Singer Lane - ABBE
Singer Lanza - MARIO
Singer Lauper - CYNDI
Singer Laura - NYRO
Singer Lavigne - AVRIL
Singer Lawrence - STEVE
Singer Leann - RIMES
Singer Lehmann - LOTTA
Singer Lehrer - TOM
Singer Lemper - LUTE
Singer Lena - HORNE
Singer Lennon - JOHN
Singer Lennox - ANNIE
Singer Lenya - LOTTE
Singer Leo - SAYER
Singer Leon - REDBONE
Singer Leontyne - PRICE
Singer Leslie - GORE
Singer Lila - MCCANN
Singer Lili - PONS
Singer Linda - EDER
Singer Lisa - LOEB
Singer Loaf - MEAT
Singer Loeb - LISA
Singer Loggins - KENNY

Singer Lola - FALANA
Singer Lonnie - MACK
Singer Lopez - TRINI
Singer Lotta - LENYA
Singer Louis - PRIMA
Singer Lovato - DEMI
Singer Love - COURTNEY
Singer Lovett - LYLE
Singer Lovich - LENE
Singer Luft - LORNA
Singer Lyle - LOVETT
Singer Lynn - LORETTA
　　or VERA
Singer Mabel - MERCER
Singer Mahal - TAJ
Singer Makeba - MIRIAM
Singer Manfred - MAN
Singer Mann - AIMEE
Singer Manson - SHIRLEY
Singer Margaret -
　　LEANN RIMES
Singer Maria - MCKEE
Singer Marie - TEENA
Singer Marilyn - MCCOO
Singer Mario - WINANS
Singer Martha - REEVES
Singer Martina - MCBRIDE
Singer Marvin - GAYE
Singer Martin - DEAN
　　or RICKY
Singer Masor - MILA
Singer Mathews - DAVE

Singer Mayfield - CURTIS

Singer McBride - MARTINA

Singer McCann – LES or LILA

Singer McCoy - NEAL

Singer McEntire - REBA

Singer McGraw - TIM

Singer McLachlan - SARAH

Singer McPhatter - CLYDE

Singer Mel - TILLIS

Singer Melba - MOORE

Singer Mercer - MABEL

Singer Merchant - NATALIE

Singer Mercury - FREDDIE

Singer Merman - ETHEL

Singer Michael - STIPE

Singer Midler - BETTE

Singer Mills - ERIE

Siinger Minaj - NICKI

Singer Minoque - KYLIE

Singer Miriam - MAKEBA

Singer Misalucha - LANI

Singer Mitchell - JONI

Singer Moffo - ANNA

Singer Moore - MELBA

Singer Morgan - LORRIE

Singer Morgana - KING

Singer Morissette - ALANIS

Singer Morrison - JIM or VAN

Singer Morse - ELLAMAE

Singer Mouskouri - NANA

Singer Murray - ANNE

Singer Nancy - AMES

Singer Naomi - JUDD

Singer Neil - SEDAKA

Singer Nelly - Melba

Singer Nelson - RICKEY

Singer Neville - AARON

Singer Micki - MINAJ

Singer Nicks - STEVIE

Singer Nightingale - MAXINE

Singer Nina - SIMONE

Singer Nixon - MARNI

Singer Norah or
    Normah - JONES

Singer Norman - JESSYE

Singer Nova - ALDO

Singer Nyro - LAURA

Singer Ocasek - RIC

Singer Ochs - PHIL

Singer O'Connor - SINEAD

Singer O'Day - ANITA

Singer Oleda - ADAMS

Singer Ono - YOKO

Singer Orbison - ROY

Singer Orton - BETH

Singer Osmond - MARIE

Singer Paisley - BRAD

Singer Palmer - ROBERT

Singer Pat - BOONE

Singer Patti - ADELINA,
    LABELLE or SMITH

Singer Patty - LARKINS

Singer Paul - SIMON

Singer Paula - ABDUL or COLE

Singer Payne - FREDA

Singer Peeples - NEA

Singer Peerce - JAN

Singer Percy - SLEDGE

Singer Perkins - CARL

Singer Perry - COMO or KATY

Singer Peter - TOSH

Singer Phil - OCHS

Singer Pia - ZADORA

Singer Piaf - EDITH

Singer Pinza - EZIO

Singer Pitney - GENA

Singer Pop - IGGY

Singer Priest - MAXI

Singer Quatro - SUZI

Singer Rabbitt - EDDIE

Singer Randy - OWEN, TRAVIS or TRITT

Singer Raven - EDDY

Singer Rawls - LOU

Singer Ray - EBERLE or STEVENS

Singer Redbone - LEON

Singer Redding - OTIS

Singer Reed - LOU

Singer Reeves - DEL

Singer Renata - SCOTTO

Singer Rezner - TRENT

Singer Richie - LIONEL or VALENS

Singer Rick - ASTLEY or DEES

Singer Ricky - SKAGGS

Singer Rigby - ELEANOR

Singer Rimes - LEANN

Singer Ritter - TEX

Singer Robbins - MARTY

Singer Robin - THICKE

Singer Rod - STEWART

Singer Rogers - KENNY

Singer Ronan - TYNAN

Singer Ronnie - MILSAP

Singer Ronstadt - LINDA

Singer Ross - DIANA

Singer Roy - ACUFF

Singer Rudgren - TODD

Singer Ruiz - REY

Singer Russell - LEON

Singer Ruth - ETTING

Singer Selena - PEREZ

Singer Salonga - LEA

Singer Sam - COOKE

Singer Samantha - SANG

Singer Sammy - HAGAR

Singer Sayer - LEO

Singer Scaggs - BOZ

Singer Schifrin - LALO

Singer Schipa - TITO

Singer Seeger - PETE

Singer Shania - TWAIN

Singer Shannon - DEL

Singer Sharp - DEEDEE

Singer Sheena - EASTON

Singer Shelby - LYNNE

Singer Sherry - NENEH

Singer Sheryl - CROW

Singer Shirley - BASSY

Singer Simms - GINNY

Singer Simon - CARLEY, ESTES or PAUL

Singer Simone - NINA

Singer Simpson - ASHLEE

Singer Skinnay - ENNIS

Singer Sledge - PERCY

Singer Small - MILLIE

Singer Smith - BESSIE or KATE

Singer Snider - DEE

Singer Snow - PHOEBE

Singer Sommer - DONNA

Singer Spector - RONNIE

Singer Springfield - DUSTY or RICK

Singer Staples - MAVIS

Singer Stefani - GWENN

Simger Stevie - NICKS

Singer Stranfield - LISA

Singer Starr - IRWIN or KAY

Singer Steve - EARLE

Singer Stevens - CAT, CONNIE, RISE or DODIE

Singer Stevie - NICKS

Singer Stewart - ROD

Singer Stratas - TERESA

Singer Stritch - ELAINE

Singer Stuarti - ENZO

Singer Stubbs - LEVI

Singer Sumac - YMA

Singer Susan - BOYLE

Singer Susanne - VEGA

Singer Sylvia - SYMS

Singer Taylor - DAYNE, KOKO or SWIFT

Singer Tebaldi - RENATA

Singer Tennille - TONI

Singer Terrell - TAMMI

Singer Thomas - IRMA or ROB

Singer Tillis - MEL or PAM

Singer Tim - MCGRAW

Singer Tom - JONES or WAITS

Singer Tommy - ROE

Singer Tori - AMOS

Singer Torme - MEL

Singer Travis - MERLE, RANDY or TRITT

Singer Trisha - YEARWOOD

Singer Tritt - TRAVIS

Singer Tucker - TANYA

Singer Twain - SHANIA

Singer Ulvaeus - BJORN

Singer Vallee - RUDY

Singer Vandross - LUTHER

Singer Vannelli - GINO

Singer Vanilla - ICE

Singer Vega - SUZANNE

Singer Vic - DAMONE or DANA

Singer Vickers - JON
Singer Waits - TOM
Singer Walter - EGAN
Singer Warren - EVON
Singer Warwick - DIONNE
Singer Washington - DINAH
Singer Watley - JODY
Singer Waters - ETHEL
Singer Wayne - NEWTON
Singer Webster - Katie
Singer West - DOTTIE
    or SHELLY
Singer Whitman - SLIM
Singer Williams - ANDY, DAR,
    DENIECE or HANK
Singer Winans - CECE
Singer Winehouse - AMY
Singer Womack - LEEANN
Singer Wooley - SHEB
Singer Yearwood - TRISHA
Singer Young - ACE or NEIL
Singer Yma - SUMAC
Singer Zayn - MALIK
Singing satiriest Tom - LEHRER
Sister-in-law of
    Prometheus - PANDORA
Sir Laurence - OLIVIER
Sitarist Shankar - RAVI
Skateboarder Hawk - TONY
Skater Alois - LUTZ
Skater _____Anton
    Ohno - APOLO

Skater Asada - MAO
Skater Babilonia - TAI
Skater Baiul - OKSANA
Skater Berezhnaya - ELENA
Skater Boitano - BRIAN
Skater Bonnie - BLAIR
Skater Brian - ORSER
Skater Button - DICK
Skater Carol - HEISS
Skater Chris - WITTY
Skater Cohen - SASHA
Skater Cranston - TOLLER
Skater Dan - JENSEN
Skater Eldridge - TODD
Skater Grinkov - SERGEI
Skater Hamilton - SCOTT
Skater Harding - TANYA
Skater Heiden - ERIC
Skater Henie - SONJA
Skater Hughes - SARAH
Skater Inoue - RENA
Skater Janet - LYNN
Skater
    Johann_____Koss - OLAV
Skater Karen - ENKE
Skater Katarina - WITT
Skater Kulik - ILIA
Skater Limpinski - TARA
Skater Mao - ASADA
Skater Michelle - KWAN
Skater Midori - ITO

Skater Nobun - ODA

Skater Oksana - BAIUL

Skater Ohno - APOLO

Skater Parra - DEREK

Skater Paulson - AXEL

Skater Protopopov - OLEG

Skater Rodnina - IRINI

Skater Sasha - COHEN

Skater Slutskaya - IRINA

Skater Sokolova - ELENA

Skater Sonjja - HENIE

Skater Starbuck - JOJO

Skater Stojko - ELVIS

Skater Thomas - DEBI

Skater Tiffany - CHIN

Skater Toller - CRANSTON

Skater Torvill - JAYNE

Skater Uzova - MAIA

Skater Valova - ELENA

Skater Witt - KATARINA

Skater Yagudin - ALEXEI

Skater Yamaguchi - KRISTI

Skater Young - SHEILA

Skater Zayak - ELAINE

Skating great Henie - SONJA

Skating metalist
      Flemming - PEGGY

Skier Alberto - TOMBA

Skier Girardelli - MARC

Skier Hermann - MAIER

Skier Maentyranta - EERO

Skier McKinney - TAMARA

Skier Miller - BODE

Skier Phil - MAHRE

Skier Skaadal - ATLE

Skier Tommy - MOE

Sleuth Vance - PHILO

Slugger Canseco - JOSE

Slugger Griffey Jr. - KEN

Slugger Hillenbrand - SHEA

Slugger Killebrew - HARMON

Soccer great Rossi - PAOLO

Soccer player Fernando - ACRE

Soccer star Brandi - CHASTAIN

Soccer star Hamm - MIA

Soccer star Michelle - AKERS

Socialite Maxwell - ELSA

Socialite Mesta - PERLE

Socialite Peggy - EATON

Sociologist Durkheim - EMILE

Sociologist Max - WEBER

Songbird McEntire - REBA

Songstress Laine - CLEO

Songstress McLachlan - SARAH

Songwriter Arlen - HAROLD

Song writer Bacharat - BURT

Song writer Bayer
      Sager - CAROLE

Song writer Blake - EUBIE

Song writer Chris - REA

Song writer Davis - ALANA

Song writer Farrell - WES

Song writer Frank - LOESSER

Song writer Green - CEELO

Song writer Greenwich - ELLIE

Song writer Harold -
ARLEN or ROME

Song writer Hart - LORENZ

Song writer Jaques - BREL

Song writer Jerome - KERN

Song writer Jimmy - WEBB

Song writer Kahn - GUS

Song writer Keys - ALICIA

Song writer Laura - NYRO

Song writer Leonard - COHEN

Song writer Milton - AGER

Song writer Mitchell - JONI

Song writer Newman - RANDY

Songwriter Orton - BETH

Song writer Paul - SIMON

Song write Phair - LIZ

Song writer Porter - COLE

Song writer Raymond - EGAN

Song writer Reed - LOU

Song writer Robin - LEO

Song writer Rogers - JIMMIE

Song writer Silverstein - SHEL

Song writer
Sondheim - STEPHEN

Song writer Taupin - BERNIE

Song writer Tom - LEHRER

Song writer Wilder - ALEX

Sophia of films - LOREN

Soprano Adelina - PATTI

Soprano Anna - MOFFO

Soprano Auger – ARLEE

Soprano Benzell - MIMI

Soprano Berger - ERNA

Soprano Birgit - NILSSON

Soprano Callas - MARIA

Soprano Calne - EMMA

Soprano Dale - CLAMMA

Soprano Della Casa - LISA

Soprano Emma - CALVE
or EAMES

Soprano Farrell - EILEEN

Soprano Flagstad - KIRSTEN

Soprano Fleming - RENEE

Soprano Frances - ALDA

Soprano Geraldine - FARRAR

Soprano Gluck - ALMA

Soprano Grist - RERI

Soprano Jenny - LIND

Soprano Kirsten - FLAGSTAD

Soprano Lear - EVELYN

Soprano Lehmann - LILLE
or LOTTE

Soprano Lily - PONS

Soprano Lucine - AMARA

Soprano Lucrezia - BORI

Soprano Marilyn - HORNE

Soprano Marton - EVA

Soprano Melba - Nellie

Soprano Mills - ERIE

Soprano Mitchell - LEONA

Soprano Moffo - ANNA

Soprano Nilsson - Birgit

Soprano Norma - JESSYE

Soprano Petina - IRRA

Soprano Ponselle - ROSA

Soprano Price - LEONTYNE

Soprano Scotto - RENATA

Soprano Tebaldi - RENATA

Soprano Tekanawa - KIRI

Soprano Tetrazzini - LUISA

Soprano Troyanos - TATIANA

Soprano Upshaw - DAWN

Soul singer Adams - OLETA

Southern of Hollywood - ANN

Spanish artist Salvador - DALI

Speaker of baseball - TRIS

Speed-skater Gustavson - SVEN

Spice girl Halliwell - GERI

Sportscaster Albert - MARV

Sportscaster Allen - MEL

Sportscaster Berman - LEN

Sportscaster Bob - LEY

Sportscaster Burk - DORIS

Sportscaster Cross - IRV

Sportscaster Dick - ENDBERG
   or VITALE

Sportscaster Hannah -
   AMES or STORM

Sportscaster Howard - COSELL

Sportscaster Jim - MCKAY
   or NANCE

Sportscaster McCarver - TIM

Sportscaster
   Musburger - BRENT

Sportscaster Rashad - AHMAD

Sportsctaster Rich - EISEN

Sportscaster Scully - VIN

Sprinter Deevers - GAIL

Statesman Salinger - PIERRE

Statesman Thurmond - STROM

Stimpy's pal - REN

Stoic philosopher - CATO

Stravinski - IGOR

Sufragist Bloomer - AMELIA

Sufragist Carrie
   Chapman - CATT

Sufragist Stone - LUCY

Supermodel Banks - TYRA

Supermodel Bundchen - GIZELE

Supermodel Campbell - NAOMI

Supermodel Carangi - GIA

Supermodel Carol - ALT

Supermodel Carre - OTIS

Supermodel Cheryl - TIEGS

Supermodeel Elsa - BENITEZ

Supermodel Evangelista - LINDA

Supermodel Heatherton - ERIN

Supermodel Heidi - KLUM

Supermodel Moss - KATE

Supermodel Sastre - INES

Supermodel Schiffer - CLAUDIA

Supermodel Taylor - NIKI

Supermodel Veronica - WEBB
Supermodel Wek - ALEK
Surrealist Joan - MIRO
Surrealist Magritte - RENE
Surrealist Max - ERNST
Surrealist Tanguy - YVES
Surveyor Elmo - ROPER
Surveyor Jeremiah - DIXON
Suzanne of TV - SOMERS
Swedish actress Anderson - BIBI
Swimmer Bionde - MATT
Swimmer Debbie - MEYER
Swimmer Diana - NYAD
Swimmer Eleanor - HOLM
Swimmer Evans - JANET
Swimmer Gertrude - EDERLE
Swimmer Janet - EVANS
Swimmer Kristin - OTTO
Swimmer Thorp - IAN
Swimmer Tom - DOLAN
Swimmer Torres - DARA
Swimmer Vicki - KEITH
Swiss mathematician
    Leonhart - EULER
Swiss painter Klee - PAUL
Syngman of Seoul - RHEE
Tanner of tennis - ROSCOE
Tarkenton - FRAN
Telejournalist Roberts - COKIE
Television's Gibbons - LEEZA
Tennis ace Rafael - NADAL

Tennis Champ Fred - STOLLE
Tennis Champ
    Mandlikova - HANA
Tennis Champ Maria - BUENO
Tennis Champ -
    Roddick - ANDY
Tennis coach Tiriac - ION
Tennis great Arthur - ASHE
Tennis great Chris - EVERT
Tennis great
    Gonzolez - PANCHO
Tennis great Keith - EMERSON
Tennis great Marble - ALICE
Tennis great Marie - BUENO
Tennis great Monica - SELES
Tennis player Agassi - ANDRE
Tennis player Andy - RODDICK
Tennis player Becker - BORIS
Tennis player
    Capriati - JENNIFER
Tennis player Chandra - RUBIN
Tennis player
    Coetzer - AMANDA
Tennis player Edberg - STEFAN
Tennis player Emmerson - ROY
Tennis player Fraser - NEALE
Tennis player
    Goolagong - EVONNE
Tennis player
    Gustavo - KUERTEN
Tennis player
    Hingus - MARTINA

Tennis player Hoad - LEW
Tennis player Huber - ANKE
Tennis player Ian - AYRE
Tennis player Irina - SPIRLEA
Tennis player Ivanavic - ANA
Tennis player Korda - PETR
Tennis player
    Kournikova - ANNA
Tennis player
    Krickstein - AARON
Tennis player LaCosta - RENE
Tennis player Lew - HOAD
Tennis player
    Likhovtsevva - HELENA
Tennis player
    Makarova - ELENA
Tennis player
    Mandlikova - HANA
Tennis player Martina - HINGIS
Tennis player Nadal - RAFAEL
Tennis player Nastase - ILIE
Tennis player
    Oudin - MELANIE
Tennis player Ramirez - RAUL
Tennis player Roddick - ANDY
Tennis player Roscoe - TANNER
Tennis player Rosewall - KEN
Tennis player Rosie - CASALS
Tennis player Safin - MARAT
Tennis player Shriver - PAM
Tennis player Smith - STAN
Tennis player Sukova - HELENA

Tennis player Tilden - BILL
Tennis player Tiriac - ION
Tennis player Virginia - WADE
Tennis player
    Wawarinka - STAN
Tennis player Wilander - MATS
Tennis player Williams -
    SERENA or VENUS
Tennis player Yannick - NOAH
Tennis pro Dementieva - ELENA
Tennis pro Roddick - ANDY
Tennis star Corda - PETR
Tennis star Fraser - NEALE
Tennis star Garrison - ZINA
Tennis star Gerulaitis - VITAS
Tennis star Gibson - ALTHEA
Tennis star Gussie - MORAN
Tennis star Huber - ANKE
Tennis star Ilie - NASTASE
Tennis star Ivanovic - ANA
Tennis star Kournikova - ANNA
Tennis star Lendl - IVAN
Tennis star Marcelo - RIOS
Tennis star Michael - CHANG
Tennis star Novotna - JANA
Tennis star Pam - SHRIVER
Tennis star Poncho - SEGURA
Tennis star Ramirez - RAUL
Tennis star Sampras - PETE
Tennis star Sharapova - MARIA
Tennis star Stefan - EDBERG

Tennis star Tanner - ROSCOE

Tennis star Tommy - HAAS

Tennis star
ZVEREVA - NATASHA

Tennis winner Rafael - OSUNA

Tenor Andrea - BOCELLI

Tenor Bocelli - ANDREA

Tenor Carreras - JOSE

Tenor Caruso - ENRICO

Tenor Domingo - PLACIDO

Tenor Gigli - BENIAMINO

Tenor Mario - LANZA

Tenor Pavarotti - LUCIANO

Tenor Peter - PEARS

Test pilot Chuck - YEAGER

Theologian Charles - HODGE

Theologian John - WESLEY

Theologian Kiergaard - SOREN

Theologian Martin - DIBELIUS
or LUTHER

Theologian Thomas - AQUINAS

Thermos inventor
James - DEWAR

Thomas or Herbie - MANN

Tiger great McLain - DENNY

Tony winner Diana - RIGG

Tony winner Huffman - CADY

Tony winnner Judith - IVEY

Tony winner Lane - NATHAN

Tony winner Salongna - LEA

Track legend Moses - EDWIN

Track star Devers - GAIL

Track star - Wyomia - TYUS

Trumpeter Baker - CHET

Trumpeter
Chuck - MANGIONE

Trumpeter
Marsalis - WYNTON

Trumpeter Miles - DAVIS

Trumpeter Red - ALLEN

Trumpeter Williams - COOTIE

Turkish statesman - INONU

Turner of Hollywood - LANA

Turner of song - TINA

Turner or Koppel - TED

Tushingham or Moreno - RITA

TV actor Gulaher - CLU

TV actor Reiser - PAUL

TV actress Cassie - YATES

TV actress Plumb - EVE

TV anchor Newman - EDWIN

TV anchorman
Peter - JENNINGS

TV anchorman Roger - MUDD

TV's Degeneres - ELLEN

TV host Gibbons - LEEZA

TV host Hugh - DOWNES

TV host John - TESH

TV host Matt - LAUER

TV newswoman
Elizabeth - VARGAS

TV producer Arlege - ROONE

TV reporter Van
Susteren - GRETA

Tyson - MIKE

Uncle Miltie - BERLE

University founder
Cornel - EZRA

Uriah - HEEP

U.S. Attorney General
Janet - RENO

U.S. open champ
Curtis - STRANGE

Van Gogh's brother - THEO

Vanna of TV - WHITE

Vaudeville entertainer
Bayes - NORA

Ventriloquist Bergen - EDGAR

Ventriloquist Lewis - SHARI

Verdugo of TV - ELENA

Verne's Fogg - PHILEAS

Vibraphonist
Hampton - LIONEL

Violin maker Amati -
ANDREA or NICOLO

Violinist Bull - OLE

Violinist Camilla - URSO

Violinist Elman - MISCHA

Violinist Francescatti - ZINO

Violinist Georges - ENESCO

Violinist Heifetz - JASCHA

Violinist Isaac - STERN

Violinist Itzhak - PERLMAN

Violinist
Jean_____Ponty - LUC

Violinist Kafanian - IDA

Violinist Kavafian - ANI

Violinist Kreisler - FRITZ

Violinist Leopold - AUER

Violinist Menuhin - YEHUDI

Violinist Milstein - NATHAN

Violinist Mischa - AUER
or ELMAN

Violinist Niccolo - PAGANINI

Violinist Oistrakh - IGOR

Violinist Pearlman - ITZHAK

Violinist Ruggiero - RICCI

Violinist Stern - ISAAC

Violinist Zimbalist - EFRAM

Violinist
Zuckerman - PINCHAS

Violin maker Nicolo - AMATI

Virologist Albert - SABIN

Vocalist Vaughan - SARAH

Wallace - MIKE

Watercolorist_____Liu - LENA

Weatherman Willard - SCOTT

Webster or Wyle - NOAH

Welles or Bean - ORSON

Welsh poet Thomas - DYLAN

West or Murray - MAE

Whitlinger of tennis - TAMI

Whodunit's Gardner - ERLE

Williams of tennis - SERENA

Wimbleton champ
Fraser - NEALE

Wimbleton champ
Gibson - ATHEA

Wimbleton champ
  Goolagong - EVONNE
Wimbleton winner
  Novotna - JANA
Wonder of music - STEVIE
Writer Adams - CECIL
Writer Aleichem - SHOLOM
Writer Allende - ISABEL
Writer Almed - SALMAN
  RUSHDIE
Writer Alther - LISA
Writer Ambler - ERIC
Writer Andric - IVO
Writer Angelou - MAYA
Writer Ann or Elmer -
  RICE or TYLER
Writer Arch - OBOLER
Writer Arthur - KOESTLER
Writer Asais - TEGNER
Writer Ashworth - ADELE
Writer Asimov - ISAAC
Writer Babel - ISAAC
Writer Barker - CLIVE
Writer Beattie - ANN
Writer Bellows - SAUL
Writer Best - EDNA
Writer Betti - UGO
Writer Bierce - AMBROSE
Writer Biggers - EARL DERR
Writer Binchy - MAEVE
Writer Blyton - ENID
Writer Bochco - STEVEN

Writer Borges - JORGE
Writer Bova - BEN
Writer Bradbury - RAY
Writer Braun - LILLIAN
Writer Bret - HARTE
Write Brown - DAN
Writer Bruckner - ANITA
Writer Buchanan - EDNA
Writer Buntline - NED
Writer Burrow - ABE
Writer Buscaglia - LEO
Writer Caldwell - ERSKINE
Writer Calvino - ITALO
Writer Canetti - ELIAS
Writer Capek - KAREL
Writer Carl - SAGEN
Writer Carroll - LEWIS
Writer Cendrars - BLAISE
Writer Chaim - POTOK
Writer Chekhov - ANTON
Writer Chomsky - NOAM
Writer Christie - AGATHA
Writer Claude - ANET
Writer Cleaver - ELDRIDGE
Writer Cleveland - AMORY
Writer Cocteau - JEAN
Writer Connell - EVAN
Writer Conrad - AIKEN
Writer Conroy - PAT
Writer Cornwell - PATRICIA
Writer Cynthia - OZICK

Writer Dahl - ROALD

Writer Damon - RUNYON

Writer Daniel - DEFOE

Writer Danielle - STEELE

Writer David - GROSSMAN
   or MAMET

Writer de Balzac - HONORE

Writer de Beauvoir - SIMONE

Writer de la Roche - MAZO

Writer Defoe - DANIEL

Writer Deighton - LEN

Writer Derr Biggers - EARL

Writer Dinesen - ISAK

Writer Dominick - DUNNE

Writer Dorothea - SAYERS

Writer Dostoevsky - FYODOR

Writer Drummond - IVOR

Writer Drury - ALLEN

Writer du Maurier - DAPHNE

Writer Dunn- OLAV

Writer Elaine - MAY

Writer Ellison - HARLAN

Writer Elmer - RICE

Writer Ephron - DELIA
   or NORA

Writer Erik - POHL

Writer Eugene - FODOR

Writer Fallaci - ORIANA

Writer Fannie - HURST

Writer Felix - ADLER

Writer Ferber - EDNA

Writer Gerritsen - TESS

Writer Kierkegaard - SOREN

Writer Fleming - IAN

Writer Follett - KEN

Writer France - ANATOLE

Writer Francoise - SEGAN

Writer Frederico
   Garcia - LORCA

Writer Frederik - POHL

Writer Gardner - ERLE

Writer Gallant - MAVIS

Writer George - ADE or PERAC

Writer Georgette - HEYER

Writer Germaine - GREER

Writer Gerritsen - TESS

Writer Gertrude - STEIN

Writer Gide ANDRE

Writer Gilbert - ADAIR

Writer Gogol - NIKOLAI

Writer Gordiner - NADINE

Write Grafton - SUE

Write Grey - ZANE

Writer H. H. - MUNRO (SAKI)

Writer H. L. - MRNCKEN

Write Hamsum - KNUT

Writer Hannah - ARENDT

Writer Harte - BRE

Writer Helen - BEATRIX
   POTTER

Writer Heinrich - HEINE

Writer Henley - BETH

Writer Henry - ROTH

Writer Hentoff - NAT

Writer Hilaire - ELLOC

Writer Hobson - LAURA

Writer Hoffer - ERIC

Writer Hubbard - LRON

Writer Huffington - ARIANNA

Writer Hughes - LANGSTON

Writer Hunter - EVAN

Writer Huxley - ALDOUS

Writer Huxtable - ADA

Writer Irwin - SHAW

Writer Isaac - ASIMOV

Writer Ishmael - REED

Writer Ivan - BUNIN

Writer Jack - ABBOTT

Writer Jacob - RIIS

Writer James - AGEE

Writer Janowitz - TAMA

Write Jeph - LOEB

Writer Joe - HAN

Writer John
     DICKENSON - CARR

Writer John Le - CARRE

Writer Jones - LEROI

Writer Josephine - TEY

Write Joyce Carol - OATES

Writer Kathleen - NORRIS

Writer Kerouac - Jack

Writer Kesey - KEN

Writer Kierkegaard - SOREN

Writer Kilmer - JOYCE

Writer Kingsley - AMIS

Write Klima - IVAN

Writer Kureishi - HANIF

Writer Lardner - RING

Writer Lathem - EMMA

Writer Laura - NYRO

Writer Laurie - ALISON

Writer Lebowitz - FRAN

Writer Lee Masters - EDGAR

Writer Leo - ROSTEN

Writer Leonard - COHEN

Writer LeSage - ALAIN

Writer Leshan - EDA

Writer Leslie - EGAN

Writer LeGuin - URSALA

Writer Leshan - EDA

Writer Levin - IRA

Writer Lindbergh - ANNE

Writer Lofts - NORAH

Writer Lola - MONTEZ

Writer Lowell - AMY

Writer Ludwig - EMIL

Writer Madame de - STAEL

Writer Madeleine
     L'_____ - ENGEL

Writer Maksirr - GORKI

Writer
     Mansfield - KATHERINE

Writer Marcel - PROUST

Writer March - NGAIO

Writer _____Maria
    Remarque - ERICH

Writer Mario Vargas - LLOSA

Writer Marsh - NGAIO

Writer Martin - AMIS

Writer Marx - KARL

Writer Maurice - SENDAK

Writer Max - BEERBOHM

Writer Maxim - GORKI

Writer McEwan - IAN

Writer Monroe - ALICE

Writer Montagu - ASHLEY

Writer Moravia - ALBERTO

Writer Morrison - TONI

Writer Mumford - THAD

Writer Murdock - IRIS

Writer_____Neale
    Hurston - ZORA

Writer Nevada - BARR

Writer Ngao - MARSH

Writer Nicholas - ROWE

Writer Nikolai - GOGOL

Writer Nora - EPHROM

Writer Norman - MAILER

Writer Novello - IVOR

Writer Oates - JOYCE CAROL

Writer O'Brien - EDNA

Writer O'Casey - SEAN

Writer Octavio - PAZ

Writer O'Faolain - SEAN

Writer O'Flaherty - LIAM

Writer Oscar - WILDE

Writer Oz - AMOS

Writer P. J. - PROURKE

Writer Paresky - SARA

Writer Pascal - BLAISE

Writer Paten - ALAN

Writer Peggy - NOONAN

Writer Pera - PIA

Writer Peters - ELLIS

Writer Philip - ROTH
    or WHALEN

Writer Phillpotts - EDEN

Writer Pierre - LOTI

Writer Plath - SYLVIA

Writer Pollitt - KATHA

Writer Primo - LEVI

Writer Proust - MARCEL

Writer Quindlen - ANNA

Writer Rand - AYN

Writer Raymond - CHANDLER

Writer Rendell - RUTH

Writer Rita_____Brown - MAE

Writer Roald - DAHL

Writer Robb - INEZ

Writer Robert - CRAIS

Writer Roberts - NORA

Writer Robertson - DAVIES

Writer Robinson - EDEN
    or SPIDER

Writer Rogers StJohns - ADELA

Writer Rohmer - SAX

Writer Rolland - ROMAIN

Writer Rombauer - IRMA

Writer Rosten - LEO

Writer Roth - PHILIP

Writer Rule - ANN

Writer Runyan - DAMON

Writer Sackville West - VITA

Writer Sagan - CARL

Writer Samuel - DASHIELL HAMMETT

Writer Santha Rama - RAU

Writer

    Sarah_____Jewett - ORNE

Writer Saroyan - ARAM

Writer Schoemperien - DIANE

Writer Segal - ERICH

Writer Seton - ANYA

Writer Sewell - ANNA

Writer Sexton - ANNE

Writer Shaw - IRWIN

Writer Sheehan - NEIL

Writer Shelley - MARY

Writer Shere - HITE

Writer Sholem - ASCH

Writer Shreve - ANITA

Writer Shute - NEVIL

Write Sidney – SHELDON

Writer Sillitoe - ALAN

Writer Silverstein - SHEL

Writer Sinclair - LEWIS
    or UPTON

Writer Sir Richard - STEELE

Writer Solzhenitsyn -
    ALEKSANDR

Writer Sontag - SUSAN

Writer St. Johns - ADELA

Writer Steel - DANIELLE

Writer Stout - REX

Write Susan - SONTAG

Writer Syner - OMARR

Writer Talese - GAY

Writer Tami - HOAG

Writer Tarbell - IDA

Writer Terkel - STUDS

Writer Tertz - ABRAM

Writer Thomas - PAINE

Writer Toffler - ALVIN

Writer Tom - CLANCY
    or WOLFF

Writer Trilling - LIONEL

Writer Turgenev - IVAN

Writer Turkel - STUDS

Writer Tyler - ANNE

Writer Umberto - ECO

Writer Uris - LEON

Writer Victor - HUGO

Writer Vittorini - ELIO

Writer Vonnegut - KURT

Writer Wallace - LEW

Writer Walton - IZAAC

Writer Waugh - ALEC
    or EVELYN

Writer Welty - EUDORA

Writer Wharton - EDITH

Writer Wiesel - ELIE

Writer Wilder - LAURA
    INGALLS

Writer Wilhelm - KATE

Writer William - INGE

Writer Willy - LEY

Writer Wister - LOESS
    or OWEN

Writer Yutang - LIN

Writer Zimmer
    Bradley - MARION

Writer Zora _____Hurston -
    NEALE

Whodunit writer
    Gardner - ERLE

Wimbleton champ
    Gibson - ATHEA

Wimbleton champ
    Goolagong - EVONNE

Wimbleton winner
    Novotna - JANA

Wrestler Flair - RIC

Yachtsman Dennis - CONNOR

Yeats - WILLIAM BUTLE

Yeltsin - BORIS

Zedong - MAO

Zola - EMILE

Zora_____Huston - NEALE

PUZZLERS

Erik Agard

Anne Allison

Alan Arbesfeld

Martin Ashwood-Smith

Richard Auer

Carla Azur

Joeseph Baumgartner

Jorge Beche

Jerry Berns

Patrick Berry

Patrick Blindauer

Bill Bob

Cory Bowers

Agnes Brown

Tim Burr

Jeff Chen

Tom Cobb

Adam Cohen

Alex Cole

Lucia Cole

Gary Cooper

Kay Daniels

Hank Dellman

Ruby Deswit

Carlin Dewars

Robert A Doll

Kay Drummond

Emery K. Duncan

Dennis D Dwight

Jonathan Dwyer

Karin Easterly

Jerry Edelstein

James Q. Ellis

Lucille Everstone

Harvey Estes

Lewis Forte

Richard H Frankland

Nellie G. Giles

Gia Gilroy

Alice Goodwin

Gail Grabowski

Kimberly Grant

Mitchell G. Grant

Joseph Groa

Henry Guarters

Norm Guttenbiller

Lester Hamm

Frank R Hammond

Jeffery Harris

Randal J. Hartman

Lewis Harper

Jordan Haversham

Jude Henry

Ritchie Hearne

Wesley Holeman

PeterM. Hollins

Kenneth Holt

Ronald D. Jefferson

Mary Jersey

Patrick Jordan

Marie Judy

Gia Kilroy

Bob Klahn

Della Knightley

Theodore Lansing

Rob Lee

Lynn Lempel

Donna S. Levin

Ian Livengood

Morgan Luck

Joseph Mantell

Todd McClary

Patrick McConville

McVann & Fleming

Joel T Meyers

Miles. Mitchum

Stanley Newman

Rich Norris

Mike Nothnagel

Tony Orbach

Michael Palmer

Timothy Parker

Jill Pepper

Doug Peterson

Fred Piscop

George Pompey

Paul J Preminger

Oscar Puma

Henry Quarters

Meerle Reagle

Margorie Richter

Philip C Riley

Ella G. Rose

Randoph Ross

David Steinberg

Hank Tellman

Ben Tusig

George N Vandy

Patti Varol

Bruce Venzke

Alice Walker

Judith K. Walker

Jeffrey Wechsler

Peter Wentz

Brad Wilber

Leonard Williams

Norman Wize

Candice Wolf

PHUNNY PHASES

Ab_____ - OVO

_____Ababa - ADDIS

ABU_____ - DHABI

_____accompli - FAIT

_____acid - IODIC or PICRIC

_____acte - ENTR

Ad_____per aspera - ASTRA

Addis_____ - ABABA

Adrien_____ - ARPEL

_____Adronicus - TITUS

Affaire de - COEUR

Aglior_____- OLIO

Agni_____ - DEVA

"Agnus_____" - DEI

_____Alamitos - LOS

_____Alba - TERRA

_____Alcohol - METHYL

_____Alegre - PORTO

Allegro_____ASSAI

_____Alighieri - DANTE

Alla_____ - BREVE
    or ROMAN

_____Alla scala - TEATRO

Allegro_____ - ASSAI

Allegro con_____ - BRIO

Allegro non _____ - TROPPO

_____- Aller - PIS

_____Al pomororo- PAPPA

_____Alte - DER

_____Alto - PALO

_____Amatoria - ARS

Amino_____ - ACID

Amious_____ - CURIAE

Amo, Amas, _____-AMAT

_____Amours - ANOS

_____and penates - LARES

_____and
    Principe - SAOTOME

Andria_____- DORIA

_____Andronicus - TITUS

_____Angelico - FRA

_____Anglais - COR

Ankor_____ - WAT

Apres_____- SKI

_____Apso - LHASA

Aqua_____ - FORRTUS,
    PURA, REGIA or VITAE

Arroz con_____ - POLLO

Ars_____Artis - GRATIS

Ars_____POETICA

Ars_____vita brevis - LONGA

_____Artery - ILIAC

_____Aryan - INDO

_____Asada - CARNE

_____Atque vale - AVE

_____au Haut, Maine - ISLE

_____au lait - CAFE

Au_____ - NATUREL

_____aurhum - BABA

Aurora_____BOREALIS

Auto_____ - DA-FE

_____- Au-vent - VOL

Ave_____Vale - ATQUE

_____Avis - RARA

Avant_____ - GARDE

_____Aviv - TELE

A votre_____ - SANTE

Baba au_____ - RHUM

_____Bagatelle - AMERE

_____Ballerina - PRIMA

Bali_____ - HAI

Ballet_____ - RUSSE

_____-Barr virus - EPSTEIN

Basse_____ - Mer (low tide)

_____Bator - ULAN

_____bean - FAVA

Beau_____ - IDEAL

Beaux_____ - ARTS

_____- beche - TETE

_____Bede - ADAM

Bel_____cheese - PAESE

Bel_____- AMI or CANTO

_____Belli - CASUS

_____bene - NOTA

Beta_____ - CAROTENE

Bete_____ - NOIRE

_____bien - TRES

Billet_____ - DOUX

Biscuit_____ - TORONI

Bitter_____- ALOES

_____Blanc - CHENIN

_____Blanco - OSO

_____Blas - GIL

Bois_____ - DARC

Bon_____ - MOT

_____Bono - CUI

Bono_____ - DEA

_____Borealis - AURORA

Bouquet_____ - GARNI

_____Brava - COSTA

_____breve - ALLA

_____brevis, ars longa - VITA

_____B'rith - BNAI

Broccoli_____ - RABE

_____broche - ALA

Broom_____ - HILDA

Bryn_____ - MAWR

_____Brulee - CREME

_____Bucci - OSSI

_____Buco - OSSO

_____Buena (herb) - YERBA

Buenos_____- DIAS

_____Buffa - OPERA

Buona_____ - NOTTE
    or SERA

Burkina_____ - FASO

Cabo_____Lucas - SAN

Cafe au_____- LAIT

Cafe_____ - NOIR

Calcium_____ - NITRATE

_____Cantata - MISSA

_____Canto - BEL

Card_____ - NOME

Carne_____ - ASADA

Carpe_____ - DIUM

_____Carta - MAGNA

_____carte - ALA

_____cava - VENA

Cave_____ - CANEM

Caveat_____ - EMPTOR

Cedant_____Togae - ARMA

Celeste_____ - AIDA

_____Centari - PROXIMA

_____Central – MASSIF

Cest_____ - AVIE

Chacun a son_____ - GOUT

Chaise_____ - LONGUE

Champs_____ - ELYSEES

_____ - Chandon - MOET

_____chango - PRESTO

_____Chat - PASDE

Chemin de _____- FER

Chennin_____ - BLAC

_____Chi - TAI

Childe_____ - HAROLD

Chili con_____ - CARNE
  or QUESO

Chou en _____ - LAI

_____Choy - BOK

_____Ciria - AMICUS

_____Citato - OPERE

Citta_____vaticano - DEL

Claire de_____ - LUNE

_____Coast - ADELIE

_____- Coburg - Gotha - SAXE

_____ - Cochere - PORTE

_____Codicil - ADDA

Coeur d'_____,id -ALENE

_____coeur - SACRE

Cogito_____sum - ERGO

_____Comic - SERIO

Commedia dell'_____ - ARTE

Comme il_____ - FAUT

Como_____ - ESTA

_____Compos mentis - NON

Concerto_____ - GROSSO

_____concors - HORS

Conde_____ - NAST

_____Contendere - NOLO

Coq au_____- VIN

_____Con dios - VAYA

_____Corda - UNA

_____Cordiale - ENTENTE

Cordon_____ - BLEU

Corgi_____ - WELSH

_____Corner - AMEN

_____corpus - HABEAS

Cosi fan _____ - TUTTE

Cote_____ - DOR

Cote d'_____ - AZUR

Coup d'_____-ETAT or OEIL

_____Creole - ALA

_____Crayon – CONTE

Creme_____ - FRAICHE

_____CRI - DERNIER

Croix de_____ - GUERRE

Cruella de _____ - VIL

_____Cuantos - UNOS

_____culotte - SANS

_____Culpa - MEA

Cum grano_____ - SALIS

_____cum laude - MAGNA

_____Cupid - DAN

_____Curiea - AMICUS

Curriculum_____ - VITAE

Cyma_____ - (molding type) RECTA

Da_____ - CAPO

_____d'alene - COEUR

_____Dahaka - ASI

_____Dame - NOTRE

_____d'Amore - OBOE

_____Dance - ANITRAS

Dar Es_____ - SALAAM

_____d"alene - COEUR

_____d'art - OBJECT

_____d'Athur - MORTE

_____d'azur - COTE

_____Darya - AMU

Das Lied von der_____ - ERDE

_____Dazs - HAAGEN

_____de Balzac - HONORE

De Bene _____ - ESSE

_____de-boeuf - OEIL

_____de camera - SONATA

_____de-camp - AIDE

_____de chose - PEU

_____de coeur - CRI

_____de cologne - EAU or BOIS

_____de combat - HORS

_____de corps - ESPRIT

_____de deux - PAS

_____de escrivir - ERTE

_____Deferens - VAS

_____de foie gras - PATE

_____de Force - TOUR

_____de Fraise - CREME

_____de Frannce - TOUR

_____de Gourmond - REMY

_____de Guerre - CROIX or NOM

_____Dei - AGNUS

_____de javelle - EAU

_____de-lance - FER

_____de la societe - ILES

_____de la paix - RUE

_____Del Corso - VIA

_____Del Este - PUNTA

_____del fuego - TIERRA

_____de - LUXE

_____de malaise - ETAT

De_____ - NOVO

De_____(sumptuous) - LUXE

_____de mayo - CINCO

_____de mer - MAL

_____de parfum - EAU

_____de pascua - ISLA

_____de siege - LETAT

_____de soie - PEAU

_____de toilette - EAU

De_____ - TROP

_____del fuego - TIERRA

_____del sol - COSTA

Depeche_____ - MODE

_____de plume - NOM

Der_____ - ALTE

Dernier_____ - CRI

_____Desperandum - NIL

_____de tourne - DEMI

_____de veau - RIS

_____de vente - ERTE

_____de Viande - GLACE

_____de vivre - JOIE

_____Dhabi - ABU

_____d'honneur - AFFAIRES

_____Diavolo - FRA

_____Dicit - NIHIL

_____Dicta or
    Dictum - OBITER

_____die - SINE

Dies_____- IRAE

_____Diem - CARPE

_____dieu - PRIE

_____di Lammermoor - LUCIA

_____dimittis - NUNC

_____Dinh Diem - NGO

_____Dire - VOIR

_____Disant - SOI

Ditat_____ - DEUS

_____dium - CARPE

_____dixit - IPSE

_____d'oeuves - HORS

_____doble - PASO

Dolce far_____ - NIENTE

_____Dolorosa - VIA

_____Domingo - SANTO

_____Domini - ANNO

Dona_____Pacem - NOBIS

_____donna - PRIMA

_____d'Orsay - QUAI

_____dos aquas - ENTRE

Duchess of _____ - ELBA

_____du Diable - ILE
    or SACRE

_____du jour - CARTE
    or PLAT

_____du lieber - ACH

_____du Salut - ILES

_____du seigneur - DROIT

_____du tout - PAS

_____du Vent - ILES

_____Eberhart - FABER

Ecce_____- HOMO

_____ed euridice - ORFEO

Emerald Point _____ - NAS

_____Emptor - CAVEAT

_____En Lai - CHOU

Enola_____- GAY

_____En Provence - AIX

_____en Rose - LA VIE

_____en scene - MISE

Entr'_____(intermission) - ACTE

Entre_____- NOUS

_____equinox - VERNAL

ESSE_____Percipi - EST

_____-Es-Salaam - DAR

Et_____ - ALII or ESQ

_____Et Laboro - ORA

_____et mon droit - DIEU

_____ex machina - DEUS

Ex_____(one-sided) - PARTE

_____Face (turnabout) - VOLTE

_____Facia - SCIRE

_____facto - IPSO

_____faire - LAISSEZ or SAVOIR

Fait_____ - ACCOMPLI

_____fan tutti - COSI

Fata_____ - MORGANA

_____Fatuus - IGNIS

Faux_____ - PAS

_____Favor - POR

_____Fein - SINN

Femme_____ - FATALE

Feng_____ - SHUI

Festina_____ - LENTE

_____Fide - MALA

_____Fideles - ADESTE

_____Filipinas - ISLAS

Fin De_____ - SIECLE

_____firma - TERRA

_____fixe - IDEE or PRIX

_____Flask - DEWAR

Fleur de _____ - LYS

_____Flow - SCAPA

Fontana de_____ - TREVI

_____Forma - PRO

_____Fortis - AQUA

Fra_____Lippi - LIPPO

_____Franca - LINGUA

_____Francaise - COMEDIE

_____fratres - ORATE

Fruits de_____ - MER

Fur_____ - ELISE

_____ghanuj - BABA

_____Garde - AVANT

_____Garou - LOUP

_____Gatherum - OMNIUM

_____Gatos - LOS

_____Gauche - RIVE

_____generis - SUI

_____Gestae - RES

_____ghanouj - BABA

_____Giorno - BUON

Gloria_____ - PATRI

_____Go Bragh - ERIN

_____Gorda - PUNTA

_____Gorde - OLDUVAI

Graf_____ - SPEE

Grand_____ - CRU

_____gratia artis - ARS

_____gratia - DEI

_____gratias - DUO

_____gravure - ROTO

_____grecque - ALA

Gregorian_____ - CHANT

Gum_____ - ARABIC

_____Guofeng - HUA

Guy de _____ - MAUPASSANT

_____Habilis - HOMO

_____Hashana - ROSH

Haute_____- MONDE

_____Heights - GOLAN

_____homo - ECCE

Hors_____ D'OEUVES

Id_____ - EST

Idee_____ - FIXE

_____impasse - ATAN

_____Incognita - TERRA

_____In Egitto - MOSE

In_____ - ESSE (living)

_____In Horto - URBS

In medias_____ - RES

In_____ - SITU

In_____(completely) - TOTO

In_____ - UTERO

In_____Verites - VINO

In_____ - VIVO

_____Incognita – TERRA

Inter_____- ALIA

Inter_____ - ALIOS

In vino_____VERITAS

_____Ipsa Loquitur - RES

_____Irae - DIES

_____Irish rose - ABIES

Iron_____OXIDE

Itar_____ - TASS

_____Jacet - HIC

_____Jahan - SHAH

Jai_____ - ALAI

Jeanne d'_____ - ARC

Je ne_____quois - SAIS

Johnny_____- REB

_____Jong - MAH

_____judicata - RES

_____Jure - IPSO

Junipero_____ - SERRA

_____Juris - SUI

Kama_____ - SUTRA

Karmann_____ - GHIA

Knight_____ - ERRANT

Kofi_____Annan - ATTA

_____Kogo - JINGU

Kol_____ - NIDRE

_____Kum (desert) - KARA

_____Kwon do - TAE

La Belle_____ - EPOQUE

La_____gauche - RIVE

Lag B'_____ - OMER

La_____Bonita - ISLA

277

_____Lahm - BATU

Laissez_____ - FAIRE

_____Lama - DALAI

_____Lance - FERDA

Land o' - GOSHEN

Lao_____ - TZU

_____la paix - RUE DE

Lapis_____ - LAZULI

_____la-Vallee - MARNE

_____la vie - CEST

_____la vista - HASTA

La_____vita - DOLCE

_____law - SALIC

_____lazuli - LAPIS

Le belle et la_____- BETE

Le_____du Printemps - SACRE

_____Lepton - TAU

_____Lescaut - MANON

Lesages_____Blas - GIL

Lignum_____ - VITAE

_____lily - SEGO

Lingua_____ - FRANCA

_____Lingus - AER

Linzer_____ - TORTE

_____Lisa - MONA

_____Lisboa - NOVA

Livin' la_____Loca - VIDA

Lobster_____Diavolo - FRA

Logum_____ - TENENS

_____L'oeil - TROMPE

_____Longa - ALBA

_____Longa, vita brevis - ARS

_____Longue - CHAISE

_____Lorraine - ALSACE

Los_____Reyes - TRES

_____Luego - HASTA

_____Lumpur - KUALA

Luna_____ - MOTH

_____macabre - DANSE

_____ - Mache - PAPIER

Madam De_____ - STAEL

_____Magica - ARS

Magister_____ - LUD

Magna_____- CARTA

_____Magnon - CRO

Magnum_____ - OPUS

_____Mahal - TAJ

Mai_____ - TAI

Mais_____ - OUI

_____majesty - LESE

_____major - CANIS,
URSA or VIS

Major_____-DOMO

_____Mal - PETIT

Mal de_____- MER or TETE

_____Malvinas - ISLAS

Mao_____tung - TSE

_____Marbles - ELGIN

Mardi _____- GRAS

_____Martin - ASTON

_____Masque - BAL

_____Massif- VINSON

Mata_____ - HARI

_____mate - YERBA

_____Mater - ALMA,
DURA, PIA or STABAT

Mato_____ - GROSSO

Mauna_____ - KEA or LOA

_____Mawr - BRYN

Mazel_____ - TOV

Mea_____ - COLPA

_____Medica - MATERIA

_____Membrane - TYMPANIC

Memento _____- MORI

Meno_____ - MOSSO

Mens_____in corpore - SANA

Mens_____ - REA

Mesa_____ - VERDE

_____Metabolism - BASAL

_____me tangere - NOLI

_____minerale - EAU

_____minor - LEO

_____Mirabilis - ANNUS

_____Mitzvah - BAR or BAS

Mobutu_____ SEKO - SESE

_____moi le deluge - APRES

Molto_____ - BENE

_____Momento - UNO

Mon_____ - DIEU

_____Monde - HAUT

_____monster - GILA

Moon_____Zappa - UNIT

_____morgana - FATA

_____Mot (wittism) - BON

_____mundi - ANNO

_____Myrtle - CRAPE

_____Nacht - STILLE

Ne plus_____ - ULTRA

_____Neisse Line - ODER

_____Nidre - KOL

_____Nisi Bonum - NIL

_____Nitrate - AMYL

_____Noir - BETE

Nom de _____ - GUERRE

_____Nome - CARO

_____Nostra - COSA

Nota_____- BENE

Nous_____ - ENTRE

Nouveau_____ - RICHE

_____nova - ARS or BOSSA

_____Novo - PORTO

Novus_____sectorum - ORDO

_____nui - RAPA

_____oblige - NOBLESS

Oder_____Line - NEISSE

_____of Iwo Jima - SANDS

_____of Kashmir - VALE

_____of Lebanon - CEDAR

Olla_____ - PODRIA

_____Omnia vincit - AMOR

_____on parle Francais - ICI

Opera_____SERIA

_____operendi - MODUS

_____orange - OSAGE

_____ordinaire - VIN

_____Oro - RIO de

_____Ovo - LACTO

_____Pacis - ARA

_____Paese (cheese) - BEL

_____Pareil - SANS

_____Park, Cal. - BUENA

Pas de_____ - DEAU

_____Pasa - QUE

Pasta_____ - FASOOL

Pater_____ - NOSTER

Pathet_____ - LAO

_____patriac - AMOR

_____Paulo - SAO

Pearl_____ - DAIO

Peau de _____ - SOIE

_____Pei – SHAR

_____Penee - ARRIERE

_____Penh - PHNOM

_____pentameter - IAMBIC

Per_____Ad astra - ARDUA

Per_____ - CAPITA

_____perpetua - ESTO

_____personae - DRAMATIS

Personae non _____ - GRATAE

Peut_____ - (perhaps) ETRE

_____Philippe - PATEK

_____Phraya - CHAO

Pico de_____ - ANETO

Pie_____mode - ALA or CAPA

Pied_____ - A-TERRE

_____perpetua - ESTO

Pis_____ - ALLER

_____Plaid - GLEN

_____Plaisir - AVEC

_____platter - PU PU

Plaza de _____ - TOROS

_____podrida - OLLA

_____poetica - ARS

_____Pointe- DEMI

Poli_____ - SCI

_____polloi - HOI

_____pompilius - NUMA

_____populi - VOX

Por_____FAVOR

_____Porsena - LARS

Port du_____ - SALUT

Post_____ - MORTEM

Pot-au-_____ - FEU

Pousse _____ - CAFE

_____Pradesh - UTTAR

Prie_____(kneeler) - DIEU

Prima_____ - FACIE

_____Prius - NISI

Prix_____ - FIXE

Pro bono_____- PUBLICO

Procol_____ - HARUM

_____Profundo - BASSO

_____ pro nobis - ORA

_____pro quo - QUID

Pro_____- RATA

_____prosequi - NOLLE

Pro_____-TEM

_____Publica - RES

Punta del _____- ESTE

_____Pura - AQUA

_____Purchase - GADSDEN

_____qua non - SINE

_____quam videri - ESSE

Quattro cinque_____ - SEI

Que_____ - SERA or TAL

_____Qui Peut - SAUVE

Quid pro_____- QUO

Quien_____SABE

Quod____Demonstradum -
    ERAT

Quod_____Faciendum - ERAT

Raison d'_____- ETRE

Rapa_____ - NUI

Rara_____ - AVIS

Rarae_____ - AVES

_____Rasa - TABULA

_____Razor - OCCAMS

_____Rea - MENS

_____Regni - ANNO

_____relief - BAS

_____Relievo - ALTO

Res_____Loquitur - IPSA

_____Resartus - SARTOR

Richard_____de
    Lion - COEUR

_____Riche - NOUVEAU

_____Rima – OTTAVA
    or TERSA

Rio de La_____ - PLATA

Rio_____ - NEGRO

_____Rios - OCHO

_____Rivera, CA - PICO

_____Rogas - UTI

_____Romagna - EMILIA

_____Roman - GRAECO

_____Romana - PAX

_____Rosenkavalier - DER

_____Rouge - BATON

_____Royale - ISLE

Sacro_____ - ILIAC

_____Sahib - PUKKA

San_____, CA - ANSELMO

_____sana in corpore
    sano - MENS

_____Sanctorum - ACTA

_____Sanctum - INNER

Sang_____ - GROID

Sans_____ - EGAL

_____Sans in corpore
    sano - MENS

_____Sanskritt - VERIC

Sao_____- PAULO

_____Sapians - HOMO

_____Saud - IBN

Sauve_____Peut - QUI

_____Savant - IDIOT

Savoir_____ - FAIRE

_____scale of
    hardness - MOHS

_____segno - DAL

_____Semper tyrannis - SIC

_____sequitor - NON

_____serif - SANS

_____Seul - PAS

_____show - RAREE

_____Shue - FENG

_____ Shuffle - LIDO

Sierra_____ - LEONE,
   MADRE or MIST

_____Signum - ECCE

_____Simbel - ABU

Sine_____non - QUA

_____Ski - APRES

Soave_____ - BOLLA

_____soda - SAL

_____Soit qui mal y
   pense - HONI

_____solemnis - MISSA

Soto_____ - VOCE

Sphagnum _____ - MOSS

_____spumante - ASTI

Status_____QUO

Status quo_____ - ANTE

St. Philip_____ - NERI

Sturm_____drang - UND

Sub_____ - ROSA

Suma cum_____ - LAUDE

Sun_____ - YAT-SEN

_____Supuesto - POR

Sword of _____ - DAMOCLES

Tabula_____- RASA

_____Tafari - RAS

_____-Tass - ITAR

_____Tai - MAI

_____Tartare - STEAK

Te_____ - DEUM

Tel_____ - AVIV

Temple of _____ - ARES

Tempus_____ - FUGIT

_____Tenure - UDAL

_____Terrier - CAIRN
   or SKYE

Tersa_____ - RIMA

Tetro alla_____ - SCALA

_____Thule - ULTIMA

Tierra del_____ - FUEGO

_____Tiki - KON

_____Tome- SAO

_____Torte - SACHER

_____Tranquillautis - MARE

_____Trasit gloria mundi - SIC

Tres_____- BIEN

_____Triste - VALSE

_____Trouve - OBJECT

_____Tse or Tzu - LAO

_____Tsu - SHIH

Tu_____ - ERI

_____Tu – ERES or ERI

Ulan_____-BATOR or UDE

Una_____ Poco Fa - VOCE

_____un drang - STURM

Urticaria - HIVES

Val d'_____ - ISERE

Valse_____ - TRISTE

_____vapeur (steamed) - ALA

Vega_____ - ALTA

Vena_____ - CAVA

_____Veneto - VIA

Veni_____Vici - VIDI

_____Venner (Holmes work) - ELSIE

_____vera - ALOE

Verbum_____ - DEI

_____Verde - PALO

_____Verte - TERRE

Vidi_____ - ISAT

_____vie - EAUDE

Villa d'_____ - ESTE

_____vincit omnia - AMOR

Vingt_____ - ETUN '

Viola da_____ - GAMBA

_____virumque cano - ARMA

Vissi d'_____ - ARTE

_____Vista - ALTI

_____Vital - ELAN

_____Vivant - BON

_____Vive - QUI

Vive le _____- ROI

_____Voce-SOTTO

_____voce (orally) - VIVA

Voir_____ - DIRE

_____volatile - SAL

_____Volens - NOLENS

_____volente - DEO

_____Von der erde - LIED

_____Vore - EATE

Vox_____ - DEI or POPULI

_____Vu - DEJA

_____way - APPIAN

_____whale – SEI

_____Wiedersehan - AUF

_____Xiaoping - DENG

_____Yoga - HATHA

_____Zedong - MAO

Zend_____ - AVESTA

Zeno of_____ - ELEA

Zhou_____ - ENLAI